Queer TV

How can we queerly theorise and understand television? How can the realms of television studies and queer theory be brought together, in a manner beneficial and productive for both?

Queer TV: Theories, Histories, Politics is the first book to explore television in all its scope and complexity – its industry, production, texts, audiences, pleasures and politics – in relation to queerness. With contributions from distinguished authors working in film/television studies and the study of gender/sexuality, it offers a unique contribution to both disciplines.

An introductory chapter by the editors charts the key debates and issues addressed within the book, followed by three sections, each central to an understanding of the relationships between queerness and television: 'theories and approaches', 'histories and genres', and 'television itself'. Individual essays examine the relationships between queers, queerness and television across the multiple sites of production, consumption, reception, interpretation and theorisation, as well as the textual and aesthetic dimensions of television and the televisual. The book crucially moves beyond lesbian and gay textual analyses of specific TV shows that have often focused on evaluations of positive/negative representations and identities. Rather, the essays in *Queer TV* theorise not just the queerness in/on television – the production personnel, the representations it offers – but also the queerness of television as a distinct medium.

Glyn Davis is Academic Coordinator of Postgraduate Studies at the Glasgow School of Art. He is the author of monographs on *Queer as Folk* (2007), *Superstar: The Karen Carpenter Story* (2008) and *Far from Heaven* (2009).

Gary Needham is Lecturer in Media and Cultural Studies at Nottingham Trent University. He is the co-editor, with Dimitris Eleftheriotis, of *Asian Cinemas: A Reader and Guide* (2006) and the author of a monograph on *Brokeback Mountain* (2009).

Queer TV

Theories, Histories, Politics

Edited by Glyn Davis and Gary Needham

Routledge
Taylor & Francis Group

LONDON AND NEW YORK

First published 2009
by Routledge
2 Park Square, Milton Park, Abingdon, Oxon, OX14 4RN

Simultaneously published in the USA and Canada
by Routledge
270 Madison Ave, New York, NY 10016

*Routledge is an imprint of the Taylor & Francis Group,
an informa business*

Typeset in Bembo by Keyword Group Ltd
Printed and bound in Great Britain by CPI Antony Rowe, Chippenham,
Wiltshire

British Library Cataloguing in Publication Data
A catalogue record for this book is available from the British Library

Library of Congress Cataloguing in Publication Data
Queer TV : theories, histories, politics / edited by Glyn Davis and
Gary Needham.
    p. cm.
    Includes bibliographical references and index.
    1. Homosexuality and television. 2. Homosexuality on television.
    I. Davis, Glyn, Dr. II. Needham, Gary. III. Title: Queer television.
    PN1992.8.H64Q47 2008
    791.45'653–dc22   2008028829

ISBN10: 0-415-45045-4 (hbk)
ISBN10: 0-415-45046-2 (pbk)
ISBN10: 0-203-88422-1 (ebk)

ISBN13: 978-0-415-45045-4 (hbk)
ISBN13: 978-0-415-45046-1 (pbk)
ISBN13: 978-0-203-88422-5 (ebk)

Contents

Acknowledgements

A large number of individuals have contributed to the development of this project, first and foremost our contributors to this collection. We would like to thank the following for providing probing insights, moral support and intellectual provocations: Jane Arthurs, Karen Boyle, Steve Cohan, Kay Dickinson, Alex Doty, Jane Feuer, Judith Halberstam, Julia Hallam, Ellis Hanson, Amelie Hastie, Joanne Hollows, Christine Holmlund, Karen Lury, Anna McCarthy, Alan McKee, Mandy Merck, Roberta Pearson, Julianne Pidduck, Christopher Pullen, Julie Russo, Chris Straayer, Sarah Street, Yvonne Tasker, Matthew Tinkcom, Yannis Tzioumakis, Dave Woods and Gregory Woods.

Special thanks to Andy Medhurst and Lynne Joyrich, who kindly allowed us to reprint previously published pieces of work, and who generously furnished them with perceptive and pithy new prefaces. Andy Medhurst's essay 'One Queen and His Screen' was initially published in Emma Healey and Angela Mason, eds. (1994), *Stonewall 25: The Making of the Lesbian and Gay Community in Britain* (London: Virago Press): 238–50; its re-appearance here was made possible by a small grant from the University of Bristol, for which we thank David Punter. Lynne Joyrich's 'The Epistemology of the Console' first appeared in *Critical Inquiry* 27(3) (Spring 2001): 439–67.

At Nottingham Trent University we would like to thank the MCS team for providing space to explore some of the issues examined in this book, and for taking on some of the stress during May 2008. We also thank Seema Sharma for sourcing for us some difficult-to-find television programmes. We have benefited from generous comments by participants at the conferences *Console-ing Passions* (Milwaukee 2006) and *Screen* (Glasgow 2007) where we first presented some of this material. At Routledge, we'd like to thank Natalie Foster and Charlie Wood for their championing of this book, and their unflagging assistance and encouragement.

Finally, thanks to David Oswald who provided us with the images that adorn this book's cover.

This book is dedicated to Iain Barbour and David Oswald, without whom television just wouldn't be the same.

Contributors

Michele Aaron is Lecturer in the Department of American and Canadian Studies, University of Birmingham. She is the author of *Spectatorship: The Power of Looking On* (Wallflower, 2007) and has edited the collections *The Body's Perilous Pleasures* (Edinburgh University Press, 1999) and *New Queer Cinema: A Critical Reader* (Edinburgh University Press, 2004). She is currently preparing a monograph entitled *Death and the Moving Image*.

Ron Becker is Assistant Professor in Mass Communication, Miami University. He has published widely on the subject of television in *The Historical Journal of Film, Radio and Television*, *The Velvet Light Trap* and *Television and New Media*. He is the author of *Gay TV and Straight America* (Rutgers University Press, 2006).

Glyn Davis is Academic Coordinator of Postgraduate Studies, Glasgow School of Art. He is the co-editor (with Kay Dickinson) of *Teen TV: Genre, Consumption and Identity* (BFI, 2004) and the author of monographs on *Queer as Folk* (BFI, 2007), *Superstar: The Karen Carpenter Story* (Wallflower, 2008) and *Far from Heaven* (Edinburgh University Press, forthcoming).

Lynne Joyrich is Associate Professor of Modern Culture and Media, Brown University, and an editor of the journal *Camera Obscura*. She is the author of *Re-Viewing Reception: Television, Gender and Postmodern Culture* (Indiana University Press, 1996) and has published extensively in the areas of film, television, feminist, queer and cultural studies.

Jaap Kooijman is Associate Professor of Media and Culture, University of Amsterdam. He is the author of *Fabricating the Absolute Fake: American Contemporary Pop Culture* (University of Amsterdam Press, 2008). He has published in numerous journals including *The Velvet Light Trap*, *European Journal of Cultural Studies*, *Post Script* and *GLQ*.

Andy Medhurst is Senior Lecturer in Media, Film and Cultural Studies, University of Sussex. He is the author of *A National Joke: Popular Comedy and English Cultural Identities* (Routledge, 2007), *Coronation Street* (BFI, forthcoming) and the co-editor of *Lesbian and Gay Studies: A Critical Introduction* (Cassell, 1997).

He has published extensively in the areas of gay and lesbian studies, popular culture, film and television.

Gary Needham is Lecturer in Media and Cultural Studies, Nottingham Trent University. He is the author of *Brokeback Mountain* (Edinburgh University Press, 2009), co-editor of *Asian Cinemas: A Reader and Guide* (Edinburgh University Press, 2006) and has published in the areas of television, film and queer theory.

Amy Villarejo is Associate Professor of Film and Feminist, Gender, and Sexuality Studies, Cornell University. She is the author of the award winning *Lesbian Rule: Cultural Criticism and the Value of Desire* (Duke University Press, 2003), *Film Studies: The Basics* (Routledge, 2007), and is the co-author of *Queen Christina* (BFI, 1995). She is the co-editor of *Keyframes: Popular Film and Cultural Studies* (Routledge, 2001) and *Capital Q: Marxism after Queer Theory* (New York University Press, forthcoming). She is currently preparing a monograph titled *Ethereal Queer: Television, Historicity, Desire*.

Joe Wlodarz teaches in the Department of Film Studies, University of Western Ontario. He has published on television and film in the journals *Camera Obscura* and *The Velvet Light Trap*, and contributed to the collection *Masculinities: Bodies, Movies, Culture* (Routledge, 2001). He is currently writing a monograph called *Unmaking Macho: Race, Gender and Stardom in 1970s American Film and Culture* (University of Minnesota Press, forthcoming).

Gregory Woods is Professor of Gay and Lesbian Studies, Nottingham Trent University. His was the first such appointment in the UK. His publications include *Articulate Flesh: Male Homo-eroticism and Modern Poetry* (1987) and *A History of Gay Literature: The Male Tradition* (1998), both from Yale University Press. He has published many essays on queer literature and culture. He is also an established poet published by Carcanet Press. His latest poetry collection is *Quidnunc* (2007).

Introduction

The pleasures of the tube

Glyn Davis and Gary Needham

When Charlotte Brunsdon (1997) first asked 'What is the "television" of television studies?' she was attempting to define, specify, and historicise not only what 'television' refers to but also the divergent approaches, assumptions, influential discourses, and disciplinary backgrounds and tensions which have sought to theorise this thing we call TV. In a similar vein we want to articulate the same kind of epistemological strategy, although less broadly and with less retrospection, in asking: 'what might the "queer" of a queer television studies be?' From this first central question arise a host of others. How can we queerly theorise and understand television? How can we as queers make sense of television? What might it mean to think through (and about) the medium of television and its distinctive characteristics from the perspective of queerness – queerness, that is, as a location of sexual alterity, as desire, and as a praxis of dissidence and political abrasion? And how can the realms of television studies and queer theory – both large bodies of output that have only occasionally made contact with each other – be brought together, in ways that are hopefully beneficial and productive for both? These queries and concerns serve as the driving force of this collection as a whole, and link together the disparate essays contained within its pages.

To a significant extent, this volume originated in particular frustrations felt by both editors. First, there is the neglect of television in debates about queer media and queer screen culture; the ascendancy of queer theory in the 1990s seemed to bypass television almost entirely. Certainly, there is nothing that could be thought of as equivalent to the wealth of books devoted to queer film. Second, the perennially text-centred focus adopted by queer writings about television (and, indeed, writings about queer television) often tell us little about television, let alone the relationship between queerness and the medium. A large number of articles and books have been produced over preceding decades that interrogate individual instances of programming, exploring the ramifications and nuances of particular lesbian/gay/bisexual/trans/queer characters and their associated plots and narratives. A large percentage of these pieces of writing ultimately offer evaluative comments on the 'positive' or 'negative' representations in these shows, denouncing or advocating certain strategies of depiction and articulation; this is what Ellis Hanson has called the 'moralistic politics of representation' (Hanson 1999: 5).

The problem with such a mode of criticism is, of course, that it assumes an agreed-upon 'party line' (and my, what a dull party *that* would be to attend), and presumes not only that all audiences will read representations of queer characters in similar (if not identical) ways but that the only programmes of interest to queer viewers are those in which queers are represented. Queer cinema and queer film criticism, as Hanson proposes, has only come to terms with this relatively recently. Long locked into a politics of representations whose quintessential logic is evaluative – and Vito Russo's *The Celluloid Closet* (1981) is the exemplary text here – queer film scholars are still in a process of negotiating the complexity of, and varied responses to, films like *Cruising* (1980) and *Personal Best* (1982), *Basic Instinct* (1992) and *Swoon* (1992). In contrast, queer television scholars, for the most part, are still clamped into the evaluative paradigm.

It is important to identify that we are not denouncing or ignoring the history of critical writing on queer television. Not only has it been politically necessary (and continues to be so) to scrutinise the depictions of queerness offered up by television, but many of these texts have contributed to the creation of a 'queer television studies' library. Steven Capsuto's *Alternate Channels* (2000), Larry Gross's *Up From Invisibility* (2001), and Stephen Tropiano's *The Primetime Closet* (2002) all detail instances of queer programming which may otherwise have disappeared into obscurity (or been lost forever, through being erased), and attempt to construct historical narratives of progression and enlightenment. Keith Howes' enormous pink slab *Broadcasting It* (1993) serves as an invaluable encyclopedic resource. Recent collections of essays on instances of programming – Kim Akass and Janet McCabe's *Reading* The L Word (2006), James R. Keller and Leslie Stratyner's *The New Queer Aesthetic in Television* (2006), Rebecca Beirne's *Televising Queer Women* (2008) – subject individual series to intense scrutiny from a variety of perspectives, with many authors offering up perceptive and original insights. Authors have pounced on individual programmes (Sasha Torres on *Heartbeat* (1993), Joe Wlodarz on *thirtysomething* (1995) and *Oz* (2005), Anna McCarthy on *Ellen* (2001), Glyn Davis on *Queer as Folk* (2007)) that they perceive as offering an alternative (however fleeting) to fixed, pervasive, and conservative televisual modes of representation. Even the websites afterellen.com and its sibling afterelton.com, while largely adhering to the 'positive/negative' evaluation mode in relation to prime time television, do afford space for interactive discussion between editors, bloggers, and readers which problematises the construction of definitive and 'closed' readings of individual media texts.

This book appears at a time of relative visibility for queer characters and people on television, at least in the US and the UK. Admittedly, the number of ongoing queer characters in US fictional series on the main networks remains relatively low, but these include well-crafted figures on series such as *Ugly Betty*, *Desperate Housewives*, and *Brothers and Sisters* – and a much larger number of populate dramas on cable channels. Queer characters proliferate across fictional British television, most notably in soaps such as *EastEnders*, *Emmerdale*, and *Hollyoaks*. Reality television series like *America's Next Top Model* and *Top Chef* remain key televisual 'spaces' for the representation of queerness. And non-hetero hosts and entertainers, from Ellen DeGeneres to Graham Norton, continue to garner sizeable audiences. Of course, there are limits to this tele-queerness in terms of what is allowed by network bosses, advertising regulators, standards bodies, and audiences: queer characters and people on television remain largely white; gay men appear more than lesbians, bisexuals, and trans individuals; sex scenes are still all too rare, and same sex kissing can still generate controversy. Identifying these limits in order to trouble them must continue to be a main aim of any queer TV studies political project. And in cultures where religious and political conservatism still prosper, and homophobia remains rife, all depictions of sexual minorities in the mass media require scrutiny and interrogation.

However, one of the guiding imperatives behind this collection was the basic assumption that focusing solely on one aspect of television – the programmes it broadcasts, and specifically those shows' handlings of queer people, characters, and stories – ignores the complexity of the medium, and the ways in which it is designed, produced, distributed, and consumed in queer ways. Indeed, to briefly adopt just one perspective on TV's complexity, we would argue that viewers' experiences of television as queer are prolific, difficult to chart or contain, because of their often personal and idiosyncratic nature, and certainly not always – or even usually – anchored in depictions of non-heterosexual characters on screen. The occurrence of such queer TV experiences by audiences may be influenced by (and this list is in no way exhaustive): the placement of the monitor or screen, and the reception of its images and sounds, in a particular environment; the other embodied audience members with whom viewing occurs; the phenomenology of interactions with the screen, the remote, and the technologies of transmission and broadcast; (mis)readings, appropriations, and re-encounters with individual texts; inflections of, or confrontations with, particular components of the televisual landscape, from 'liveness' to 'intimacy', from the cancelled television series to the regulated timescape of the ordered schedule. Here, perhaps, it is worth saying a little about some of these factors, in order to flesh out – if only through examples – possible frameworks through which television's queerness can be thought and conceptualised.

Televisions frequently appear in commercial spaces of queer consumption: bars, clubs, stores, and saunas. When screening regular broadcast content, these monitors and boxes may serve solely as ambient sound and light, largely ignored, or the programming being shown may be viewed and consumed in a manner similar to much television grazing. However, the space may also inflect the reception of the screen and its content. An afternoon visit to a gay male sauna may bring into contact hardcore pornography, scarcely dressed bodies, and mainstream shows, as patrons often take time out from sex to catch up with their favourite soaps; bar trips can combine intoxication, blaring disco remixes and images of dragalicious newsreaders; sex store visits could collide DVD booths, a polyglot array of toys and devices, and footage of *American Idol* (in fact, pornography and popular television often sit side by side in the DVD section of many sex stores). The queerness of these amalgamations or juxtapositions as instances of 'queer TV' might not be located solely in the placement of screens in non-straight spaces, but precisely in (or in-between) the pile-up of their constituent components. Consider also that programmes which enjoy mass appeal across various demographic groupings – *The Eurovision Song Contest*, say, or *Desperate Housewives* – may have their queerness foregrounded, or made more transparent, when consumed by a large gay/lesbian audience in a queer bar. The queer cultural status of particular programmes – such as the Australian prison drama *Prisoner: Cell Block H* – may even be forged in such locations. *Prisoner* is actually a key text here: not only did stars of the series make guest appearances in gay and lesbian venues across the UK, but dance remixes of its title theme were produced and played in queer clubs, both extratextual extensions that bled the experience and consumption of the original television series out into new spaces, including the dance floor. More recently the 'Puppy Episode' of *Ellen*, the first instalment of *Queer as Folk*, and the finale of *Will and Grace* were all consumed in queer bars in ways markedly (and affectively) distinct from domestic viewing, ways that imbued them with additional import.

What of the technology itself, as a set of objects? The rubber buttons of the remote and the ergonomics of the handset's design, the red/green standby power light, the curve of the cathode ray television screen or the flatness of the plasma, the size of the iPod's mobile window and the limitations of its earphones, the positioning of television's screen and speakers within the environment of consumption … Is there such a thing as a queer interaction with these aspects of television's hardware? Certainly, we do not wish here to endorse a simplistic essentialist model in which all queers engage 'differently' (whatever that might mean) with the television set and its peripheral technologies as a collection of objects. But it might theoretically be possible to identify a queer individual, whether child or adult, from their notably perverse uses of televisual hardware. Indeed, perhaps particular aspects of television-as-object afford the potential for queer appropriation. Markedly distinct relationships – of touch, of haptic and somatic connectivity, of sensuous play within the wash of noise and light – might distinguish the queer encounter with the set.

Further, are there ways in which specific elements of TV, identified by television theorists as particular to the medium, can be thought or explored queerly? Is there something queer about flow, or the 'intimacy' associated with the small screen and its modes of address and consumption? Jane Feuer, in her essay 'The Concept of Live Television: Ontology as Ideology' (1983), identified liveness as a key characteristic of television – and it continues to be, whether examples of programmes are actually live (increasingly rare) or merely constructed and broadcast as though they are. Useful theoretical connections could be made between television as 'live' and specific conceptualisations of queerness – as unpredictable, evanescent, immediate, and uncontainable. In a pre-watershed 2007 live broadcast from the reality television series *I'm a Celebrity … Get Me Out of Here*, one of the celebrity participants, former supermodel Janice Dickinson (and didn't they know the risks involved in casting her?) could be heard pointing out to her camp co-participant Christopher Biggins a nook in a wall, which she (quite correctly) identified as resembling a glory hole. This reference – arguably obscene, definitely queer – escaped the regulation of the live broadcast, which is subject to a time delay to bleep bad language; perhaps the censors didn't understand Dickinson's reference, or presumed that most audiences at home wouldn't. And yet its very occurrence – and such delicious moments are not rare – highlights the ways in which forms of TV queerness can materialise through liveness, an association that demands further critical scrutiny. As an additional example of medium specificity here, the cancelled television series, left hanging without resolution (although possibly rescued for posterity and fan consumption by a DVD release) could be seen as one of the queerest aspects of television programming and experience.[1] The sense of conclusion and satisfaction delivered by the closed text – which arguably serves to valourise conservative and patriarchal ideologies – is not provided, replaced instead by a formless open-ended yearning, a realm of possibilities without barricades.

Even if we return to instances of programming – and it is crucial to note that most of the essays in this collection do include analyses and discussions of specific programmes, although these are in no way the hermetic readings which dominate collections on contemporary series – it could be argued that theorists have also been focusing on the wrong shows. Might it be that the queerest programmes on television are not necessarily those that centrally feature queer characters and storylines? Lynne Joyrich, in a short essay entitled 'Closet Archives', comments of *Veronica Mars*:

> I would … argue that, beyond the identified queer characters in some plots, there is an overarching queerness to *Veronica Mars*'s very approach to televisual norms and viewing experiences – more so than with many programmes that claim to be about gay or lesbian life – because of its de- and re-construction of (if not stealth attack on) precisely those norms. (2006: 142)

The same argument could be made about a number of comedy titles in which queer characters, if present, have only a marginal presence: *The Comeback*, *Arrested Development*, *30 Rock*. The drama series *Invasion*, despite focusing on familial relations and featuring no characters openly acknowledged as non-straight, regularly adopted a refractory and unsettling affective tone which provided it with a queer register and appeal. The show's narrative, a reworking of *Invasion of the Body Snatchers* tropes in which the denizens of a small community are replaced by human/alien hybrids, made knowledge about any individual character's 'true nature' difficult to secure – for both audiences and other characters in the series. Beyond this epistemological problematic, however, there was something else queer about the show – a structure of feeling, perhaps, augmented by a particularly vivid and claustrophobic use of mise-en-scène, and the casting of actors with an aura of sexual otherness (Eddie Cibrian's hyper masculinity, Kari Matchett's glacial poise). Similarly, in numerous programmes including *Smallville* and *Lost*, a tension between secrecy and disclosure is a key narrative organisational strategy. This has strong resonances with Sedgwick's discussion of the concept of the closet, and with other theorists' interrogations of the narrativization of queer experience, making possible a queer understanding of the series despite their absence of non-hetero characters (Sedgwick 1990; Battis 2006; Davis and Needham 2008).

In raising all of these concerns, we recognise that there is a considerable literature – and, indeed, a history of theorisation – that complicates any attempts to perceive television through a queer optic. Broadly speaking, television has regularly been configured as a domestic medium and, as such, closely associated with the home, the family, the quotidian; in other words, the heteronormative. Foundational television studies texts have identified the ways in which a space was made for television within the post-war home (Lynn Spigel's *Make Room for TV* (1992)), and the imbrications of the medium in domestic familial disputes around power and authority (David Morley's *The Nationwide Audience* (1980)). Roger Silverstone, in his book *Television and Everyday Life* (1994), discussed in detail the affiliations between the medium and conceptions of the home and family – including the representations of both within a range of specific programmes. And yet these perspectives are open to interrogation and question: all queers have families, and all are raised within domestic environs; the nuclear family has been knocked from its position at the apex of 'normality' with the proliferation of single-occupant homes, single-parent families, blended families, queer families with kids of their own, and so on; and queers may be just as domestic as (if not more so than) their heterosexual counterparts.

At a more personal and anecdotal level, the editors are also reminded that their first confrontations with queer images were almost solely through television, and that many of these encounters now serve as cherished, fond memories. In our respective childhood/adolescent bedrooms – for we both grew up in homes with multiple televisions – TV contributed significantly to our emerging queer subjectivities. An indicative sample of key programmes, images, moments, and characters here would include: being aroused by the homoeroticism of '*CHiPs*' and muscular cartoon heroes like *He Man*; Channel 4's late night screening of Derek Jarman's *Sebastiane*; identification with powerful (and maleficent) television divas such as Jane Badder in *V* (one editor's particular fascination); and being introduced to the breadth of queer culture and the importance of lesbian and gay politics through the magazine programme *Out on Tuesday*. This list is not included here for reasons of lazy nostalgia: rather, we suspect that our attachment to the medium – forged as we scanned ruthlessly for representations of ourselves and our kin in secluded privacy during our formative years – is not rare among queer viewers. For us, at the very least, the place of film in queer life is frankly overstated and overrated.

And yet the relationship between queerness and television is often theorised as a fraught one. Indeed, a number of queer scholars have criticised television as an inadequate medium for handling non-heterosexual sexualities and identities. Joe Wlodarz (1995) discusses the normalising discourses of *thirtysomething* and Anna McCarthy (2001) in an essay on *Ellen* has noted that TV's quotidian flows and predictable rhythms afford little in the way of possibility for queer audiences, representations, and politics:

> *Ellen* demonstrated that the problem of queerness on television is not simply a matter of difficult "adult content." Rather, same-sex desire plays a deeply agonistic role in the unfolding of temporal structures associated with television's modes of (auto)historiography – the media event, the television schedule, the season run, the final episode. (2001: 597)

McCarthy identifies 'the problem that queerness poses for television's representational politics: the difficulty of making same-sex desire uneventful, serial, everyday' (609). As television regularly configures queerness as excessive, as spectacle, as interruption, sexual alterity cannot be accommodated by the medium into its dominant and pervasive time structures – regulated chronotypes which are intricately interwoven with its representational protocols. A similar argument is made by Dennis W. Allen in an essay on *Melrose Place* (1995), in which he identifies that television's queer characters are only allowed one narrative role: the revelation of their sexual identity:

> *Melrose Place* assumes heterosexuality to be self-evident, the unproblematic ground that motivates the straight characters to manufacture the secrets that it is the function of the plot to reveal in time. In contrast, homosexuality is conceived here as itself a secret. As such, any gay narrative on the show collapses in upon itself because the discovery of homosexuality that must, formally, mark the beginning of the gay plot is also the Aristotelian "recognition scene" that is the beginning of the end of that story. (1995: 610)

In other words, it is narrative form per se, as much as melodramatic fictional television's serial structures, that is at fault here; how, fundamentally, can one tell a queer story? It is worth mentioning here how often the revelation of a character's homosexuality quickly leads to narrative redundancy after said disclosure. Most of the gay and lesbian characters in television soaps have little to do after they come out, and more often than not they eventually get written out; this was the fate of *Coronation Street*'s Todd Grimshaw (Bruno Langley) who left in 2007, obviously for queerer pastures beyond the world of Weatherfield. When provided with post-closet narratives, the fate of such characters is often to have the queer aspects of their lives (sex, love, queer friends and spaces, homophobia) elided. However, the ongoing narrativisation of queer life is possible, as is evidenced by other examples of programmes already mentioned: *Brothers and Sisters*, *Hollyoaks*, *The L Word*.

While the essays collected in this book do treat television with some scepticism, and with good reason, recognising the manifold limitations of the medium such as those outlined by McCarthy, Wlodarz, and Allen, they also approach TV with passion and, for want of a better word, love. As much as we're drawn by a necessity to theorise television queerly, this book also stems from our passion for television and the place it occupies in our queer lives, how we share the television experience with our partners and friends. One of the crucial issues that most of the 'positive images' writings often avoid mentioning or discussing is the emotional bond that many queer audiences feel for their television – for its programmes and characters, certainly, and also for the medium as a whole. While we would not want to argue that queer TV fans are any more invested in the box than their straight counterparts, the overall impression produced by much of what has constituted 'queer TV studies' to date is that television deals gay, lesbian, bisexual, and trans individuals a poor hand – and that all queers could therefore be forgiven for rightly spurning the medium. For this collection, then, we felt that it was politically important to reinstate the queer TV audience as an engaged and affectively involved demographic. Of course, television also infuriates many queer viewers – and bores them, angers them, arouses them, just like any other audience. But as a significant proportion of the essays here suggest – and the inclusion of the word 'pleasures' in the title of this introduction makes especially clear – many queers adore television, are committed to it, and pledge their allegiance to the box over and above other media.

This book is divided into three parts – 'Theories and Approaches', 'Histories and Genres', 'Television Itself' – although the thematic and conceptual concerns addressed by individual authors cross the nominal boundaries between these sections. In 'Theories and Approaches', three scholars explore the bringing together of queerness and television central to this book, and the ways in which the meeting or confrontation can be most usefully conceptualised and interrogated. Lynne Joyrich, in her essay 'Epistemology of the Console' (first published in 2001, reprinted here with a new preface), drawing in particular on the writings of Eve Kosofsky Sedgwick, utilises the notion of the closet as a model for understanding the operations of television: its representational protocols, its complex political strategies, its revelations, and dark spaces. Although Joyrich discusses exemplar texts (*Roseanne*, *Ellen*) and particular episodes, the arguments she makes have a broader potency and relevance, as well as offering a clear and sustained example of one way in which queer theory and television studies can be productively brought together.

Amy Villarejo, in 'Ethereal Queer: Notes on Method', offers up a range of provocative ruminations and insights on tele-queerness. Taking flight from the upcoming move from analogue to digital broadcasting, she explores the implications of recent technological shifts in TV as an industry – and their influence on audiences, programmes, and so on – in constructing and formulating a queer form of television theory. Finally, Michele Aaron, in 'Towards Queer Television Theory', asks whether observations from queer film theory can provide insights and modes of analysis of pertinence to queer TV studies. She identifies three specific trajectories of theorisation: interrogations of individual contemporary texts; historical, archaeological, and retrospective unearthings; and investigations of the queerness of TV itself. Aaron offers comments on each of these routes and, in line with the approach adopted by this book, argues 'it is this third avenue that, I believe, presents the greatest challenge and is most needful of attention'.

Four essays appear in the 'Histories and Genres' block. Andy Medhurst's essay 'One Queen and his Screen' (which was first published in 1994, and appears here with an appropriately cheeky new introduction), offers a number of insightful contributions to the construction of any kind of 'queer TV studies'. Medhurst takes the 'positive images' debate to task, and offers up his own personal and perverse history of British TV's queerness. In doing so, he highlights a number of concerns that queer TV studies need to address: how do lesbians, gay men, bisexuals, and trans people learn to watch television? What is it about specific texts that may solicit queer attention in a manner imperceptible to straight viewers? Can a comprehensive account of queer TV history ever be constructed? Joe Wlodarz, in 'We're Not All So Obvious', also problematises the 'doing' of queer history. He revisits US fictional TV series of the 1970s, a decade which has often been criticised for its limited and negative representations of queer characters. Wlodarz identifies the recurrence of specific queer character types – in particular, the athlete and the adolescent – and explores the ramifications of these figures. He also proposes a new model of queer viewership that takes account of selective cross-text and cross-channel consumption, in which perceptive viewers mentally connect, combine and compare solitary episodes.

Both Greg Woods and Ron Becker, in their respective essays, examine recent moments of Western television history, and shifts in representational protocols that expose the working through of significant cultural anxieties. Woods, in 'Something for Everyone', revisits examples of 1990s British gay magazine shows, and the ways in which this specific generic programming format attempted to accommodate queerness as its defining component. Although they failed (some of us were probably out on 'the scene' when it was scheduled in the UK), magazine programmes such as *Gaytime TV* are representative of a crucial political moment in which a mainstream form of gayness was being formulated and disseminated – and as such, they expose the machinations of the culture industry in attempting to identify, shape, and capitalise on such a movement. Ron Becker, in 'Guy Love', explores the representation in some recent US texts (and beyond, in other media) of a queer form of bonding between straight men (what has been termed, in some journalistic writings, the 'bromance' or 'man crush'). The borders of homosociality, masculinity, and acceptable physical affection are troubled and toyed with in these series, which are indicative of a wider cultural awareness of sexual identity fluidity. This does not mean they are utopian, of course – these texts, Becker acknowledges, are politically problematic for a host of reasons – but, like the queer magazine programmes discussed by Woods, they mark a notable cultural and historical turn in television.

In the final, third part, 'Television Itself', three authors consider specific aspects of television as a distinct medium through queer theory and philosophy. In his essay 'Scheduling Normativity', Gary Needham explores television's temporal structures, positioning these in relation to recent theorisations of time by queer scholars such as Judith Halberstam and Lee Edelman. Needham reveals temporal organisation – evident, for instance, in scheduling practices – as key to the normative operations of television, and the ways in which TV's time is closely interconnected with the family (as both embodied group and ideological force). He also identifies queer pleasures and articulations of same-sex desire that manifest themselves on television as moments out-of-time, out of synch with normative conceptions of television's temporal logic and experience. Jaap Kooijman, in his article on zapping, examines the queer potential of the remote control. Drawing suggestive and provocative connections between the flâneur, the gay male activity of cruising, and the practice of zapping between channels, Kooijman argues for a queer politics of remote use and televisual viewing. Finally, in 'Hearing Queerly', Glyn Davis examines TV's queer uses of sound. Beginning from Altman's assertion that television sound is more important than the image, with audiences only watching the screen for around half of the time that the TV is switched on, he identifies a range of aural strategies that have manifested across a variety of programming forms – the live interruption, the unpredictable collision, the scripted interjection, stretches of silence – that have queer potential both affectively and politically.

Of course, this collection of necessity has some gaps in its content. What collection doesn't? There are some subjects that we would have liked to discuss in additional detail, in order to do justice to the richness of both queer theory and television studies, and the ways in which they may work together. These would include: queer considerations of the transnational trade in programme formats and the international channels of capital and commerce by which television now operates; additional exploration of the concept of 'space' and geography for queer TV studies; ethnographic interrogations of the queer audience (if such a thing is even identifiable or possible to categorise). However, we prefer to see this collection as a first set of provocations, an intervention in the theorisation of both queerness and TV, a setting of the stage, and we hope that it will inspire other writers and thinkers into exploring and investigating tele-queerness further.

Notes

1. We would like to acknowledge and thank Amelie Hastie for proposing this particular argument and perspective to us.

References

Akass, K. and McCabe, J. (eds) (2006) Reading The L Word: Outing Contemporary Television, London: I. B. Tauris.

Allen, D.W. (1995) 'Homosexuality and Narrative', Modern Fiction Studies 41(3-4, Fall–Winter): 609–34.

Battis, J. (2006) 'The Kryptonite Closet: Silence and Queer Secrecy in Smallville', Jump Cut 48. Online: http://www.ejumpcut.org/archive/jc48.2006/gaySmallville/index.html [accessed 25 May 2008].

Beirne, R. (ed.) (2008) Televising Queer Women: A Reader, New York: Palgrave Macmillan.

Brunsdon, C. (1997) 'What Is the "Television" of Television Studies?' in D. Lusted and C. Geraghty (eds) The Television Studies Book, London: Hodder Arnold, 95–113.

Capsuto, S. (2000) *Alternate Channels: The Uncensored Story of Gay and Lesbian Images on Radio and Television, 1930s to the Present*, New York: Ballantine Books.

Davis, G. (2007) *Queer as Folk*, London: BFI.

Davis, G. and Needham, G. (2008) 'Queer(ying) *Lost*' in R. Pearson (ed.) *Reading Lost: Perspectives on a Hit Television Show*, London: I.B. Tauris, 277–96.

Feuer, J. (1983) 'The Concept of Live Television: Ontology as Ideology' in E. A. Kaplan (ed.) *Regarding Television*, Frederick, MD: University Publications of America, 12–21.

Gross, L. (2001) *Up from Invisibility: Lesbians, Gay Men and the Media in America*, New York: Columbia University Press.

Hanson, E. (1999) 'Introduction: Out Takes' in E. Hanson (ed.) *Out Takes: Essays on Queer Theory and Film*, Durham, NC: Duke University Press, 1–19.

Howes, K. (1993) *Broadcasting It: An Encyclopedia of Homosexuality on Film, Radio and TV in the UK, 1923–93*, London: Cassell.

Joyrich, L. (2006) 'Closet Archives', *Camera Obscura* 21(3): 136–43.

Keller, J.R. and Stratyner, L. (eds) (2006) *The New Queer Aesthetic on Television: Essays on Recent Programming*, New York: McFarland.

McCarthy, A. (2001) '*Ellen*: Making Queer Television History', *GLQ: A Journal of Lesbian and Gay Studies* 7(4): 593–620.

Morley, D. (1980) *The Nationwide Audience*, London: BFI.

Russo, V. (1981) *The Celluloid Closet: Homosexuality in the Movies*, London: Harper Collins.

Sedgwick, E.K. (1990) *Epistemology of the Closet*, New York: Penguin.

Silverstone, R. (1994) *Television and Everyday Life*, London: Routledge.

Spigel, L. (1992) *Make Room for TV: Television and the Family Ideal*, Chicago: University of Chicago Press.

Torres, S. (1993) 'Television/Feminism: *Heartbeat* and Prime Time Lesbianism' in H. Abelove, M. A. Barale and D. M. Halperin (eds) *The Lesbian and Gay Studies Reader*, London and New York: Routledge, 176–85.

Tropiano, S. (2002) *The Prime Time Closet: A History of Gays and Lesbians on TV*, New York: Applause Theatre and Cinema Books.

Wlodarz, J. (1995) 'Smokin' Tokens: *thirtysomething* and TV's Queer Dilemma', *Camera Obscura* (33–34): 193–211.

—— (2005) 'Maximum Insecurity: Genre Trouble and Closet Erotics in and out of HBO's *Oz*', *Camera Obscura* 20(1): 58–105.

Part I

Theories and approaches

Chapter 1

Epistemology of the console

Lynne Joyrich

PREFACE, A RE-VIEW

Seeing at a distance

In the US around 1997, there was a lot of buzz among both those who work in and those who watch TV (i.e. among almost everyone) proclaiming a new (tele-)vision of sexuality, instigated by the simultaneous 'coming out' of star Ellen DeGeneres and the character, Ellen Morgan, whom she played on her eponymous sitcom, *Ellen*. Did this herald a new age in American televisual treatments of sexuality, and, if so, how? And a new age of what, exactly? No one could answer this precisely … but industry insiders, critics, and viewers began looking for and/or lauding changes in the ways in which US TV might recognize and represent sexuality – particularly queer sexualities. After all, not only was ABC's *Ellen* giving us the first openly gay fictional character in a prime-time network programme, but – for 'good' or 'bad,' in 'open' or 'veiled' ways, as 'significant' and/or 'secondary' figures – LGBTQ folks had been turning up, more and more, in programming ranging from news and talk shows to soaps and sitcoms, from inexpensive reality shows to 'quality' pay-channel dramas. And the greater disclosure and variety of sexualities that this seemed to announce affected not only tele-visions and tele-epistemologies of homosexuality but of heterosexuality as well. Just to give one, though particularly telling, example: in the midst of the non-stop media coverage that spurred the country's explicit discussion of sexual acts engaged in by then President Bill Clinton (from when the first reports of rumours about an affair with White House intern Monica Lewinsky emerged in mid-January 1998 until Clinton at last acknowledged the 'improper physical relationship' in grand jury testimony on 17 August 1998 and then, that same night, in a televised address to the nation), *Sex and the City* premiered (6 June 1998), also attracting the American viewing public (or at least those who could afford HBO) with its blow-by-blow account of the sex lives – and, not unrelated, consumption habits – of four stylish New York City gal-pals. Something certainly seemed like it was happening … and all we had to do was look at our screens to know it.

But what does it mean just to look at our TV sets and 'to know' – particularly when this means 'knowing sexuality'? This was the question that I attempted to address in writing 'Epistemology of the Console,' in which I explored how television is both caught up in and helps to create the contradictions of knowledge and sexuality by which we – gay and straight; on the screen, behind it, or in front of it – are simultaneously placed and displaced. Looking back at this essay now for *Queer TV* gives me a unique opportunity to produce my own 'tele-vision' (a seeing at a distance – in this case, of approximately a decade) of that reading of how TV produces, and immerses us within, its strangely distanced yet also enclosing sight. Or, one might say, it is a chance to look back both at TV's paradoxical both near- and far-sightedness when it comes to knowing sexuality and at my own view of that nexus. I appreciatively take this opportunity, not to attempt to bring my examples up to date (an impossible project, given the ever-changing stream of TV programming – the flow, constitutive of the desires and knowledges we entertain, that thus demands analysis more than any particular examples), nor to proclaim TV's recent progress in that flow (for, while I wouldn't want to argue that there has been 'regress,' the logic that I attempt to unravel would make such a proclamation self-defeating); rather, this preface allows me briefly to reflect again on that televisual logic so as to re-interrogate these very discourses of reflection and progression, vision and visibility by which we typically describe knowledge, sexuality, and television.

Blue light district

The phrase 'blue light district' has contrary meanings: in some places, it signifies an area where one might buy sex for money (a synonym for 'red light district'); in other places, it means almost the opposite: an area filled with surveillance cameras and heavily patrolled by police so as to impede the selling of sex and other 'harmful substances.' Perhaps, then, it's the perfect, paradoxical metaphor for TV, a medium defined by its own contradictions (flow through segmentation, continuity via its discontinuous texts, distanced yet overly close) – a medium that, through its glowing blue light, marks out an area for both the commodification of sexuality and its surveillance and policing.

We are accustomed, in Western society, to thinking about knowledge through metaphors of light – of illumination; of enlightenment; of making things visible; in effect, of shining a beacon (like a searchlight, or TV's electron scan beam) of truth. These tropes, while applied to all sorts of 'knowing' (to a notion of knowledge in general), have been particularly significant in relation to knowing sexuality, especially given the appeals to visibility that have structured most recent LGBTQ movements. Yet I would argue that such appeals are paradoxically based on precisely the view of sexuality, vision, and knowledge against which they struggle: that is, while relying so heavily on discourses of enlightened visibility is certainly understandable in this post-Enlightenment society of the image, this nonetheless means that queer political and cultural opposition becomes framed in the same terms as the dominant ones that we'd like to challenge, thus undermining the effectivity of that opposition. For rather than universal knowledge that sheds light, there are specific knowledges that simultaneously both illuminate and obscure, produced by specific discourses and modes of signification (of which, as I elaborate in the following essay, discourses of sexuality and mass-mediated modes of signification are key); and rather than identities always already existing, even if in the shadows, waiting to be brought to view, subjectivities and sexualities are only formed (and deformed; formed *as* deformed) through those specific knowledges.[1]

Within our culture's construction of knowledge, sexuality is considered something 'inside' of each subject – permanent yet invisible unless brought to light, and thus calls to make it visible (not only as a strategy for each person coming out, but as a demand for public representation) have been central in LGBTQ politics. Not coincidentally, this demand also aims to make alignments between a politics of sexuality and politics of gender and race – clearly an important goal, but troubling when articulated in this way, in that an alignment based on the idea that sexual orientation should be made as indelibly 'visible' as race and gender (supposedly) are carries dangerous assumptions, taking this visibility for granted and not acknowledging it as itself a construction.[2] (And an inadequate one at that – obviously, we can't necessarily simply 'see' gender and race identifications, nor would it be at all helpful to demand that we should, as this ignores the many complex ways in which subject and social positions might be experienced, claimed, and understood.)

The language of visibility, as a particular discourse of knowledge, a particular mode of mediation, and a particular political programme, thus retains its own blind spots. And when it comes to thinking about TV's treatment of sexuality, and where we'd like it to go, we also have to consider whether 'visibility' is even the primary register. Television may be 'seeing at a distance,' but it has also been variously labeled 'radio with pictures' (emphasizing the central role of sound in TV programming) and 'moving wallpaper' (emphasizing its environmental, not just representational aspect), and, in today's world of 'media integration,' it is just as likely to be experienced on a computer as a TV set, thereby even further increasing the already existing cross-media possibilities for multiple readings and writings, fantasy games and fan productions, ancillary texts and (of course) commodity tie-ins across numerous signifying and sensory modes.

It is for these reasons that, in attempting to understand television and sexuality, I focused on the question of knowledge – on the epistemology of the console – rather than on the more usual target of visibility. That is, rather than looking at how TV looks at (or away from) queer folks, I tried to understand how TV comes to know sexuality, how it comes to construct what we even count as knowledge about sexuality. Yet the danger for the academic or the TV critic – that is, for someone whose professional responsibilities are supposed to include the production of knowledge – also lies precisely here: what kind of knowledge can we produce about the formation of knowledge; what kind of logic should we use in analyzing TV's logic? Is there a way to 'think TV' without thinking just like it, a way to understand how we literally 'think through' its epistemological forms without only reproducing the forms of this mass-reproduced medium?

Across the channel, down the stream

A critique that has been leveled at the essay, 'Epistemology of the Console,' is that, in parts, it may be a little too schematic: that, in outlining some of US TV's typical strategies for knowing sexuality, it risks presenting them as simple options offered by television producers among which viewers might then select (much like, if planning an evening of viewing sustenance, one can choose a soap opera or a sitcom, a reality show or a drama, or, in the case of literal consumption, one can pick dishes, from among various categories, off a menu). In some ways, such heuristic categorization may be appropriate for an essay on television, given TV's own conventions; indeed, in contrasting television to cinema, Rick Altman has famously argued that while 'attention to classical Hollywood narrative is in large part *goal-driven*, ...attention to American television narrative is mainly *menu-driven*.' (1986: 45, italics in original). That is, given its structure of flow and segmentation, television seems to offer a variety of tasty little bits, arranged by the networks but still available to be mixed and matched at the viewer-consumer's own channel-changing discretion. Nonetheless, while my 'menu-like' attention to television's strategies might thus seem fitting to its subject, this is also, I recognize, a potential pitfall – or a paradox.

As still the dominant media form in our culture (and today in most cultures around the globe), it is hardly surprising that television is, at least to a great degree, constitutive of the very ways in which we think – including the ways in which the television theorist thinks. Yet this is not only inevitable; it is also, I would argue, oftentimes instructive. In saying this, I am not trying to make an apologist case for television's 'educational' (vs. purely 'entertainment') value; in fact, in my thinking about television's thinking, I argue that TV undoes this binary (along with many others – continuation/interruption, totalization/fragmentation, protraction/immediacy, stability/instability, inside/outside, domestic/social, public/private, real/virtual, and so on). Rather, I am suggesting both that it is important for television critics to acknowledge their kinship (indeed, shared identity) with television viewers and even with television textuality itself, which, as just indicated (and elaborated in more detail in the main body of the essay) engages a logic that confounds our usual categorical oppositions – thus offering, in the best case scenario, a productive model for theory (though, in the worst case scenario, a spiral of only increasing consumption and diminishing returns). But this 'worst case' also points to the problem with thinking only within TV's own terms – to, then, the necessity to think beyond, beside, and/or between television's texts so as to interrogate its epistemology with our own.

Yet what does it mean to think beyond, beside, or between TV texts? With a medium in which 'the text' itself is almost impossible to define – comprised as it is by an ever-growing temporal and spatial flow, with continuity created from discontinuity, unity from division (and vice-versa) – *is* there a beyond, between, besides? As I've been attempting to stress, television's logic (and, I hope, my own in thinking through it) is more complicated and contradictory than it initially appears, not really operating by a simple 'menu' channel structure but as a complex, mobile field – one that cannot be assessed in simple textual (or, as I argue, sexual) terms. This is suggested by the very insufficiency of presuming firm categorical differences (as in the shorthand used above) between 'a soap opera or a sitcom, a reality show or a drama,' given the ways in which, for example, many TV series have become serialized in form, soaps include comic moments, reality shows are certainly as 'dramatic' as they are 'real,' and dramas market their 'ripped from the headlines' realism – that is, the ways in which TV crosses its own divides and links its texts in dynamic interaction. This too is suggested by that other use of the term 'menu' in today's digital, hypertextual world. If TV (and, to return to Altman's phrase, our attention to it) is 'menu-driven,' this thus needn't mean that it is purely schematic, but, rather, that television constructs a multi-faceted, multi-accented, multi-meaning universe, where the usual distinctions we are likely to make (between programme types, media strategies, viewer investments, ideological effects) don't necessarily hold in the usual ways. And this may be even more the case today than when the essay was originally written, with TV in our era of 'media convergence' even further combining and recombining its strategies just as we combine and recombine television texts in our viewings, thinking, lives.

Nonetheless, the breakdown of categorical discriminations on television certainly doesn't mean an end to political and social discrimination; clearly, US TV is still a heterosexist (and sexist, racist, classist, ageist, etc., etc.) institution. In other words, while, as I argue, television's logic may be one in which binaries become blurred – with, strangely, exclusion sometimes operating via inclusion, obscurity sometimes generated by obviousness, the 'screened' produced by exactly what's screened – this doesn't, of course, at all mean that it's a 'liberating' medium, the model of Marshall McLuhan's (1962; 1964) egalitarian 'global village.' But it does mean that instead of assuming that we know how and what TV knows, we truly subject its complex epistemology to scrutiny. As those interested in queer TV, it is critical to keep making demands of television; but articulating these in the usual terms (more truth vs. falsehood, more visibility vs. invisibility, more presence vs. absence), while marking important goals, may also contribute to the problem of a limited schema if these are the only ways in which we frame our demands.

This, ultimately, I would argue, is what TV logic can teach us: its paradoxes, spiralings, and double movements can ensnare us … but they can also criss-cross themselves, sometimes reinforcing ways of thinking that we want to move beyond but sometimes, maybe, re-envisioning categories in ways that allow us to see differently (or, as I say in the essay, that reveal how the logic can explode itself). In this, then, there is value not simply to tracing TV's epistemology but to considering how its tracings can assist our own epistemologies; not only training our sights on television but allowing it, perhaps, to train our sight – and other means of knowledge – anew. In this way I continue to hope we might strive to expose the epistemology of the console so that it needn't be just a consolidated box of our culture's ignorance and fears.

– *Lynne Joyrich, 2008*

EPISTEMOLOGY OF THE CONSOLE

Outbursts? Exploding closets and epistemological crises

The 1994 Halloween episode of *Roseanne* exhibits the Connor family and their friends playing a series of Halloween tricks on one another, each attempting to outdo the others. The plot focuses in particular on two extended pranks, both of which are referenced by the episode's title, 'Skeleton in the Closet.' The most elaborate involves a ploy to persuade Roseanne that her brother-in-law Fred is gay. Roseanne 'accidently' witnesses Fred's apparent familiarity with several gay men at a beauty salon and then at a costume party (in which he appears as Batman to his wife's Robin); notes his discomfort at male attention that seems to allude to a secret history; and is spurred to recall her own memories of Fred's past that include his hairstyle experimentation and a desire to see the film *That's Entertainment*. After this series of coded references allows Roseanne to 'recognize' Fred as homosexual, the prank reaches its climax when Roseanne and her sister Jackie storm into the bedroom, only to find Fred in bed with Roseanne's own husband Dan. Jumping out of the bedroom closet, family friends Leon and Nancy, two of the programme's queer characters (and here dressed as Hillary Rodham Clinton and Marilyn Monroe, respectively), shout 'we are everywhere,' as Roseanne (dressed as Prince) runs off to find a camera with which to capture this sexual surprise. An interwoven subplot – articulating a connection between anxieties over the uncertainties of sexual bodies with anxieties over the uncertainties of aging bodies – provides the material for the second prank. After having been an object of coiffeusorial scrutiny across the episode, Roseanne's mother uncovers her own 'secret,' whipping off a wig to reveal a balding head. In a joke that may hint at the death drive underpinning television's illusion of liveness, all members of the Connor family then remove wigs or file in bald-headed, a group of TV's talking heads transformed into talking skulls. Faced with these two Halloween tricks (one metaphorical and one literal unmasking), Roseanne resorts to the only thing that might top such stunning pranks: she removes some dynamite from underneath the kitchen sink and blows up the house.

I start with this anecdote from *Roseanne* because I believe that it dramatizes in an especially instructive way the dynamics – explosive yet banal – that I would like to discuss: the way in which US television both impedes and constructs, exposes and buries, a particular knowledge of sexuality. While *Roseanne* had been at the forefront of queer representation throughout its network run (as indeed this episode – with its assorted cast of gay, lesbian, bisexual, trans, and straight characters – indicates), the episode nonetheless demonstrates the stakes of such representation: discovering that Dan is gay would be tantamount to exploding the familiar and familial TV diegesis. That is, bringing what typically exists outside TV's representational space into its very core creates an epistemological crisis that threatens, both literally and figuratively, to blow this space up. Or does it? After all, though Nancy announces 'we are everywhere,' the episode actually assures us that 'we' are not: the outing of such central characters can only function as a successful prank because of its patent absurdity. And though Roseanne really does seem to blow the house up at the show's end, suggesting a final limit to its ongoing flow, she and the rest of the family return the next week as usual – domestic as well as epistemological and sexual spaces intact. Marking a difference that is promptly forgotten through a gag that is equally daring and trite, the homosexualization of television is here, as I will argue it is in much recent programming, both envisioned and erased.[3]

In this way, 'Skeleton in the Closet' exemplifies a peculiar logic of knowing (or not knowing) sexuality. In interrogating this logic – that is, in considering the ways in which the televisual apparatus attempts to know sexual (particularly, though not only, homosexual) subjects and the ways in which we, as viewing subjects, come to know sexuality through television's scanning look – my emphasis may at first seem atypical for those exploring epistemologies of television. For rather than analyzing the construction of knowledge in television studies, I am attempting to analyze a construction of knowledge in television itself. This construction is what I have termed the 'epistemology of the console,' a term obviously indebted to Eve Sedgwick's remarkable study of the 'epistemology of the closet,' itself indebted to Michel Foucault's study of the disciplinary effects of discourses of knowledge. Arguing that sexual relations are inextricable from those questions of knowledge that drive and discipline modern culture, Sedgwick considers how sexuality constitutes a privileged but fraught epistemological field – indeed, how sexuality (particularly the hetero/homosexual binary) is fully entangled in what now registers as knowledge. According to Sedgwick, the division imposed between heterosexuality and homosexuality is central to our very conceptual universe, acting as a structuring device – albeit an unstable one – in our culture's epistemology; it is used, for instance, to mark such divisions as same/different, inside/outside, public/private, secrecy/disclosure, health/illness, life/death (Sedgwick 1990). Given this defining relation to founding conceptions of truth, identity, and knowledge, the hetero/homo division is then not just relevant to a select few (those identified under its regime as homosexual), but to everyone because we are all catalogued according to these contested axes. In fact, it is precisely because these categories *are* contested that such enormous (though often contradictory) efforts are made to police their borders.

Coding and mediation: framing film and television

In cinema studies, such border crossings and policing have been explored in readings of a number of films that, as D. A. Miller says of *Rope*, allow 'homosexuality to be elided even as it is also being elaborated' (1991: 124).[4] This is particularly the case in films made during the era of the Motion Picture Production Code (MPPC) when explicit reference to 'sex perversion' and 'aberrations' was forbidden (see Russo 1987: 120–1). Unable to be denotatively presented, homosexuality came to be connotatively played (and vice-versa, as knowing allusion came to signify not just secrets in general but this particular one; not just an attitude of suggestive innuendo, but a specific gay sensibility). While this strategy may have allowed code-era Hollywood to maximize audience address, accommodating both 'knowing' and 'naïve' viewers at once (because some might easily find meanings that others might just as easily deny), it minimized the possibility of epistemological certainty. Held 'definitionally in suspense' through connotation, homosexuality became impossible either to confirm or to disprove, with the unsettling (or heartening) effect that heterosexuality itself could no longer be absolutely guaranteed (Miller 1991: 125).

Even after the MPPC was dismantled in favor of an age-based rating system that segmented the audience according to degrees of expected understanding, the logic of the closet – in which sexuality is always suspect – did not simply fade away;[5] if anything, Sedgwick suggests, its drama is even 'heightened in surprise and delectability ... by the increasingly intense atmosphere of public articulations of and about the love that is famous for daring not speak its name' (Sedgwick 1990: 67).[6] In the post-Code era, then, this epistemic/erotic nexus has continued to construct homosexuality as both desired and disavowed. By setting up gay characters as foils for straight ones even as it closes down possibilities for their narrative development, recent Hollywood film seems to require representations of homosexuality no more and no less than it requires their effacement or dismissal.[7] How we supposedly 'know' that we are seeing homo, bi-, or even heterosexuality, how exactly these sexualities are made to appear: these remain questions that demand attention. Certainly, they appear and disappear differently for different subjects; that is, what is knowable and unknowable about men and women is not the same. For example, while historically film and television have approached gay men's sexuality through connotation – making male homosexuality uncertain in any specific case but presumably knowable as a general category – they seem to have approached lesbianism in almost a reverse fashion. Here, particular women may explicitly be shown engaging in same sex eroticism (typically framed, to be sure, for the benefit of a presumed male spectator), yet lesbianism as a sexuality in and of itself remains unimaginable and hence an unknowable desire (raising the classic question, What do lesbians do in bed? – other than wait for a man to join them). Despite these distinctions in erotic and epistemological categories, it nonetheless can be politically and theoretically useful to consider them in tandem because within mass culture the two are often made to stand in for one another – as demonstrated, for instance, by the mass-mediated paranoia displayed around both gay men and lesbians at the dawning of the age of AIDS.

As that example suggests, an analysis of the lingering logic of the closet is no less relevant for contemporary television than for film. In fact, given the US TV industry's recent move to rate and regulate its adult content so as to avoid outside regulation, it might even be more relevant. At just about the same time in television history that viewers were endlessly speculating about when, how, and why (or why not) the title character of ABC's situation comedy *Ellen* would come out of the closet, the television industry initiated the first in a series of stages in such self-regulation, adopting a rating system that, though age-based, was more likely to reproduce the connotative uncertainty of the MPPC than the denotative alternative, initially rejected by programmers and distributors, of designating and quantifying TV's sexual and violent acts. More recently, amid discussion over standards (both technical and moral) for the 'V-chip' (a technology designed to give parents the ability to block programming deemed 'harmful' due to its language, violence, or sexual content), the industry has moved toward just such a denotative content code, displaying notations during programme title sequences that, in addition to giving age guidelines, also warn of potentially troublesome dialogue, images, and situations.[8]

Yet this system too fails to provide anything like 'full disclosure' or epistemological clarity. It is unevenly applied across television's output; the symbols are not clearly defined nor explained; and most important (and obviously), such content evaluation necessarily depends upon textual and contextual interpretation.[9] How one perceives a television episode (even if paying much attention to it) depends upon the reading strategies, intertextual references, and extratextual discourses brought to bear upon the show, and these of course vary for different viewers – or even for the same viewer at different moments or in different aspects. Writing on classical cinema, Richard Maltby (1996) has argued that the Production Code functioned as an enabling mechanism to allow Hollywood films to speak simultaneously to both 'the innocent' and 'the sophisticated,' thereby promoting, as previously noted, the industry's presumption of a universal audience (unlike the later film rating system that divided the audience into age categories). I am suggesting that something similar occurs in television, though rather than personifying the 'sophisticated' and 'innocent' readings in distinct viewers as Maltby does, I would argue that television's particular epistemology often allows the same viewer to assume both positions at once, so that, for instance, a viewer might be expert at decoding TV conventions without necessarily being particularly 'knowing' about the stakes and implications of this very decoding (that is, one might be a 'clever' viewer but not a 'critical' one).

Thus encouraging viewers to defer their judgment (however the industry deems to judge itself through self-determined ratings), television operates, as Judith Mayne (1998) has described it, as 'a door that swings both ways' (a closet door, perhaps?). Indeed, television is a crucial site for the exploration of the logic of the closet not only because of its central role in establishing (and suspending) knowledge in postmodern culture but also because US television itself is located at the intersection of many of the same conceptual divisions that Sedgwick has described. By both mediating historic events for familial consumption and presenting the stuff of 'private life' to the viewing public, the institutional organization of US broadcasting situates television precisely on the precarious border of public and private, 'inside' and 'outside.' Here it constructs knowledges identified as both secret (domestically received) and shared (defined as part of a collective national culture).[10]

The resulting epistemological structure may make even banal sexual situations – commonplace, if sometimes unsavoury, heterosexual exchange – appear scandalous. Take, for instance, the Anita Hill/Clarence Thomas hearings in which television's intercrossings of the public and the private produced the all-too-familiar allusions to sex, not to mention sexism, as somehow strange and shocking, bringing suspicion on the one who dared disrupt the open-secret structure rather than on the one who

simply disavowed it. A more recent example of television's activation of this structure is, of course, provided by the Clinton sex scandals. This political 'crisis'/media
boon provoked endless TV talk and an equally incessant demurral about just what
sex is (or more accurately, how exactly one defines sexual relations). While not
the only issue at stake in the scandal and its coverage, that question of sex came
to be seen as both origin and obstacle, and as such it was both omnipresent and
deflected through televisual diversion – at work within each joke or press debate,
yet not quite posed as such. Skipping back in time to a more fantastic instance of
media diversion (here, literally a diversion from real politics to television fantasy),
another example of how television both constructs the explicit as unsayable and
authorizes an excess of talk about that which is ostensibly beyond what we should
know is furnished by Dan Quayle's 1992 attack on TV character Murphy Brown's
decision to have a child outside of marriage. The widespread news coverage of this
condemnation of an imaginary newscaster for her (lack of) sexual and family values
again demonstrates the twists of a tele-epistemology that imbricates not only the
public and the private, the domestic and the social, but, more comically here, the
fictional and real. Indeed, it is only appropriate that in preparing an interview with
a recently out Ellen DeGeneres about her life and show, 20/20 attempted to get a
statement from Quayle.[11]

Real queer: playing the roles

As the previous examples indicate, US TV's location within and between conflicting
social and psychic spaces imbues its representations of sexuality (even presumptive
heterosexuality) with a certain ambivalence; this is all the more noticeable in television's representations of gay and lesbian sexualities. It is no surprise then that the
aforementioned tension between the fictional and real, the live and the recorded,
is particularly noteworthy in television's treatment of queer subjects. This might be
suggested by another example literally (that is, temporally in TV's flow) contiguous
with that of *Ellen*. On the *Grace Under Fire* episode that aired on ABC immediately
before *Ellen*'s (in)famous coming out show on 30 April 1997, there was a moment
of rupture between television's always already tenuous line between the fictional
and real, the diegetic and extradiegetic, when the programme's narrative was cut
short by a 'real live' marriage proposal from one of the show's actors to one of its
camerawomen. Such a public announcement of heterosexuality – coming moments
before *Ellen*'s much more critiqued public announcement of homosexuality – both
demonstrates the ways in which the relationship between these textual registers has
historically been more fraught for television's queer than straight subjects and serves
as a graphic reminder to the many critics of the (supposed over-)attention given to
the events on/around *Ellen* that homosexuality hardly has a stranglehold on media
recognition.

Indeed, how narrative attention is televisually orchestrated reveals that it is often
heterosexuality that is in fact realized through such 'recognitions.' As in many films,
it is not unusual for television programmes to establish characters who, diegetically,

are 'really' gay in order to establish (not always successfully) that the other characters are not. Ironically, it is television's own logic of the closet that requires this realization; the televisual production of sexuality (even in its heteronormative forms) may rely less on portrayals of love, desire, and erotic behavior (which threaten to exceed TV's domesticated space) than on practices of oppositional location and defense, however self-defeating. This, for example, is what Sasha Torres argues about the short-lived *HeartBeat* and its predecessors *Kate and Allie*, *The Golden Girls*, *Cagney and Lacey*, and *L.A. Law*, all of which have introduced specific gay or lesbian characters so as to 'localiz[e] the homosexuality which might otherwise pervade these homosocial spaces' (Torres 1993: 179). A similar, though more vertiginous operation occurs in shows, as in a recent episode of *Spin City*, in which a straight character masquerades as gay for the benefit of the 'real' queer, inverting the dynamics of the closet in order (supposedly) to mark the differences between hetero and homo, identity and role, but of course always threatening to erase these very partitions.

The ambiguity of the situation becomes even further pronounced when moving between textual and extratextual levels. TV may attempt to employ 'diegetically real queers' to assure audiences of the distinctions between gay and straight, identity and mask, yet 'non-diegetic real queers' (i.e., gay and lesbian actors) may simply provoke epistemological crises along these same fault lines. There are countless cases in which actors cast in gay roles strive to create an unassailable division between the person and the part; in the case of *Ellen*, the situation is reversed. Here, television meets the demand that we recognize the difference between straight and gay precisely by refusing to allow us to recognize the difference between character and actor. By having Ellen DeGeneres come out of the closet just shortly before Ellen Morgan did, television assures us that we can recognize homosexuality through and through when we see it, that it can't be faked – despite the competing corollary admission that this conflated Ellens' sexuality had been faked until this point.

Of course, there is something particularly odd about the idea that one can 'out' a fictional character in the first place – as if this character might have been sneaking off to the bars or parks during commercial breaks when our attention was otherwise diverted – that both plays on and further produces television's spiraling dynamic of the fictional and real. Though Ellen the sitcom character bears a striking resemblance to Ellen the sitcom actor, to ask, as *Time* magazine among many others did, whether Ellen Morgan was 'really gay all along,' even before DeGeneres and the writers knew it, suggests a level of autonomous televisual existence that proves TV's epistemology to be much 'queerer' than that of other media forms (Handy 1997: 82).[12]

Needless to say, television does not always play this out. The example of *Ellen* demonstrates particularly well the potentially bizarre permutations of a tele-epistemology that mixes fact and fiction, inside the text and out, more so than, for instance, those moments of disclosure about figures who have an historical existence beyond TV, as in the made-for-TV movie *Breaking the Surface: The Greg Louganis Story*, or, though this example itself points to television's oddities,

Dr. Quinn, Medicine Woman's 'outing' of Walt Whitman.[13] Of the many both facile and difficult aspects of the latter example, consider the case of *Dr. Quinn* actor Chad Allen, who himself was outed not long before this episode and who appears in it as one of Whitman's few supporters. At key points in the narrative, the camera cuts to his concerned and empathetic face, bearing silent witness to the town's condemnation and to Whitman's persevering spirit. In a double displacement (from current issue to historical drama, and from the fantasy of bodily activity to the contemplation of a face in halting close-up), the episode thus positions Allen precisely at the point of its erotic/epistemic collapse. His very silence is itself suggestive of the way in which television's construction of the fictional and real may create a closet door that swings both ways, on the one hand entrapping gay actors in a redoubled logic of the closet (for how can this in-character-actor speak out?) and, on the other, opening a space (however small) for them to stand in visible if unvocalized condemnation of this logic.

In couched terms: television and therapeutic discourse

This display of an erasure (or, conversely, the erasure of display) is indicative of the epistemological spiral provoked by television's treatment of the 'reality' of homosexuality both in its texts and in the information that circulates around them. Yet, as stated above, the effects of revealing the true sexuality of fictional characters is, if less poignant, even more perplexing. The suggestion that a character like Ellen Morgan was gay before anyone creating her was (at least consciously) aware of this – her broadcasting family is indeed the last to know – perhaps only makes sense in the light of another aspect of television that reinforces its link to the logic of the closet: the dominance of therapeutic discourse in and for TV, across both its real and its fictional forms.

As Mimi White (1992) has demonstrated, therapeutic and confessional strategies centrally figure in US television, providing not just subjects for narratives but TV's very mode of narrativization. In this light, it is only fitting that, in the season-long prelude to *Ellen*'s coming-out episode, Ellen's inability to fix on her sexuality would be matched by an equal inability to fix on a therapist, a gag that helped drive the programme's (and its lead character's) 'progress' toward sexual revelation. Making this perfectly clear was the opening to the episode 'Bowl, Baby, Bowl' (4 December 1996) in which Ellen, reclining on a therapist's couch, states:

> Well, um, the first time, I was, um … I was with a man, and then I was with a woman for a little while. And then I was with a man again, and then with another man, and let's see, then woman, woman, man, woman, and then another man. And you know, lately I'm beginning to think it doesn't really matter if it's a man or a woman, you know? It's the person that counts. But one thing I know for sure … I can't keep going from therapist to therapist like this.

Coming a few months into the 1997 season, this joke not only perpetuated the programme's continuing gag of (barely concealed) hints and clues but displaced the sexual mystery supposedly behind this set of clues onto a therapeutic one, fully collapsing object choice onto analyst choice. Is it then any wonder that the shrink on whom Ellen finally settles, the one who actually helps her uncover the 'truth,' should be played by none other than Oprah Winfrey, the exemplar of TV's therapeutic regime?

What follows from this analytic equation is that sexual indecision is treated in such couched terms, the stakes of which are circled around but not yet quite named. Given its institutional determinants, US television's therapeutic discourses have been wedded to familial and consumer ideology, but, as Foucault (1978b) has shown in his analysis of confessional strategies, it is precisely sexuality as an 'implantation of perversion' that their deployment produces as the secret of the self. Homosexuality – *the* mark of diacritical sexual difference in our society – would thus be both an effect of and obstacle to television's confessional, familial, and consumer regime, the sexuality produced precisely *as* obstacle, necessarily inside and outside the televisual domain. If then, as White argues, television not only transmits but transforms our understanding of confessional and therapeutic relations, it also not only transmits but transforms our understanding of sexual relations.[14] That is, US television does not simply reflect an already closeted sexuality but actually helps organize sexuality as closeted, as positioned in the epistemic centrality yet fraught with an incoherency that I am attempting to map here.

It is therefore not surprising that the epistemology of the closet is such a notable structure in recent television, even – or especially – in an era of more detailed articulation. With sexual disclosure seemingly compulsory yet forbidden, demanded yet contained, television constructs illicit sexualities ambivalently as both known and unknown; in the epistemology of the console, some things are apparently better not really apprehended even as this ignorance is maintained and betrayed by an attitude of smug knowingness about things supposedly beyond our need to fully comprehend. Thus, whether by making homosexuality as *the* secret knowledge to be gleaned or difficult seriously to entertain, television typically creates a classic epistemic double bind. In other words, though narratives that explicitly deal with the closet are marked as exceptions, for reasons I've given, the closet becomes an implicit TV form – a logic governing not only the ways in which gays and lesbians are represented but also the generation of narratives and positions on and for TV even in the absence of openly gay characters (or gay characters at all).

The dynamics of the closet for TV's queers must therefore be read alongside television's ambivalent construction of sexuality in general. Because it exceeds television's domesticated world, sexuality, even in its heterosexual varieties, can only appear as such – as sexuality – through assorted impasses and inversions (for instance, all those romantic reversals in television drama and humorous mismatches in television comedy). Rather than focus, then, on only one example – *Ellen's* manifest story of self-discovery and coming out – it is interesting to consider some of the permutations of television's ways of 'knowing' sexuality, which might be schematized as in the following 'case studies.'

Test patterns: broadcasting it

Inferring sexuality

One example from our not-too-distant TV past often claimed by those interested in queer representations – though the programme itself never made any such claims – is the prototypical case of *Love, Sidney*. This early 1980s programme typifies the 'Who knows?' brand of homosexual (non)performance.[15] Though lead character Sidney Shorr (played by Tony Randall) had what one directory of television programmes calls the 'distinctive trait' of being gay in the TV movie on which the situation comedy was based, the series itself refrained from ever mentioning homosexuality, though, as this same directory put it, 'it could have been inferred' (Brooks and Marsh 1992: 527).

More recent television texts, aiming for new material and audiences, may no longer depend on such consummate evasion, but a structure of hints and allusions – an articulation of the unarticulated – often still prevails. Indeed, by shifting the site of elision from identity to the eroticism it supposedly names – if *gay* or *lesbian* is established as description but not desire – evasion might still be the operative strategy even when a gay man or lesbian is labeled as such. In this way, homosexuality might be known but not as sexuality; it occupies a position in the narrative but one that entails no cultural performance.[16] (Another way of putting this would be to restate the obvious point that sexual identity is different from sexual desire – and perhaps nowhere are they more different than on television, given the industry's attempts to define sexuality as product while retaining its simultaneous anxiety around sexuality as practice.) This method of holding queer representation at a distance (a kind of tele-containment, if you will) was evident, for instance, in the treatment of the character Matt Fielding on FOX's *Melrose Place* – the only character in the early days of this steamy prime-time soap not seen engaging in a string of scandalous affairs. Though one of TV's first long-running gay characters, Matt seemed to hold this position (at least initially) precisely by desexualizing it. Other examples of desexualization are even more dismally provided by television's treatment of people with AIDS, indicatively linked in the media – again, often through allusion – to homo- and bi-sexuality.[17]

Detecting sexuality

While non-heterosexual subjectivities may now be named on television, this does not mean that a logic of detection and discovery – in which hints of sexuality are offered as clues to be traced – has simply been eclipsed. This may be best demonstrated today by the hermeneutic of suspicion found in several cop/detective shows that are characterized by their direct enactment of the drive to know.

In this epistemological exercise, solving the mystery of sexual ambiguity and/or identification may overtake even the drive toward solving the crime. For instance, in recent episodes of *Homicide, Law and Order*, and *New York Undercover*, locating homosexuality (usually in the crime victim) is posed as *the* key to 'case' closure (in both senses of the term).

The 17 November 1995 episode of NBC's *Homicide: Life on the Street* is particularly instructive in this regard. In this episode, homicide detectives Tim Bayliss and Frank Pembleton investigate the death of a man killed outside a gay bar, apparently the victim of a gay bashing. Early in the episode, they discover who the murderer is but continue the investigation, merely, it seems, to discover if the victim was, in fact, gay (a 'charge' disputed by his college buddies and one that leads the victim's father to believe that his son is better off dead). The mystery of sexual orientation seems most to disturb Bayliss, who questions his partner about how and at what age a homosexual knows that he is gay. 'Age twenty-six,' Frank matter-of-factly replies. 'At twenty-six, every man determines his sexual preference,' he continues before at last concluding the conversation by pointing out that the very question is 'nonsense.' Nonetheless, the question seems to obsess Bayliss; he insists against Pembleton's wishes on prolonging the investigation and so turns his attention to the 'clues' – not of criminal, but of sexual, behaviour (as occurs, for example, when he visits the home of a family friend of the victim and, noticing the guests at a Thanksgiving celebration that the cops have interrupted, interrogates a woman about her lesbianism).

In the end, the detectives discover that the victim was not gay – that, as Bayliss tells the father, the gay bashing was 'a mistake.' This double-edged assessment of mistaken identity is refined through Bayliss's final understanding of the situation, and it is clear that the moral of the story is that any such confusion doesn't matter: a crime is still a crime. But the amount of narrative energy that has gone into reaching this conclusion seems to belie it, perhaps suggesting (as Frank Pembleton has suggested all along) that any way of asking – and attempting definitively to answer – a question of sexual identity leads to its own absurdities, undoings, and erasures (even if these are not always as dramatic as the literal erasure of a life or the symbolic erasure of what the media like to refer to as a lifestyle). Interestingly, in a later season of *Homicide*, Bayliss begins to question the mystery of his own sexuality and erotic identifications, spurred on by the knowledge of past amorous mistakes. Yet however much the programme might play with and/or critique policing procedures of 'suspect identification' (by, for instance, reversing the roles of suspect and victim or suspect and cop), the very narrative drive of the detective programme incites a desire to solve its enigmas, be these criminal or sexual – or frequently, as elaborated above, a conflation of both.

Conferring sexuality

In contrast, more comic texts may make no effort whatsoever to follow such sexual 'clues' to a conclusion; rather, by holding the question in permanent suspension, these texts encourage an epistemology (and erotics) of 'knowing viewers.' I'm thinking of a programme like *Xena: Warrior Princess*, whose creators acknowledge the centrality of sexual ambiguity to that show's campy fantasy appeal. In commenting on lead character Xena and her sidekick Gabrielle, the couple whose emotional and eroticized bond defines the tenor of the programme even though some episodes feature them in narrative and/or sexual clinches with men, producer Liz Friedman has stated, 'I don't have any interest in 'saying they're heterosexuals.'[18] That she also shows no interest in actually saying that they're lesbians or bisexuals while still providing numerous teasing opportunities for just such readings is equally as clear.

Another notable example of a programme that cheerfully permits viewers to prick at its ostensibly heterosexual surface is the sitcom *Frasier*, which features straight characters created and performed by a number of out-writers and actors, leading to a sense of humour that, if not out-and-out campy, has been seen by some fans as expressing a gay sensibility through its wit and 'knowing' style. Indeed, the style of these two otherwise quite different programmes has been the subject of much debate on, for instance, the internet newsgroups devoted to television or showbiz gossip. The discussions often stress the 'gay feeling' that pervades the shows even – or especially – in the absence of denoted gay characters. In other words, it is precisely the keen and artful presence of a certain absence in the texts – and the accompanying logic of undecidability, incongruity, and allusion – that seems most to mark them as somehow queer. Their queerness is external to these shows in another way as well. That is, as my reference to gossip forums indicates, finding evidence of marginalized sexualities within the episodes may rely as much on intertextual knowledge and extratextual context as it does on the texts themselves; bringing them out depends on what audience group (or set of intertexts) the viewer (or programme) is in. Watching *Xena* alongside an uproarious crowd at a lesbian bar or enjoying *Frasier* in tandem with writer Joe Keenan's comic gay novels (1992; 1988) focuses attention onto certain charged moments in the programmes that seem to nod to those viewers in the know. Such viewers are then reinforced in their interpretations, spurred on to ever more imaginative (or perhaps much more plausible) explanations of the characterological and narrative dynamics.

Enlightening sexuality

Shows that aren't based on a logic of detection (whether tragic or comic, with solvable mysteries or not) may partake in what I see as one of the more interesting permutations of the epistemology of the console, that of the 'knowing character.' Several television shows today feature 'openly' gay or lesbian secondary characters – characters for whom homosexuality is so matter-of-fact that they divest viewers of the self-satisfying pleasure of figuring it out by reading the codes.[19] What they offer instead is their own positioning as repositories of knowledge: we may never know too much about them (after all, they're only secondary characters), but they seem to have privileged access to information or wisdom that other figures lack.

Inverting the trope in which gay characters are introduced only as questions and problems for straight ones to deal with, today's queers may be known without mystery, and this, in fact, seems to make them the most comfortably centered in knowledge of all.[20]

A relatively early (and therefore somewhat fraught) example of this relationship between homosexuality and knowledge is suggested by Sasha Torres's reading of the lesbian character on *HeartBeat* (the first continuous lesbian character in US prime time, introduced in 1988).[21] As Torres explains, the programme generally took a 'universalizing' view of lesbianism, linking Marilyn's homosexuality to the homosociality of the women's clinic at which the characters all worked. In the one episode that did explore Marilyn's 'difference' from the others, however, this difference was displaced 'from her sexual status as a lesbian to her professional status as a nurse practitioner' – a displacement that I would name as precisely the one from sexuality to knowledge because, as Torres elaborates, it involved Marilyn's positive valuation of midwifery as a form of 'women's ways of knowing' over the patriarchal knowledge of conventional medicine (Torres 1993: 181–2). Other examples of TV's treatment of such characters are less conflicted, demonstrating a smoother shift from positioning queers as enigmas commanding some sort of spectatorial curiosity to positioning them as educators (of the viewer as well as of other characters) who need make no such demands.

Consider, for instance, the use of queer men and lesbians on shows as different as *Mad About You*, *My So-Called Life*, *Murder One*, *Party Girl*, *The Real World*, *Dawson's Creek*, *All My Children*, *Party of Five*, *Spin City*, and *Buffy the Vampire Slayer*. *Spin City*'s Carter Heywood, a black gay man, was hired by the mayor to inform him on 'minority issues,' but because of his own sensible perspective among a senseless crowd he's inevitably ignored. School teacher Michael Delany, *All My Children*'s only character in possession of a PhD, acts as the wise confidant for everyone else in the town of Pine Valley, but his own life is never narratively elaborated – not because it's marked as exotically unknowable but precisely because it's presented as already known. It's as if we simply understand the smooth progression of his relationship with his lover, as opposed to the events in the lives of heterosexual characters that are deemed so surprising that they require detailed explication (again suggesting the complications provoked by *any* performance of desire).

In this way, these 'knowing' gay characters of the 1990s are comparable to many African–American characters of the 1980s and still today; though they may have power *within* their narrative worlds, they lack power *over* them, the ability to command narrative attention. Indeed, one of *Ellen*'s producers observes that homosexuals 'have become the new stock character, like the African–American pal at the workplace' (quoted in Handy 1997: 80). An almost identical observation is offered by Rob Epstein, co-director of the documentary film *The Celluloid Closet*: 'It's become a stock character – like what blacks were on television 15 years ago … It seems mandatory to have a gay sidekick' (quoted in Jacobs 1996: 21). Yet these are not just any sidekicks; the particular roles that these secondary characters play reveal something of the complex and crisis-ridden ways in which race and sexuality signify in the American imaginary. The 1980s and early 1990s initiated a number of crime dramas in which blacks and Latinos were presented as police chiefs, minor characters with institutional though rarely narrative authority. In this way, programmes like *Miami Vice*, *21 Jump Street*, *NYPD Blue*, *Law and Order*, and *Homicide: Life on the Street* have maintained an association between people of colour and criminality despite the reversal of positions within the media's usual equation.[22] Overseeing instead of surveilled by the cops (though the latter position has hardly disappeared, merely existing alongside of this new permutation), such characters do not exactly redouble but rather double back on television's discourse on race.

Similarly, television's queer characters may not necessarily play the (still often common) role of obscure objects, loci of mystery, scandal, and uncertainty; instead, they may be figured as devoid of all mystery (and thus potentially of all dramatic interest), more pedagogic than puzzling. But whether enlighteners or enigmas, knowing readers or riddles to be known (however impossible this task is taken to be), TV's gay characters are constructed as epistemological nodal points – crucial in some ways to the production of knowledge if not to the dramas that drive the TV productions. Their position might then even be compared to the problematic place of queers within critical theory itself; as those who most embody a disruption in the logic of binary sexual division, queers can function, to borrow Katie King's (1986) term for another context, as a 'magical sign' of theoretical (particularly deconstructive) knowledge – even if gay, lesbian, bisexual, and transgender people are still disempowered in the actual halls of academe.

Disclosing sexuality

Finally, there is the previously mentioned case of *Ellen*, whose breakout lesbian character seemed to be 'the last to know.' Though there is much more to be said about this case than I can say here (and so I'll engage in a bit of epistemic elision myself and presume that most readers already know at least some things about one of TV's most talked about shows), I'd argue that the most fascinating thing about this programme is the way that it took TV's underlying logic of the closet and actually narrativized it across its (in)famous season. It is then not surprising that, even in its 'uncloseting,' it enacted a return to the epistemology of allusion governing earlier TV texts (in this, it might be seen as a return of the repressed). Indeed, in a replay of many of the tropes outlined above, the series teased viewers with an elaborate game of catch-the-queer, or at least the queer references, long before the lead character's homosexuality was ever explicitly designated or displayed.

That this was a game – an enactment of familiar scenarios, even if its direct engagement with them made *Ellen* stand out as unique – was evident from the way in which the programme both recognized yet rehearsed the rules. In fact, among the 1996–7 season's many hints and allusions, *Ellen* also included moments that seemed to comment on its very deployment of hints and allusions – a self-reflexivity through which the text elaborated as well as narrativized its relation to the logic of the closet.[23] One such instance occurred even in the 1996 season premiere entitled 'Give Me Equity or Give Me Death' (the episode that contains the frequently referenced opening in which Ellen sings to herself in the mirror, 'I feel pretty and witty and ... hey,' when her morning ritual is interrupted by a plumbing problem in her bathroom).[24] Envious of her gay male friends, Peter and Barrett, who have purchased a home, Ellen is tempted to buy a house herself; to encourage her, Peter brings his realtor over to Ellen's apartment to show her pictures of houses for sale. The realtor sets up a slide show in Ellen's living room and provides a running narration for the images, including references to the realtor's own (hetero)sexual exploits, as Peter and Ellen watch on the couch eating popcorn. This home viewing experience (in both senses of the term) is thus set up from the very beginning of the scene as an analogue to television (also primarily a viewing of domestic spaces from within our own domestic space).

The comparison becomes even more pronounced when the realtor attempts to persuade Ellen of the possibilities of her place within this picture by acting out a scene with little dolls (enthusiastically described by Peter as 'like a puppet show of your life'). To the realtor's, 'Just think Ellen; this could be you, walking up to your new home ... and here's your husband coming home from work ... ' Ellen replies 'oh, I think that puppet's in the wrong show,' prompting the slide show's author to toss the male doll aside. A miniature of a miniature (a puppet show of a televisual life), this show-within-the-show might be seen as mapping the trajectory that the rest of the season will take, from Ellen reconsidering her domestic/familial position to her act of coming out – in other words, a thematization of the text's unfinished movement from implicit enactment to explicit thematization of television's epistemology of the closet.

Yet even the culminating moment of Ellen's self-identification does not fully overturn the tropes by which television's treatment of gay subjects are managed; the explicit announcement does not erase TV's implicit (sexual and spectatorial) contract. The episode in which Ellen Morgan comes out of the closet is officially entitled simply 'The Episode,' suggesting that this one text epitomizes the entire *Ellen* epistemology. However, it is commonly referred to (even in some 'official' ABC venues) as 'The Puppy Episode,' supposedly a joke generated by speculation over exactly what Ellen Morgan needed to give her life meaning (perhaps a puppy?). Although 'The Episode' clearly indicates that what Ellen needs is not just a pet, in its evocation of warm and fuzzy affection, this title does hark back to TV's typically desexualizing representation of gays and lesbians. This too then suggests the way in which Ellen's unclosseting simultaneously advances from and retreats into television's conventions for treating queer subjects – most notably through the very logic of suggestion.

Both commenting on and contributing to processes of connotation, *Ellen* thus demonstrated the power and the pathos of this logic of allusion. Before 'The Episode' ever aired, the series of clues planted in interviews, publicity, and extraneous programme gags threatened to overtake the identity they indexed along with the attention paid to the television series' own storylines (most of which had to do with the heterosexual concerns of her parents and pals). Through countless hints, double-entendres, and puns made both off and on the show (Ellen as possibly 'a lefty' or maybe 'Lebanese'), 'lesbian' became an endlessly replaced and replaceable signifier. These innuendos – lines, as *The New York Times* stated, 'repeated so often that they're now familiar to people who have never watched *Ellen*' – made queer-themed 'inside' jokes available to all viewers even when Ellen's homosexuality still remained throughout most of the season 'outside' the sitcom form (Bruni 1996: 40). Curiously, then, the knowledge of the lesbian inside the text was both largely extratextual (the intense search for clues prompted by press leaks, gossip, and finally the producers' announcement that they were considering 'going in [that] direction' [ABC Entertainment President Jamie Tarses quoted in GLAAD Alert 1997]) as well as always already redundant (labeled, again by the *New York Times*, as an 'anti-climax' undermining the programme's potential sexual and epistemic charge).[25]

Of course, the 'been-there-done-that feeling' that the *New York Times* (among many others) attributed to *Ellen*'s never-before-done treatment of this issue corresponds to the programme's general epistemological construction (or lack thereof) (Bruni 1996: 1). Often described as a *Seinfeld*-clone without even that show's structuring cohesion, *Ellen* seemed to lack an epistemic center, a definitive identity for its lead to provide the programme with an organizing principle. Yet however indistinct, Ellen was the central character around which this text revolved, making the stakes of her sexual status different than those of the secondary queer characters previously named. The challenge – as well as the potential promise – for viewers may then have been found in learning how to accept a change in a well-known character, one who ironically was known for not really knowing herself.

However, this does not necessarily pose a challenge to the logic of the closet. There was still no coherent queer epistemology (whatever that might be) ordering the text; though some episodes in the last season did initiate new trajectories in Ellen's life (and, arguably, in television's treatment of sexuality), these existed in tension with the show's already established focus on Ellen's relations with her (probably needless to point out, insistently heterosexual) community of family and friends. As stated even by one of *Ellen*'s executive producers, Ellen thus became a homosexual in a 'heterosexual situation,'[26] the sitcom highlighting precisely (in an inversion of the trope of all those knowing gay sidekicks) an unsure, unsophisticated, unknowing queer. Still defined by an aura of confusion (though perhaps one now thematized rather than just acted out), *Ellen* marks an absent center within a field of knowledge, indeed marks the way in which that knowledge is always absent from itself.

For if, as Sedgwick compellingly argues, sexuality is inextricable from what counts as knowledge in our culture, then it is impossible simply to define a programme of knowing sexuality.[27] This, of course, is as true of television programmes as it is of academic ones. The question of what exactly the viewers of queer TV texts know must thus remain an open one. In considering the effects of our – and television's – pedagogical practices, however, it is nonetheless interesting to speculate on the epistemology that might govern future viewings of past *Ellens* – previous seasons that have already been sold to run on the Lifetime cable channel. For viewers of those shows, will knowing that Ellen will have already come out of a closet still closed in the rerun they're watching alter the terms of TV's epistemological contract, fully confounding the relationship between in and out? This question is difficult to answer, not least because of its formulation in the future perfect tense.[28] But this 'televisually tensed' construction does not at all suggest that such mediated acts of coming out will guarantee a perfect future; however noteworthy in television history, Ellen's revelation need not herald a new sexual nor even TV age.[29] Yet the very confounding of conventional logic that such an internally inverted formulation produces itself indicates the ways in which television might, if not actually discard, at least disturb some of the presupposed terms that delimit sexuality and our own means of knowing.

Epilogue: a buy out?

However much this last case may have begun to shift, or at least make explicit, the terms of televisual time and space, knowledge and sex, that incite the logic of the closet, there is one aspect of US commercial television unlikely to be upset by this, or any other of the permutations that I've mentioned: the logic of the commodity. Indeed, the statement made above – that Ellen has 'already been sold' – suggests more than just the fact that syndication rights to the series have been purchased; more generally, it points to the way in which the series and its star have been commodified and, from that, to larger issues of television commodification.

Despite the strange bedfellows thereby created, it is not unexpected that the intersection of Ellen's/Ellen's drama of coming out and the television industry's own drama of commodification was a matter of concern to a number of otherwise very different groups. An array of viewers and critics presumed that the programme's steady diet of clues leading up to the actual announcement episode was nothing but a bald marketing ploy on the part of Ellen's producers at ABC and Touchstone Television (both owned by the Walt Disney Company). From the initial leak to the news media ('conveniently timed,' Entertainment Weekly stated, 'to coincide with the sagging sitcom's Sept. 18 season premiere' [Jacobs 1996: 20]); through the long trajectory of publicity-generating buzz and speculation; across scheduling changes to ensure 'safe' consumption of the show (a move to a later time slot); incorporating DeGeneres' own disclosure in the 14 April issue of Time magazine; and finally to the moment when character Ellen Morgan herself proclaims she's gay during the first week of the 1997 May sweeps period (in which advertising rates are set according to a programme's Nielson ratings): to many this seemed like simply a season-long sales pitch for the series. And a successful one at that – with an estimated 42 million viewers watching, 'The Episode' was said to have reaped the year's highest ratings of both any sitcom and any ABC show).[30]

Yet there was payment as much as profit. As mentioned, the commodification of Ellen's/Ellen's yawning closet door elicited a range of reactions from a range of parties. Many people of varying political persuasions were troubled by what they saw as a harmful mix of consumerism and gay politics (either because of the harm caused by any consumption of a 'gay lifestyle,' or because of the harm caused by having such a serious issue sullied by consumer exchange).[31] DeGeneres herself seemed concerned about what this might do to her future earning power. Well aware of her own position within the TV industry, she remarked on more than one occasion that 'I'm the one who's going to get the biggest boycott. ... I'm the product here,' and even went so far as to plead in her *20/20* interview, 'Please buy me!'[32] As for others selling products, several of the programme's regular sponsors pulled their ads from 'The Episode,' including Chrysler (which set up a toll-free phone line to register reactions to their decision), General Motors, J.C. Penney, Johnson and Johnson, and Wendy's. Despite this ad soundbite-flight, ABC still refused some commercials offered in their place: a thirty second anti-discrimination appeal from the Human Rights Campaign, and an ad for Olivia Cruise Lines, a business owned by and geared toward lesbians. The last case is especially peculiar. Rejecting the ad in an apparently prophylactic segregation of TV's commercial spots from TV's (commercial) programmes, ABC stated that 'discussion about same-sex lifestyles is more appropriate in programming' (quoted by Kelty 1997: 16), thus disavowing the very fact of broadcast flow through this denial that television commercials are an intrinsic (indeed *the* most crucial) part of the programming schedule.

Yet what is missed, I would argue, by all of these reactions against the supposedly unnatural combination of *Ellen*'s story of the closet and televisual consumerism/commodification is the way in which the logic of commodity is already related to the logic of the closet. In other words, there is no pure space of gay self-disclosure uncontaminated by relations of consumerism and commodification, just as there is no pure space of consumerism uncontaminated by what we might see as closet relations. For as Marx explains in his discussion of 'The Fetishism of the Commodity and its Secret,' (1977) the commodity itself has a dual form, already exhibiting an inside/outside paradox much like the one associated with the epistemology of the closet. Though it seems as if the commodity has a pre-existent internal truth (its own self-generated identity and value), this sense of an inner reality is only created through its outer circulation, through the 'external' – that is, social – relations of production and exchange. Indeed, the 'secret' of the commodity is created precisely through what Marx calls the 'intercourse' between objects made comparable to one another – 'socially uniform,' of 'common character' and similar 'semblance,' that is, objects that are 'homo' to one another – though this social relation must itself be disavowed (or might we say closeted?) (Marx 1977). Thus, though DeGeneres stated near the beginning of the season that 'it's not just "Ellen buys a table" this year,' (quoted in Jacobs 1996: 20) she was only half right: it is not Ellen but *Ellen*'s viewers who, in effect, 'buy a table,' who consume a product perceived through an epistemology of the commodity that is very much like the epistemology of the closet itself. And like Marx's famous table that 'as soon as it emerges as a commodity ... not only stands with its feet on the ground, but, in relation to all other commodities ... stands on its head,' Ellen too necessarily becomes through this process 'a thing which transcends sensuousness,' her homosexuality now an objectified and consumable – rather than simply erotic – form (Marx 1977: 163).

Never one to miss the opportunity for a joke, DeGeneres herself spoofed this combined logic of the commodity and closet. On *The Tonight Show with Jay Leno* that aired on NBC the same night as 'The Episode' aired on a competing network, Leno interviewed actress Anne Heche, DeGeneres's girlfriend, also under fire for using their relationship as a publicity stunt. Asked whether Ellen came to the show with her, Heche replied 'Well, yeah, she's here ... she goes everywhere with me,' at which point there's a cut backstage to reveal DeGeneres, supposedly unaware of the camera, talking on the phone: I'm at the *Tonight Show* with Anne. This is ridiculous. When she approached me with the idea of, like, getting together for publicity, I thought 'fine, O.K., I'll do it for you,' but I need more money ... this is going to hurt my image, do you understand what I'm saying? I can't be seen with her like this. No, no, no, it's not over now. She wants me to stay until people know how to pronounce her last name ... Just ask for more money 'cause I can't keep this up.' She then hangs up the phone, exclaiming to herself, 'My husband and kids are going to kill me.'[33] In this extended gag that takes aim at both sales and sexual presumptions, DeGeneres exposes, through double reversals, the logic of the commodity and the logic of the closet (indeed, exposes the link between the two), suggesting in the process the ambivalent effects of this very linkage.

Still, a joke that mocks the commodification of gay identity, with whatever fatal wit, does not erase it; indeed, ultimately, it was this very commodity logic that killed *Ellen* (in the process, at least according to DeGeneres's own rhetoric, killing Ellen herself). In the 1997–8 season, the show's ratings plummeted, making it difficult, ABC executives claimed, for them to sell airtime to advertisers. Countering that explanation, DeGeneres claimed that it was ABC that failed to sell the show; they misplaced it in the network lineup and refused to advertise it with the same vigour as their other programmes.[34] There were also conflicts over content: one, for example, involved a dispute over the filming of a kiss. Making an interesting comparison, DeGeneres noted, in a *PrimeTime Live* interview with Diane Sawyer, that ABC had publicized episodes of other sitcoms with same-sex kisses – specifically, those in which the protagonists got their kisses as ploys in sexual masquerades (as occurred, for instance, on *The Drew Carey Show* and *Spin City*, both of which aired stories in which their leads pretended to be gay). Only *Ellen*, with an 'actual gay' protagonist, not only received no promotion for its 'kiss episodes' (even one in which the kiss is 'fake' even if Ellen's sexuality is 'real'), but garnered a parental advisory warning as well.[35]

The issue behind these institutional battles was, of course, whether, as Chastity Bono of the Gay and Lesbian Alliance Against Defamation put it, *Ellen* had become 'too gay'; after Ellen Morgan came to the knowledge of her sexuality, many of the 1997–8 episodes detailed her growing knowledge of gay/lesbian life (learning the ins and outs of a relationship, developing a familiarity with gay politics and people) – material that raised controversies over notions of relevancy, awareness, and audiences' ability to 'relate.'[36] According to some, in its attempt to narrativize the logic of the closet, *Ellen* had become harpingly pedagogical; according to others (including DeGeneres herself), it was important to use the programme as an educational device. Yet to attempt to use TV's famed 'intimacy' as a tool for teaching about new intimate pairings is to risk neglecting the anxiety (often siphoned off as laughter) that accompanies TV's treatment of sex. Eschewing the comedy typically found in sitcom pairings, Ellen's search for a mate was presented in more serious terms, pushing at the limits of the show's genre in order to show how gender need not be a limit to TV's vision of romance. The questions, then, over what's too gay or not gay enough, what's 'funny that way' or what's simply queer, whether the show was 'too different' or 'too all the same,' overly demonstrative or underappreciative in instructing viewers on reading the text, revealed once again that the door of the closet can swing both ways, that sexual knowingness remains a fault line for knowing TV.[37]

Both supporting and refuting the idea that *Ellen* was, as ABC president Robert Iger put it, plagued by 'sameness,' the programme's final episode inserted *Ellen* into an honoured trajectory of TV history.[38] Linking *Ellen* to past and present TV texts, the one-hour finale, a 'mockumentary' on groundbreaking television, alternated 'interviews' with cast and 'commentators' (largely other television personalities) with scenes of Ellen's 'appearances' in a number of key televisual moments (the first on-air pregnancy, à la *I Love Lucy*; the introduction of political rhetoric in situation comedy, à la *All in the Family*, and so on). Clearly, this was meant as a sort of self-congratulation for the series' groundbreaking status as the first prime-time programme to feature a gay or lesbian lead;[39] or was it? In the final moments of the show, DeGeneres explains *her* understanding of the programme's watershed event: she was the first prime-time figure ever honestly to reveal her age on television. To punctuate, DeGeneres replays lines from her famous speech in 'The Episode.' 'Why do I have to be ashamed? I mean, why can't I just see the truth? I mean, be who I am, I'm thirty-five years old' – and then abruptly stops the tape.

Which brings me back to my opening example of *Roseanne*. As I noted in describing the episode 'Skeleton in the Closet,' the Connor family pranks also couple performances of sexuality with performances of age – both of which incite anxieties over the ambiguities of body and identity (that show's bombshell that age and sexual orientation, involving not simply categorization but lived instantiation, might not be as certain and determined as we think). For commercial television, which must keep its texts both steadily familiar yet refreshingly alive, the uncertainty of the new and the inevitability of growing old pose equal threats. In their masquerades, members of the Connor family mock both fears, miming the awkward pangs of self- (and other-) discovery and the horrors of premature decline. As indicated above, in describing her rebirth and decline, DeGeneres also used a rhetoric of death. In an interview about her programme's cancellation, she told

Entertainment Weekly, 'And now I'm dead,' to which Heche, also at the interview, added: 'That's it. Being married to a dead person, it's cool, it's different. We've already done the gay thing' (quoted in Cagle 1998: 28). And so, apparently, had television. The shock of the new quickly gave rise to the tedium of the old – surely a death blow for a text in a medium that stakes its claim on up-to-date liveness.

But not to worry. As Eve Sedgwick reminds us, as long as we locate ourselves within an epistemological space mapped by the terms of life/death, inside/outside, public/private, secrecy/disclosure – as, I've suggested, US TV does – sexuality will remain a pressing issue, one both bothersome and banal.[40] The logic of the closet will thus always be available for televisual resuscitation – something more than demonstrated by the public/private, sensational/deadening drama of what even *TV Guide* came to call 'ClintonTV.'[41] A less momentous (or perhaps less monotonous) example, but one that relates more directly to the other examples I've given (because, in fact, it reiterates all of them) is the recent NBC show *Will & Grace*. Cited in many stories concerning DeGeneres's battles, *Will & Grace* was frequently brought up (or brought out) in the popular press as a demonstration that *Ellen*'s demise need not be taken as a sign of television's resistance to gay and lesbian content.

Given my argument that television has not simply been resistant to gay con-tent – that its position on the precarious border of the many oppositions I've listed demands some engagement with questions of sexuality just as it demands their disavowal – I would not necessarily disagree. But this upholds, rather than undoes, the tele-epistemology I've described. Indeed, in bringing homosexuality back to televisual life, *Will & Grace* also resuscitates the many strategies of 'know-ing sexuality' previously elaborated. Because, unlike *Ellen*, *Will & Grace*'s Will was introduced as gay from the very start, the network didn't have to imagine how to have him (and us) come to this knowledge. Yet, in revealing television's anxious attempt to draw a distinction between the attribution of sexuality and the enact-ment of desire, Will is, in effect, placed in a male/female couple, as the show is centered on his relationship with his female roommate/soulmate, the aforemen-tioned Grace. His best friend, Jack, the other gay man on the show, is also, to some degree, teamed with a woman (thematically if not emotionally), Grace's friend Karen. Further, Jack seems to combine almost all of the other strategies in one (the knowing secondary character whose life doesn't get the attention, the obvious stereotype turned into camp, the object of jokes based on hints and innuendos, and so on).

In other words, if *Ellen* can be seen as narrativizing, not just symptomatizing, TV's logic of the closet, then *Will & Grace* might be seen as spatializing this logic – adding dimension by exhibiting (whether knowingly or not) all of the permutations in one half-hour show. Perhaps, in that way, it implicitly performs the range of the textual/sexual moves that I've tried explicitly to map. But this is not to say that explicit announcement (whether of the television theorist or the television text) is a means of escaping the epistemological trajectories I've discussed; like a televi-sion console whose exterior is made to be displayed while the actual workings are hidden within, such announcements may repackage or reframe, but not necessarily short-circuit the system (though, as I've suggested, it is likely to short-circuit itself). In other words, I hope that I have demonstrated that in formulating a politics of representation, we need not – indeed, should not – simply ask for more (more disclosure, more true-to-life drama, more explicit imagery), that the explicit revelation of sexuality on commercial television need not explode the logic of the closet. For that, taking a lesson from *Roseanne*, we might just have to blow up the whole house.

Notes

1. These points are obviously indebted to both Michel Foucault's and Eve Kosofsky Sedgwick's groundbreaking work on knowledge, discourse, and sexuality, most especially to Foucault's books *Discipline and Punish* (1978a) and *The History of Sexuality, Vol.1* (1978b), and Sedgwick's books *The Epistemology of the Closet* (1990) and *Tendencies* (1993).
2. While I, unfortunately, cannot elaborate all of the arguments that have been made critiquing the association of visibility with knowledge and liberation, let me just briefly gloss my critique of the notion that sexual orientation should be as indelibly visible 'as race and gender.' For one, this is mistakenly to assume that gender and race *are* simply 'visible' and thus to accept a way of classifying sexual and racial differences that has an extremely troubling history. Second, it is to ignore theories that have demonstrated how 'visibility' certainly need not operate in any liberating way, as feminist analyses of women constructed as disempowered 'objects to be seen' have emphasized. And while the emphasis may differ in arguments about media treatments of 'racial minorities' (in that, as with queer subjects, there have been more than understandable demands for greater visibility and representation), here too we must consider how the visibility of some might operate at the detriment of others, how visual 'representation' (in the sense of depiction) need not equal political 'representation' (in the sense of delegatory democracy), and how the specific strategies of representation (rather than visible representation *per se*) are key to the production of meaning. Given these points, it may seem curious that 'visibility' has become *the* dominant rallying point in queer politics. One rationale lies in the enormous importance of visual media themselves in historically helping to articulate queer identities and communities. Another reason, I would suggest, is the association typically made between visibility and permanency (as in my use of the phrase 'indelibly visible'), which may then seem to offer more stable ground for making right claims than a 'changeable' identity can. Indeed, our society has tended to align the notions of permanent and changeable not only with visible and invisible (or only capriciously visible) but with the nature/nurture, biology/social construction, and now genetic/choice oppositions concerning 'explanations' for same-sex attractions. While queer movements have, at different times, turned to various arguments about this, today's discourses are more likely to propose that, if same-sex attraction is genetic (and thus ultimately visible to science), it must then be respected and protected as a category. Yet the violently eugenic fantasies on the part of some people that finding a 'gay gene' may offer the possibility of eradicating it are more than enough to indicate the problems here – and, of course, whether queer desires and/or identifications are changeable or not must make no difference in arguments about the right to be respected

and valued. Finally, adding to the ambivalence around these categories is the fact that today's queer communities themselves are likely to conceptualize the alignments of visibility and permanency (vs. 'trying out' the appearance and/or disappearance of an identity 'by choice') quite distinctly when it comes to making analogies with gender or making them with race: for example, transgendered people have been discussed in quite different ways than have people who are said to be attempting to 'change race' (with, for instance, media icon Michael Jackson often being used as a symbol of both impulses). Obviously, I can't (and wouldn't even want to) try to settle this ambivalence here; but any analysis of these very complex issues would have to go beyond focusing on the supposedly individual 'pathologies' – or individual bravery – of the specific subjects who may visibly seem to embody these issues instead to consider the wider social dynamics in which they are located.

3. My analysis of 'Skeleton in the Closet' (which aired on ABC on 26 October 1994) is indebted to discussions with the graduate students in my fall 1994 course titled 'Seminar in Mass Culture: Sexuality and Representation,' especially to insights provided by Amelie Hastie and Jeff King, and to King in his paper "'Skeleton in the Closet": *Roseanne* on the Limits of Gay and Lesbian Representation' (unpublished manuscript, 1995).

4. See also White (1991) and Parsi (1996).

5. The Code was abolished in favour of an age-based rating system in 1968.

6. Diana Fuss discusses the entanglement of 'in' and 'out' and the way in which even 'the first coming out was also simultaneously a closeting' (1991: 4).

7. See Paulin (1996), Dyer (1993), and the essays in the collections edited by Bad Object-Choices (1991), Burston and Richardson (1995), Creekmur and Doty (1995), and Wilton (1995).

8. Federal Communications Commission (1988): 2. The television industry first submitted a proposal for a television rating system to the Federal Communications Commission as a result of the 1996 Telecommunications Act. This was a voluntary agreement – forged, however, under the threat of mandated rule if the industry and the FCC could not agree. In 1997, programme producers and suppliers were employing a code that demarcated age-appropriate viewing: shows could be rated TV-Y (children's programming deemed appropriate for kids aged 2 and above); TV-Y7 (programmes made for older children); TV-G (shows not specifically made for children but still appropriate for a general audience); TV-PG (recommending parental guidance); TV-14 (recommending guidance for children under 14); or TV-MA (suggested for mature audiences only). After some debate initiated by citizen and children's advocacy groups, representatives of the television industry submitted a more detailed proposal, approved by the FCC in March 1998, that included the content indicators: FV (to indicate fantasy violence in children's programming); V (violence); S (sexual content); L (adult language); and D (suggestive dialogue). These codes are designed to work in conjunction with the V–chip, which will allow viewers to block programming based on either age or content indicators (or some combination of both). Television set manufacturers were required to include such blocking technology in at least half of all thirteen-inch or larger sets by 1 July 1999; all models that are thirteen inches or larger must have had the V–chip by 1 January 2000. For those who want access to V–chip technology without purchasing a new TV, there are set top converter boxes that can be hooked up to older models.

9. As of this time (2001), NBC and the cable channel BET are still displaying the suggested age categories, not the content indicators, while movie channels simply

use the film rating system (also age-based, but involving a slightly different set of symbols); news and sports programming is unrated. (The irony of this – at a time when reference to oral sex and other 'salacious' material has become a staple of news reports since the Clinton sex scandals – no doubt goes without saying). Adding to the problem of a lack of uniformity is the fact that it is the programme producers/distributors themselves who determine their shows' ratings (though, in theory, this is overseen by a monitoring board); an oft-cited example of the ensuing inconsistency is that David Letterman's late night talk show on CBS is rated TV-PG while Jay Leno's NBC show (airing during the same time slot) is rated TV-14. Finally, there is the question of viewer comprehension (how many people, for instance, understand the distinction between D, for suggestive dialogue, and L, for adult language?) *TV Guide* provides the ratings for most programmes in its schedules (though very inconsistently; the notations are sometimes included in programme advertisements, 'close-up' features, and/or actual schedule listings, but they do not always appear), but it does not include a key code that defines them; such a code is available from cable services if requested by subscribers.

10. Lynn Spigel's work has contributed a great deal toward tracing the historical negotiations around television's place within the public/private divide; see Spigel (1992).

11. Diane Sawyer, interview with Ellen DeGeneres, 25 April 1997, *20/20*.

12. This is the magazine issue in which DeGeneres announces, 'Yep, I'm Gay' in bold letters on the cover.

13. See 'The Body Electric,' 5 April 1997, *Dr. Quinn, Medicine Woman*.

14. White argues that 'the television apparatus modif[ies] and reconfigure[s] the very nature of therapy and confession as practices for producing social and individual identities and knowledge' (1992: 7; see also 8–9).

15. *Love, Sidney* ran on NBC from 1981 to 1983. This was not, however, the first prime-time television series to feature a regular gay character. Jodie Dallas (played by Billy Crystal) appeared on ABC's *Soap* from 1977 to 1981. Of course, given the way in which (as its title indicates) that programme was modeled (comically) on a soap opera, Jodie was not the lead character nor was he the only one to arouse scandal; the show received numerous complaints before it even aired. Though Jodie's identity as 'a homosexual' was explored (satirically, as with everything else on the show), *Soap* conflated issues of sexuality with issues of gender (as in a story line involving Jodie's desire to change his sex), and, like *Dynasty*'s later treatment of its 'homosexual' character Stephen Carrington (introduced on ABC in 1981), *Soap* had Jodie flip-flop in his sexual orientation. Other early representations of homosexuality on television include: *CBS Reports: The Homosexuals*, the first nationally aired documentary on the subject (CBS, 1967); *That Certain Summer*, the first made-for-TV movie with a gay theme (ABC, 1972, dir. Lamont Johnson); *All My Children*, which featured daytime television's first homosexual character (the child psychologist Lynn Carson, who was introduced to the ABC soap in 1983); and *An Early Frost*, the first TV movie about AIDS (NBC, 1985, dir. John Erman).

16. Demonstrating the struggles around this is the case of *thirtysomething*; in 1989, it showed a gay male couple in bed talking. Although the performance of their relationship consisting of nothing more than a pre-sleep discussion, this visual acknowledgement of a gay relationship (as opposed to simply naming the characters as gay) itself was considered scandalous enough to incite a boycott of the programme, and ABC pulled the episode so that it would not appear in reruns.

17. For discussions of television and homosexuality that elaborate these strategies of desexualization and/or non-performance (and offer additional television examples), see, among others, the essays by Netzhammer and Shamp, Hantzis and Lehr, Moritz and Gross in Ringer (1994); Gross (1989); and Kennedy (1997).

18. Liz Friedman, quoted in *Reuters/Variety Entertainment Summary*, www.clarinet. com, 13 April 1997.

19. Cindy Patton (1995) makes a similar argument about the lesbian character in the film *Internal Affairs*.

20. The trope of the gay character as a question or problem for the straight one may be most pronounced in TV movies about sons with AIDS; see, for example, Leo (1989).

21. Another early example is provided by daytime television's first lesbian character, *All My Children*'s Dr. Lynn Carson, a therapist who served as the wise and caring advisor for many of the show's other characters – in particular, the confused Devon McFadden. The description of the Lynn and Devon characters and plot offered by a commemorative volume put out to celebrate *All My Children*'s twenty-fifth anniversary perhaps best suggests how complex and fraught TV's strategy of the 'knowing character' can be. Found in a section of the volume titled 'Issues and Answers: Homosexuality,' the description goes as follows: 'In 1983, Devon McFadden was drawn to her doctor, Lynn Carson, daytime's first admitted lesbian character. The doctor/patient relationship grew complicated when a confused Devon declared her feelings for Lynn. The doctor proved to be an understanding friend as she gently helped Devon realize she was heterosexual' (Warner 1994: 79). In other words, the way that this 'admitted' lesbian demonstrated her wisdom and 'understanding' was precisely by convincing a woman interested in dating her that this potential lover was, in fact, heterosexual.

22. Most (but not all) of the characters in the above mentioned programmes are men; a related phenomenon involves the prevalence of, in particular, black female judges on law shows. This also articulates a connection between people of colour and criminality, but here, the terms of reversal might be seen more specifically as judgment/lack of judgment (the latter, of course, defining the common stereotype of the sexually active teenage girl and/or the unwed crack mother, both standard media images of women of colour).

23. Indeed, this self-reflexivity occurred even at the moment of coming out in 'The Episode': after struggling to actually name herself as gay, Ellen finally does manage to get the word out – while unwittingly leaning into a microphone hooked up to an airport loudspeaker. Through this enactment of a different kind of public broadcasting, the programme thus underscores the very public nature of Ellen Morgan's – and Ellen DeGeneres's – declaration; see 'The Episode,' *Ellen*, 30 April 1997.

24. 'Give Me Equity or Give Me Death,' *Ellen*, 18 September 1996.

25. The comment that *Ellen*'s premise was already an 'anticlimax' comes from Andrew Sullivan, quoted in Bruni 1996: 1.

26. 'Ellen Morgan is still in a very heterosexual situation … Almost all her friends are heterosexuals.' Dava Savel, one of *Ellen*'s three executive producers, quoted by Handy 1997: 85.

27. As Sedgwick writes, 'modern "sexuality" and hence modern homosexuality are so intimately entangled with the historically distinctive contexts and structures that now count as *knowledge* that such "knowledge" can scarcely be a transparent window onto a separate realm of sexuality but, rather, itself constitutes that sexuality' (1990: 44; see also 2 and 34).

28. The future perfect is defined as '1. perfect with respect to a temporal point of reference in time to come; completed with respect to a time in the future, esp. when incomplete with respect to the present' (Stein 1988: 537).

29. The purpose of this discussion is thus not simply to suggest more 'positive' modes of representing gay men, lesbians, bisexuals, and transgendered people on television (though it would doubtlessly be preferable to have queer characters that don't just die from murder, suicide, or AIDS – often all equated in TV representation – and that don't either just disappear from the screen or appear only asexually), but to analyze why and how TV's queers are represented as they are at this particular time. In other words, it is to question what investments – in knowledge and in sexuality – current US television has and how these investments might be transformed and/or differently performed.

30. *Reuters/Variety Entertainment Summary*, www.clarinet.com, 1 May 1997.

31. 'The Episode' itself made reference to the relationship between consumerism and gay politics, mocking in particular the fear of homosexuals as predators on – that is, untrustworthy consumers of – heterosexuals. In the story, Ellen meets Susan (played by Laura Dern), a lesbian colleague of Ellen's old boyfriend. Though growing more and more attracted to Susan across the episode, Ellen initially denies these feelings, becoming, in fact, quite defensive about their implications. When Susan assumes, from various 'clues,' that Ellen is also a lesbian, Ellen asserts, 'I think I know what's going on … It's not enough for you to be gay; you've got to recruit others.' Susan wryly replies: 'Well, I'll just call National Headquarters and tell them I lost you. Damn, just one more and I would've gotten that toaster oven.' ('The Episode,' 30 April 1997, *Ellen*). Taking aim at both sexual and commodity stereotypes, this joke thus plays on several levels, satirizing the notion of 'gay recruitment' precisely by linking it to consumer desires – and especially to a consumable object typically associated with heterosexual marriage (the toaster oven, the classic example of a wedding shower gift yet here redefined as a reward for a kind of lesbian 'consumption.').

32. DeGeneres's comments about a boycott are quoted by Handy 1997: 85; her plea to 'buy me' was made in an interview on *20/20* (Sawyer, interview with DeGeneres, 25 April 1997).

33. Jay Leno, interview with Anne Heche, 30 April 1997, *The Tonight Show with Jay Leno*.

34. See, for instance, DeGeneres's comments quoted in Jacobs (1996) in *Entertainment Weekly* (the issue with 'Yep, She's Too Gay' printed on the cover, harkening back, of course, to her previous 'Yep, I'm Gay' *Time* cover article); and Cagle 1998.

35. DeGeneres made this observation in a *PrimeTime Live* interview with Diane Sawyer, 6 May 1998.

36. Chastity Bono's comments were widely reported. For one take on the incident (and DeGeneres' reaction), see, for instance, Cagle 1998: 30.

37. Related to this question of whether *Ellen* became 'too different' or 'too all the same' is the generic and style vacillation that the show experienced in the 1997–8 season. For instance, *Entertainment Weekly* complained that 'the show fluctuated from merely poignant (Ellen visits her girlfriend in the hospital) to broadly comic (Ellen at a wake in a chicken suit)' and that the supporting cast members 'were often relegated to deep background.' (Cagle 1998: 30). Shifting between melodrama and slapstick, instruction and inanity, gay themes and heterosexual norms, the programme lacked any cohesive identity – despite the fact that the programme's mission now seemed to be to clarify an identity for its title character (and for gays and lesbians on TV in general).

38. ABC president Robert Iger made this comment to Diane Sawyer in the *Prime-Time Live* story about the cancellation of *Ellen* (Sawyer, interview with Iger, 6 May 1998, *PrimeTime Live*). To Iger's claim, 'The audience left primarily due to *sameness* – not gayness, sameness,' Sawyer responded, 'Well, she is gay every week, though... Paul Reiser is heterosexual every single week.' Sawyer then asked Iger to compare this situation concerning sexuality to one concerning race: 'You wouldn't ask a black person to be a little less black.' Iger's reply: 'Society... is more used to differences in race.' This slippage between gayness and sameness, and then, immediately thereafter, between gayness and difference, is very telling not only in light of my comments above about television's pedagogic potential through sameness and difference but also in light of Sedgwick's more general point about homosexuality and the founding conceptual oppositions (including the binary same/different) of our culture's epistemology. The exchange is also, of course, telling in the conjunctions and disjunctions it articulates between US TV's treatment of sexuality and its treatment of race.

39. Despite the self-congratulatory stance of *Ellen*'s finale, the show nonetheless once again mocked the combined logic of the commodity and closet previously discussed. For instance, to interviewer Linda Ellerbee's exclamation that 'over 40 million people watched that show ['The Puppy Episode'],' Ellen replied, 'if I had known we'd get that kind of number, I would have called it the "everybody who's watching please send me a dollar" episode.' When, later, DeGeneres suggested that the programme's groundbreaking moment involved not the announcement of her sexuality but the announcement of her age, Ellerbee, taken aback, said, 'Maybe I'm mistaken but I thought telling people you were gay was the whole point of the episode.' DeGeneres responded, 'Really? No, no, that's just the spin the network put on it. They're gay-crazy over there.' While denying that this was either her motive or her understanding of the text (though still expressing anxiety over her financial position), DeGeneres still acknowledges (however satirically) the profit that both ABC and Ellen herself might be able to accrue by capitalizing on this supposed gay-craze. ('*Ellen*: A Hollywood Tribute,' 13 May 1998, *Ellen*).

40. Thus, though DeGeneres remarked to Diane Sawyer, 'You can't just come out and then go back in the closet,' I am suggesting that such 'coming out and going back in' indeed defines television's epistemological movement (even if not the actual movement of actors in the US TV industry) – or, more accurately, that television confounds the distinctions between in and out so that these two positions cannot simply be posed as oppositions but are instead mutually implicated in the medium as it's been historically organized in this country (Sawyer, interview with DeGeneres, 6 May 1998, *PrimeTime Live*).

41. *TV Guide* introduced 'ClintonTV,' penned by Andrew Ferguson, as a new section to provide 'continuing coverage of the scandal' at the beginning of October 1998. In the inaugural column, Ferguson notes how 'the medium of television had absorbed the scandal and transformed it, making it its own ... The scandal has become great TV – and in so doing has revealed the strengths and weaknesses of TV itself' (1998: 34). What Ferguson is interested in is television's capacity for 'live' coverage, 'immediacy,' and 'speed.' According to him, 'everything was exposed, instantaneously' (35), yielding a populist free-for-all that threatens standards of legitimacy and authority; at risk, Ferguson suggests, is 'journalism as a profession, [and] journalists as specialized practitioners doing work that requires concentration and expertise and a sense of detachment' (42). While I am also interested in how television makes such sex

scandals 'its own,' thus revealing 'the strengths and weaknesses of TV itself,' I am less concerned with defending traditional journalistic standards of epistemic authority and legitimacy than in analyzing a framing tele-epistemology that leads TV critics such as Ferguson to describe television in terms of both exposure and obscurity, concentration and distraction, close participation and reasoned detachment.

References

Altman, R. (1986), 'Television/Sound' in T. Modleski (ed.) *Studies in Entertainment: Critical Approaches to Mass Culture*, Bloomington, IN: Indiana University Press, 39–54.

Bad Object-Choices (ed.) (1991), *How Do I Look? Queer Film and Video*, Seattle, WA: Bay Press.

Brooks, T. and Marsh, E. (1992), *The Complete Directory to Prime Time Network TV Shows, 1946–Present*, 5th edn, New York: Ballantine Books.

Bruni, F. (1996), 'It May Be a Closet Door, But It's Already Open,' *The New York Times*, 13 October, Arts and Leisure, Section 2, National edn, 40.

Burston, P. and Richardson, C. (eds) (1995), *A Queer Romance: Lesbians, Gay Men and Popular Culture*, London: Routledge.

Cagle, J. (1998), 'As Gay as it Gets?' *Entertainment Weekly* 431(8 May): 27–32.

Creekmur, C.K. and Doty, A. (eds) (1995), *Out in Culture: Gay, Lesbian, and Queer Essays on Popular Culture*, Durham, NC, and London: Duke University Press.

Dyer, R. (1993), *The Matter of Images: Essays on Representations*, London and New York: Routledge.

Federal Communications Commission (1988), *Commission Finds Industry Video Programming Rating System Acceptable; Adopts Technical Requirements to Enable Blocking of Video Programming*, 12 March, Rept. GN 98–3.

Ferguson, A. (1998), 'The Power of Babble,' *TV Guide*, issue 2375 (3 October): 34–5, 42.

Foucault, M. (1978a), *Discipline and Punish: The Birth of the Prison*, trans. A. Sheridan, New York: Pantheon.

—— (1978b), *The History of Sexuality, Volume 1: An Introduction*, trans. R. Hurley, New York: Pantheon.

Fuss, D. (1991), 'Inside/Out' in Fuss (ed.), *Inside/Out: Lesbian Theories, Gay Theories*, London and New York: Routledge, 1–10.

GLAAD Alert (1997), 'ABC Holding Key to Ellen's Closet, Taking Five Gay Characters Off Air', 10 January.

Gross, L. (1989), 'Out of the Mainstream: Sexual Minorities and the Mass Media' in E. Seiter et al. (eds) *Remote Control: Television, Audiences, and Cultural Power*, New York: Routledge, 130–49.

Handy, B. (1997), 'Roll Over, Ward Cleaver,' *Time*, 14 April: 80–2.

Jacobs, A.J. (1996), 'Out?' *Entertainment Weekly* 347(4 October).

Keenan, J. (1988), *Blue Heaven*, New York: Plume.

—— (1992), *Putting on the Ritz*, New York: Plume.

Kelty, M. (1997), 'The Outing of Ellen,' *LGNY* (11 May): 16.

Kennedy, R. (1997), 'The Gorgeous Lesbian in *L.A. Law*: The Present Absence?' in C. Brunsdon et al. (eds) *Feminist Television Criticism: A Reader*, Oxford: Oxford University Press, 318–24.

King, K. (1986), 'The Situation of Lesbianism as Feminism's Magical Sign: Contests for Meaning and the US Women's Movement, 1968–1972,' *Communication* 9(1): 65–91.

Leo, J. (1989), 'The Familialism of Man in American Television Melodrama' in R. R. Butters et al. (eds) *Displacing Homophobia: Gay Male Perspectives in Literature and Culture*, Durham, NC, and London: Duke University Press, 31–51.

McLuhan, M. (1962), *The Gutenberg Galaxy: The Making of Typographic Man*, Toronto: University of Toronto Press.

—— (1964), *Understanding Media: The Extensions of Man*, New York: McGraw Hill.

Maltby, R. (1996), '"A Brief Romantic Interlude": Dick and Jane Go to 3 1/2 Seconds of the Classical Hollywood Cinema' in D. Bordwell and N. Carroll (eds) *Post-Theory: Reconstructing Film Studies*, Madison, WI: University of Wisconsin Press, 434–59.

Marx, K. (1977), 'The Fetishism of the Commodity and its Secret' in Marx, *Capital Volume 1*, trans. B. Fowkes, New York: Random House, 163–77.

Mayne, J. (1998), '*L.A. Law* and Prime-Time Feminism,' *Discourse* 10(2), (Spring–Summer): 30–47.

Miller, D. A. (1991), 'Anal *Rope*' in D. Fuss (ed.) *Inside/Out: Lesbian Theories, Gay Theories*, London and New York: Routledge, 119–41.

Parsi, N. (1996), 'Projecting Heterosexuality, or What Do You Mean by "It"?' *Camera Obscura*, 38(May): 162–86.

Patton, C. (1995), 'What is a Nice Lesbian Like You Doing in a Film Like This?' in T. Wilton (ed.) *Immortal Invisible: Lesbians and the Moving Image*, London and New York: Routledge, 20–33.

Paulin, S. (1996), 'Sex and the Singled Girl: Queer Representation and Containment in *Single White Female*,' *Camera Obscura* 37(January): 32–69.

Ringer, J.R. (ed.) (1994), *Queer Words, Queer Images: Communication and the Construction of Homosexuality*, New York: New York University Press.

Russo, V. (1987), *The Celluloid Closet: Homosexuality in the Movies*, 2nd edn, New York: Harper.

Sedgwick, E.K. (1990), *Epistemology of the Closet*, Berkeley, CA: University of California Press.

—— (1993), *Tendencies*, Durham, NC: Duke University Press.

Spigel, L. (1992), *Make Room for TV: Television and the Family Ideal in Postwar America*, Chicago, IL: University of Chicago Press.

Stein, J. (ed.) (1988), *Random House Webster's Dictionary*, 2nd edn, New York: Random House.

Torres, S. (1993), 'Television/Feminism: *HeartBeat* and Prime Time Lesbianism' in H. Abelove et al. (eds) *The Lesbian and Gay Studies Reader*, London and New York: Routledge, 176–85.

Warner, G. (1994), *All My Children: The Complete Family Scrapbook*, Los Angeles, CA: General Publishing Group.

White, M. (1992), *Tele-Advising: Therapeutic Discourse in American Television*, Chapel Hill, NC: University of North Carolina Press.

White, P. (1991), 'Female Spectator, Lesbian Spectre: *The Haunting*' in D. Fuss (ed.) *Inside/Out: Lesbian Theories, Gay Theories*, London and New York: Routledge, 142–72.

Wilton, T. (ed.) (1995), *Immortal Invisible: Lesbians and the Moving Image*, London and New York: Routledge.

Chapter 2

Ethereal queer
Notes on method

Amy Villarejo

By the end of our new century's first decade, a shift of the seismic kind will have shaken the American television industry, with other national, international, and global aftershocks sure to follow. I mean, for the few of you diligent readers and spectators who will not have noticed, the conversion to the digital signal, scheduled (consistently rescheduled) to take place on 17 February 2009. (Briefly, what this means is that it will no longer be possible to receive an analogue signal through the so-called 'ether', as full-power stations will stop broadcasting in analogue on that date; a converter box will be necessary for those with analogue televisions who do not subscribe to pay television services such as cable or satellite to receive the digital signal. Most significant of all, the massive portion of the broadcast spectrum that had been devoted to broadcasting the analogue signal will become available to industry for commodification.) With the precision of a date comes an invitation for dramatic or polemical interpretation: what will this day have meant, and to whom?

The digital television transition may well be but one step in the long process Americans have devoted to giving up the commons, in this case the broadcast spectrum, for capitalist expansion. 'Enclosure', the term used to describe the historical process of private property asserting its right over common land, frequently references a movement ('the enclosure movement') or a moment ('the first enclosure'), but it unfolded over many centuries of what Marx would call 'primitive accumulation' and continues today with new forms of enclosure (intellectual property, spectacle, war) in the service of ravenous capitalist expansion.[1] Understanding the digital television transition as a new form of enclosure needn't be an exercise in nostalgia for the commons, for, as the joke has it, 'the way we never were'. From its inception, television's relation to public life has been complicated, varied, contested. But, as I will want to argue as strenuously as possible in these pages, it is essential for scholars and activists interested particularly in queer television to take a broad view of the tectonic *movements* of enclosure – that is, media policy, regulative frameworks, and evolving forms of spectacle in the processes of neoliberalist expansion – in order to calibrate our critical inventions.[2]

In what follows, then, I make a methodological case in favour of a queer cultural studies approach to television. If attachment, inspiration, attraction, recognition, desire, and identification have largely been seen as the motors of queer investments in television-as-spectacle, I wish to reintroduce the partially abandoned, rusty apparatus and its history into critical practice. (Translation: reader beware! A reading of some show you love or some incredibly-hip-show-you've-never-heard-of-but-will-pledge-forevermore-to-watch-faithfully will not, therefore, follow.) February 17, 2009 may mark nothing more than the date on which the *speed* of the morphing institutions is no longer possible to ignore; if I could make it signify, I would wish it to announce the birth of a new, urgent, queer media practice.

Queer studies/cultural studies

How we understand the complex phenomenon of television – as Raymond Williams (1974) put it, 'technology and cultural form' – depends upon the critical practice through which we frame the questions we put to and through it at this historical conjuncture. Questions filter through all that sediments in the apparatus: interest (and its obverse, boredom), information, humour, aesthetic innovation, repetition, desire, bodily response, shock, consumption, distraction, and so on. But they ultimately congeal here as a direction for thought, an *ethos* and a framework. The methodological topos I would therefore like to stress in this opening section is the sometimes marginalized legacy of cultural studies for queer studies and, in turn, for the study of television. I then, in later sections, unfold cultural studies' capacious and committed interest in histories, institutions, technology, and policy as the horizons and indeed preconditions for textual analysis or readings.

By 'sometimes marginalized', I mean that while queer study remains an emergent and mobile concatenation (queer theory; feminist theory; lesbian, gay, bisexual and transgender (LGBT) studies; and so on), it nonetheless has depended upon the motor of humanities-based close reading to propel much of its development. When I've asked my university colleagues for blurb-length characterizations of the field, they've responded, I think cogently, that it's 'the reading of sexual rhetoric'. Surely a line of Anglo-American queer thought follows, with inspiration and affection, the work of Eve Sedgwick, by consensus one of the most stunning and thoughtful readers at present of modern literature in English. Other literary scholars in the United States, including D.A. Miller, Michael Warner, Lee Edelman, and Diana Fuss (to take a few influential examples) are similarly trained in the art of close textual (literary) analysis, and bring it to bear on a variety of objects, not all literary ones (Miller and Edelman frequently write on film, Fuss has written beautifully about domestic spaces). And of course Judith Butler, to take another prominent figure in the field, ultimately reads philosophical and other 'theoretical' texts closely, whether Lacan or Levinas, Foucault or Benjamin (Jessica *and* Walter). While I wouldn't wish to overstate the case, I think it fair to say that, in the bulk of these writers' work and that which is inspired by their example, the social, industrial and political conditions of a given text's *production* (as opposed to the elaboration of its context) are simply not germane to the project of its analysis. Few are interested, as Janice Radway is in *Reading the Romance* (1984), in actual readers' practices, or, as David Morley is in

Family Television (1986), in viewer responses, preferring instead the implied reader and the hypothetical spectator.

Central to the work of cultural studies in the Birmingham tradition (if understood as a loose and mottled set of critical practices) has been an insistence on the *relation* between those hypothetical positions and actual people (even if they, in turn, are valorized too mythically as 'the working class', 'women', or 'queers'). Even many scholars currently writing on queer cinema rarely consider the edits made, in response to censorship regulation, to various DVD editions of the 'films' under consideration, or the personnel other than the director and stars who contribute to the so-called text. Such neglect characterizes also much of the work that passes under the banner of more generalized 'theory'.

This strong emphasis on textual analysis within some, not all, strains of queer studies means that it tends not to converse easily across actual disciplinary barriers. (To this I can attest having directed an academic programme seeking to do just that kind of crossing.) Unlike some of the discussions generated at Birmingham between, say, sociologists and literary scholars, these readings are a far cry from the mass communications-inflected research of someone like Larry Gross, who has had an influential role in the monitoring of queer images through the Gay and Lesbian Alliance Against Defamation (GLAAD). Frequently, social science research is taken by this crowd to be naïve, coarse, or totalizing. But, for reasons upon which I expand below, such crossing is now urgently necessary for an expansive view of queer media and its future, not least because few humanities-based scholars of television have any capacity really to understand, much less to influence, production or to understand emergent industrial practices. What intellectual and political resources do we lose in this neglect of institutional analysis?

To give it its due, television study itself seems to be casting a critical gaze on that ready-to-hand academic paper (delivered at conferences and then 'developed' into an essay) focusing on a (sometimes elegant, more often not) reading of a series or episode of a beloved series on television. To take a recent example, several contributors to the exciting volume *Cable Visions: Television Beyond Broadcasting* actually indict scholarly practices that neglect industrial, technological, and political processes in favour of hermetic textual analysis. This book provides a particularly nice example because it collects, in my view, some of the wisest scholars in television studies writing today; additionally, it takes a view of the television industry that encompasses one of the things that is distinctly queer about TV today, that is, the innovations in representations of gendered and sexual life made possible by the more lax regulatory field of subscription networks. Amanda Lotz, for example, distinguishes between ad-supported and subscription networks in her essay 'If It's Not TV, What Is It?', and concludes with if not a rousing than an insistent call for institutional analysis:

> Accounting for institutional features may not be central to textual analyses, but even examinations of programmes must acknowledge variant institutional contexts in a way that makes comparisons across situations problematic.

The institutional certainty does not resolutely determine the textual, but it provides a significant feature that evaluations too often under-emphasize.

(Lotz 2007: 100)

From a different angle, writing in the same volume about viewing the Home Box Office (HBO) original programme *The Sopranos*, Dana Polan sees television's renewable capacity for commodification as an argument against isolated textual analyses:

> As original programming moves into an uncertain future – but in which there is certainty that there are always new revenue streams to be found somewhere – we encounter another reason perhaps why interpretation of individual shows seems beside the point. In the larger economy of media circulation, culture is a mere pretext to reach consumers, and it matters only as long as it continues to do so.
>
> (Polan 2007: 281)

For Lotz, institutional analyses crucially expose the limits to comparisons, so much so that she is reluctant to speak about subscriber-supported economic models and advertiser-supported models as being in competition with one another in the same television universe. Television criticism, in her view, cannot neglect how these contexts inscribe particular configurations of art and commerce and, therefore, 'must interrogate how institutional characteristics contribute to programming possibilities because the type of programming provider and specific institutional context yield particular constraints and abilities' (Lotz 2007: 87). (To take an example germane to the current enthusiasms of some queer viewers, Showtime, a subscriber-supported network notable for the series *The L Word* and the US version of *Queer as Folk*, is part of the Viacom empire, which includes non-cable, indeed non-television concerns comprising an extremely complex economic conglomerate [I love this list]: Paramount Pictures, Paramount Home Entertainment, CBS Television, Paramount Television, the Viacom Television Stations Group which operates 29 television stations, UPN, MTV1, MTV2, Nickelodeon, BET, Nick at Nite, TVLand, NOGGIN, the N, VH1, Spike TV, CMT, Comedy Central, The Movie Channel, Flix, Sundance Channel, LOGO, Simon and Schuster, and Infinity Broadcasting which operates 185 radio stations that reach 76 million listeners daily.)[3] For Polan, the industrial tendency towards a crisis mentality and drive for new sources of revenue mean that scholarly treatments of 'quality' programmes such as *The Sopranos* may simply not matter much, as programming responds to imperatives other than those valued by academic taste. *Mutatis mutandis*, the same could be said for *The L Word, Queer as Folk, Queer Eye for the Straight Guy, Noah's Arc*, etc.

Both of these arguments ought to make a difference for our new hybrid, queer television studies, cautioning us against the simple or *self-evident* reading of what is, after all, *industrially produced* sexual rhetoric, queerness literally brought to you by Sony or GE (General Electric). Cultural studies work never loses sight of the horizon of the textual in the social. Toby Miller, in his essay in the same volume, takes these warnings much further, as he has in the past, issuing strident criticisms of the most banal forms of cultural studies. In 'Bank Tellers and Flag Wavers: Cable News in the United States', Miller charts a genealogy of television studies that returns to cultural studies in Birmingham, a genealogy that might propose a different set of precedents for queer studies, too. Let me spend a longer moment on it towards this end. Here, if you can forgive the tone and longish citation, is Miller's assessment of the field:

> My argument here is in many ways a killjoy argument in large circles of US television and cultural studies, where it is something of a *donnée* that the main-stream media are not responsible for – well, anything. This position is a virtual *nostrum* in some research into, for instance, fans of TV drama or wrestling, who are thought to construct connections with celebrities and actants in ways that mimic friendship, make sense of human interaction, and ignite cultural poli-tics. This critique commonly attacks opponents of television for failing to allot the people's machine its due as a populist apparatus that subverts patriarchy, capitalism, and other forms of oppression. Commercial TV is held to have progressive effects because its programmes are decoded by viewers in keeping with their own social situations. All this is supposedly evident to scholars from their perusal of audience conventions, web pages, discussion groups, quizzes, and rankings, or from watching television with their children. But can fans be said to resist labor exploitation, patriarchy, racism, and US neo-imperialism, or in some specifiable way make a difference to politics beyond their own selves, when they interpret texts unusually, dress up in public as men from outer space, or chat about their romantic frustrations? And why have such practices become so popular in the First World at a moment when media policy fetishizes consumption, deregulation, and self-governance? As Theodor Adorno said, while there are problems with 'cultural snobbism', populist TV disempowers audience knowledge in the key areas of public life affected by politics.
>
> (Miller 2007: 286–7)

Let me reserve a response for a moment, just to play out the full scope of his allegations. According to Miller, the *reason* for this sorry state of scholarship, if one can dignify it thus, is the *Americanization* of cultural studies: the migration of what we can all agree were venerable 'UK-based critiques of cultural pessimism, political economy, and current-affairs-oriented broadcasting' (Miller 2007: 287). In the British context in the 1970s, the television industry was a heavily regulated duopoly dripping with class prejudice and snobbery, to which, in Miller's words, it made good sense to oppose a 'playful, commercial, non-citizen address as a counter' (287). Not so when cultural study crosses the puddle and gains some institutional traction in the United States, where the television industry, again in Miller's language, is by contrast 'an amoeba' (287), by which I think he means to stress its relatively fluid and changing form over the past 40 years (from the

Big Three network broadcast television plus public broadcasting service (PBS) plus UHF independents to the 800+ channel grid of the MVPD – multichannel video programming delivery – world of today).

Miller's point appears to be that US cultural study misses Lotz's argument: it forsakes institutional analysis in its thrall to the seemingly oppositional pre-given minutiae of the text (whether text is taken as programme or elements of fan culture or whatnot). Institutional analysis, by extension, would envelop precisely those arenas of so-called First World enclosure missed by a blinkered textual focus, namely media policy (consumption, deregulation, self-governance). (Shards of Polan's argument incidentally register in Miller's position, too, since the attribution of quality also shifts with national and institutional differences.) What Miller's tone eclipses, however, is the difficulty of specifying a practice adequate to the institutional and political context. It is not so much that the tone tends towards caricature or snide dismissal, although it does, as it abandons the task of genealogy at the level of precisely those formations that would be best equipped to counter this restricted if not misplaced focus.

Elsewhere, Miller cites the 'formidable and very interdisciplinary' genealogy of television studies, and it is indeed true that television studies may be a *primary* instance of cultural studies methods (Miller 2002: 1). That is, both draw, as Andrew Lockett suggests, from 'mass literary textual traditions, from sociology and mass communication and from the diverse sources of contemporary theory – feminist theory, structuralism, post-structuralism, postcolonial studies, queer theory and Marxist critical thought' (Lockett 2002: 24). Both, however, may have lost the forest of structures of public life for the trees of audience interest, individual response, and diversity. What worries me in Miller's tone is, if you'll pardon the alliteration, a reverse reifying reaction, whereby those very structures and institutions become self-evident, whether 'media policy', 'publicness' itself, or, for Lockett, 'the stock market, government, the celebrity production machine' (2002: 24).

The best traditions of multivalent cultural studies insist that we rack our foci dramatically, not abandoning but radically resituating our object so as to meet the determinations of our moment. What resources of thought and activism can we bring to media policy? To ideas of the public? To regulatory schema? To new innovations in distribution and to new schemes of synergy? To celebrity culture? To finance capital? Our cultural studies' legacy would stress at the very least the following: questions of history and historicity; institutions (including industrial organization, industrial personnel, labour issues, etc.); technology; media policy and the forms of public life safeguarded or threatened by such policy. In the remainder of this essay, I take each in turn, sketching the directions my own work is taking but hesitating to assess too briskly its destination.

History and historicity

By the former term, history, I mean to balk at the presentism of the current study of queer programming, the unending drive to produce readings of every single new character or series, however horrendous, dubious, or trivial. One also wants to complicate the assumptions of many television scholars about the queer archive, restoring a sense of its vastness and its role in shaping contemporary queer life. Adorno, writing in the 1950s in America, already acknowledged the pervasiveness of gay *stereotypes* on television (Adorno 1954). Margo Miller observes, in her fine essay 'Masculinity and Male Intimacy in Nineties Sitcoms: *Seinfeld* and the Ironic Dismissal', that queer moments may both precede and follow the prominent display of gay and lesbian characters: 'Before prime-time television had mainstreamed gay and lesbian characters, queer pleasures were widely available in sitcoms with same-sex intimacy and unconventionally gendered characters' (Miller 2006: 147). Given the uneven circulation of television kinescopes and subsequent recordings of television broadcasts, moreover, it is difficult to know how to measure the queer archive.

What does seem clear, for all of the ostensibly 'critical' ink spilled over *Queer Eye for the Straight Guy*, is simply that many archival shelves (or whatever the metaphor will become in our digital world) remain under-explored: news coverage of LGBTQ events and issues; documentary work from *An American Family* to the short-lived experiment *Network Q* to *POV*-screened pieces such as *Word is Out*, *Silverlake Life*, *Coming Out Under Fire* (or, in the reverse direction, the work undertaken but not marked as 'GAY' by many queer makers and writers for TV such as *Jack & Bobby*, beloved apparently by only two people, me and Nancy Franklin of *The New Yorker*); series made possible by early narrowcasting in the mobilization planning data viewer (MPDV) industry, such as *The Kathy and Mo Show*, or gay and lesbian stand-up comedy; and the endless parade of queerness on talk television (on which, see Gamson 1998). And this, again, is just in the context of the United States. Revisiting *Out on Tuesday*, the magazine programme produced by Mandy Merck and others for Channel 4 in the UK in the 1990s, one is immediately struck by the presence of *critical cultural studies on TV*! The Australian series *Prisoner* (exported overseas as *Prisoner: Cell Block H*) lives on through vibrant and active fandom and clearly merits attention in the argument for the force and practices of female camp spectatorship. And so on. But to enlarge the archive is still to dwell within the logic of representations, the domain of much activist and scholarly effort, without constituting the archive as a *question*.

By the latter term I used above, 'historicity', I mean, then, to reference the very question of time in relation to television. How do instantaneity, liveness, retrieval, flow, and delay structure queer lives? How does the modern chronotope – that organization of life segmented, quantified, measured, and commodified that is characteristic of modernity and exemplified in the television grid – trump other potentially queer temporalities that may be possible or inherent in the sphere of television? If digital technologies index to many the *speed* of spectacle, the *acceleration* of capitalist expansion and the instantaneous flows between markets and information systems, some have also wanted to understand technologies that produce reflection and the collocation of diversity. In a longer version of this project, I have wanted to test a convergence between television technologies of reproduction and liveness, on the one hand, and the technologies of queer life on the other. Television, I have argued, needs to be seen as an, if not *the*, agent of forms of queer life, for example, 'coming out', rather than seeing queer representations as mere responses to gay publicness.[4] To follow this example, coming out, a 1970s technology of gay life, involves a mode that in powerful ways converges with the televisual: in most of our experiences of coming out, I would say it involves shuttling between private and public, between a sitcom and a soap opera (or between comedy and melodrama), between domestic/familial and work life. Its temporality is also televisual: a cross between a repetition (serial) and an event. Is it possible that TV made coming out the act of queer life in the 1970s, rather than the other way around? These kinds of questions find extended interlocution in recent studies of media that take temporality and historicity as primary vectors of inquiry, such as Philip Rosen's *Change Mummified* (2001) or Bliss Lim's *Translating Time* (forthcoming), and in queer studies work with similar foci, such as the special issue of *GLQ* edited by Elizabeth Freeman on *Queer Temporalities* (2007), or Lee Edelman's *No Future* (2004). They complicate the flows that dominate much writing on 'gay television': teleologies, progressive narratives, repetitions. It is difficult to intervene in a discussion in which the following, from the introduction to an already-cited anthology, might hold sway (and for this reason, I turn in the following section to examine television institutions):

> Perhaps soon, the same economic imperative that determined the success of *Will & Grace* and *Queer Eye for the Straight Guy* and the failure of *Normal, Ohio*, will legitimize more courageous televisual ventures into the present queer underground. The recognition of gay and lesbian financial power may (from a Marxist point of view) resemble (or even be) exploitation, but it is also a very powerful facilitator of civil rights in a culture that values nothing more than materialism and consumerism. From the stereotyping and overt commercialism of *Queer Eye*, one could argue that gay men are the quintessential Americans.
>
> (Keller and Stratyner 2006: 4)

This argument, this particular one would, in fact, not wish to make.

Institutions

If American television is, in Miller's word cited above, an 'amoeba', it is the most monstrous goddamn amoeba you have ever encountered. It is the largest in the world in terms of stations (more than 1,700), and it generates more than $50 billion in revenue. Rarely do humanities-based scholars encounter it directly in the form of the conglomerates that dominate electronic media: Time Warner, The Walt Disney Company, Viacom (referenced above), Comcast, Sony, DirecTV Group, Vivendi, General Electric, Fox Entertainment Group, and Gannett. These represent the top ten.[5]

These conglomerates are ready to exploit the possibilities of almost unlimited bandwidth. In the winter of 2007–8, many Americans (and audiences around the world for Hollywood-produced television) met with an aspect of the television industry rarely glimpsed as this massive amoeba teetered on the brink of a crisis: the labour of its writers in the form of a strike by the Writers' Guild of America. (As I composed this essay, the WGA was poised to begin negotiations with the Alliance of Motion Picture and Television Producers (AMPTP) over the primary issues underlying the strike.) The WGA explains this moment in terms of its consequences for workers in the industry:

> Industry experts agree that in the next 2–5 years most American televisions will be connected to the internet and the shows and movies you watch will be transmitted via an internet connection. Corporate revenue from video downloading is estimated to be $1 billion for the next three years; proceeds from video streaming will be $3 billion during the next two years.
>
> Writers are asking for Guild coverage of writing for the internet, basic residuals for internet content reuse, and the tools to enforce this agreement. These residuals are not a bonus for writers; they are a critical part of compensation. The media conglomerates are refusing to grant the Writers Guild jurisdiction over original writing for the internet, though nearly ALL writing will likely be transmitted this way in the future. (www.wga.org)

As original content finds its way from the internet to network for the first time in the United States (with Marshall Herskovitz and Ed Zwick's *Quarterlife* migrating from MySpace, although the series was cancelled after just one episode!), the writers' claim about the likely developments in transmission seem quickly to be coming true.

If this shift in distribution can function as an index of change, the new industrial climate of synergy means changes at *all* levels of production, distribution, and exhibition (even these categories need an overhaul). One industry executive I've met described a return to the practices of 'Golden Age' sponsored television production, wherein a single sponsor would underwrite a given programme, such as was the case with the anthology dramas of the 1940s and 1950s (NBC's 'Kraft Television Theatre' and subsequently 'Ford Television Theatre', 'Philco Television Playhouse', and 'The US Steel Hour'). The longevity of the Hallmark Hall of Fame (the fifty-year-old television production arm of the greeting card company, Hallmark) indicates that we haven't abandoned that model entirely, but there is a new niche for relatively low-budget serial drama ($100K to $200K per episode) that can be sold to a sponsor who then can dictate strongly its content: enter Christian programming on mainstream commercial networks. The current generation of scholars won't know what hit 'em.

One promising route for understanding these changes already comes in John Caldwell's (2008) ethnographies of production 'cultures'. His interviews and discussions with workers in the Los Angeles film and television industries reveal habits of self-understanding and critique among even 'below-the-line' labourers that, in turn, disclose some of the most salient shifts in the amoeba's form I have been describing here (in those movements of expansion such as media convergence, tense relations between labour and industry, outsourcing, the drive towards user-generated content, conglomeration, and so on). I find the level of care in this work inspiring. Another comes in fan/scholar collaborations, such as critical work on *The L Word*, that complicate denunciations of fan practices as self-absorbed indulgence or delusional flights and, simultaneously, complicate the expectation of scholarly detachment. Lotz's remark I cited above about the limits of comparison may make the case for institutional analysis the most strongly; on this massive scale, what can we say we know if we are unable conceptually to *compare*?

Technology

Constraints of space prohibit me from touching more than briefly on each of these points, but it feels most difficult to be brief in describing current changes in television technology in an essay that opens with the digital television transition. As I've tried to say, however, it is not self-evident that this transition marks anything momentous at all; neither does it disclose movements that are more obviously 'technological' than economic, social, cultural, or political. The question concerning technology, to paraphrase Heidegger (1982), is what we need to delineate for our own moment: its relation to forms of image and spectacle, its relation, above all, to power.

Let me differentiate the question first, then, from the 'technical' (not the 'merely' technical, for we needn't dismiss it). Some changes that we feel proximately in our (or richer peoples') homes belong to the technical: we seem to connect our components (no longer videotape but digital video recorders) via high-definition media interface (HDMI) cables, making it possible to transmit enormous quantities of data without conversion or compression to our televisions (now much larger liquid crystal display (LCD) or plasma monitors rather than cathode ray tube (CRT) displays). Content migrates from the internet to these displays (televisions?) in the digital world, as the striking writers know, so that distinguishing between television and cinema, between MySpace and NBC, or between advertising and (free to producers) user-generated content no longer seems fruitful.

The transition from analogue to digital television facilitates this blurring. The Benton Foundation report, 'Citizen's Guide to the Public Interest Obligations of Digital Television Broadcasters', projects a variety of uses for the new data capacities of digital signals, in addition to the improved 'accuracy' and 'clarity' (I use scare quotes here for reasons I explain below) of high-definition television (HDTV) signals:

> The data capacity of DTV makes possible services such as subscription television programming, computer software distribution, teletext and interactive services, including revenue-producing offerings such as stock prices, sports scores, classified advertising, paging services, 'zoned' news reports, advertising targeted

> to specific television sets, 'time-shifted' video programming, and closed-circuit
> television. (www.benton.org)

At this level we might, then, begin to generate significant questions about the
boundedness and nature of television itself, questions that are more properly technological insofar as they beckon towards the primary question, as philosopher Bernard
Stiegler might put it, of who we are. In whose service is this technology? What
does it make possible and for whom? How does it enable our social and political
imaginations; or our capacities for surveillance, war, and control? Where, in short,
does it take us?

   Above I've suggested, following many others' leads, that one way to understand what is different about communications technology at this moment is speed.
Stiegler, in *Technics and Time, 1*, concludes with a meditation on what he calls
light-time:

> Today memory is the object of an industrial exploitation that is also a war of
> speed: from the computer to programme industries in general, via the cog-
> nitive sciences, the technics of virtual reality and telepresence together with
> the biotechnologies, from the media event to the event of technicized life,
> via the interactive event that makes up computer real time, new conditions
> of event-ization have been put in place that characterize what we have called
> *light-time*.
>
> (Stiegler 1998: 276)

A politics of memory, such as he calls for in response to this 'war of speed', responds
to a host of questions about what I would frame as a question about technology
through the problematic of 'liveness', by which I mean, again too briefly: (1) the
ideological effects that follow from claims of presence, instantaneity, simultaneity,
'reality' (including those insistently spun by digital television broadcasters about
accuracy and clarity); (2) the back and forth operations of recognition, misrecognition, simplification (Laurence Rickels [1991: 113] calls it 'miniaturization'), and
spectacle that characterize television viewing wherein we imagine that we see ourselves or versions of our lives 'on' TV; (3) questions about how we frame 'life'
itself, from Giorgio Agamben's (2000) resuscitation of the distinction between *zoe*
and *bios*, to live performance and media events, to the guarantee of justice through
a live trial, to theatres of war. Queerness can, I think, lie at the centre of this
problematic just as it prompts new thinking about time, provided that our frames
are encompassing enough, expansive enough, to confront the scale and speed of
changes configuring, and brought about through, technology.

Media policy

In the midst of these changes, current thinking about media policy seems, at
best, limited. In the United States, massive deregulation of media industries has

led to huge gaps between the original intent and language of regulatory schema, including the charge for those industries to operate in the 'public interest, convenience, or necessity' (from the 1934 Telecommunications Act). Previously, such language obliged broadcasters to (1) localism (i.e. local news and information), (2) education (broadcasting sufficient and appropriate material for children), and (3) diversity (represented by independent rather than conglomerate ownership of media, access for disabled viewers via closed captioning, and a loose sense that diversity serves democracy by disseminating information about candidates for elections).

Repeated in the most recent major Telecommunications Act (of 1996) is this mantra of localism, education, and diversity, and it's 'diversity', not surprisingly, that has become the most vexing to define. Take diversity of ownership. Ownership of television stations by women and people of colour (or queers or the disabled) seems now like laughable crazy talk: in what world would we simply buy a television station in order to circulate our 'diverse' views? (People of colour, by the way, own 1.5% of television stations, according to www.benton.org.) Closed captioning is widely available, and educational television remains a contested but at least imaginable domain. If it's true that the digital transition provides an opportunity, it seems less and less true that television broadcasters have any *obligation* whatsoever, as the Benton folks put it, to 'bring a broader range of community voices – representing the full gamut of American viewpoints, background, and ethnic diversity that makes America America' (www.benton.org). Ultimately, even these so-called media activists revert to boasts about the size of the Hispanic *market* in a bid to plead that broadcasters cannot afford to ignore them/it.

Media activists cite struggles on a number of different fronts to diversify mass media, but they consistently propose a political model that is derived from the past and requires new thinking. Robert McChesney's string is a good example: 'reasoned, coherent, consistent, democratic socialist, pro-labour, or even old-fashioned New Deal Democratic' (McChesney 1997: 78). Habermas (philosopher proponent of the rational public sphere) meets Joe Hill (radical, itinerant, organizer, Wobbly, and left-wing martyr). In this assessment, and this isn't much of a caricature, if 'the people' just had the opportunity to hear oppositional and progressive voices, they would join hands and retake the media for democracy.

But 'the people' have never been very pro-queer, especially those in 'the labour movement' (what labour movement, by the way?) McChesney hopes will lead the digital revolution. Neither do many media activists want to remake educational television into sexual education, or into a haven for gender nonconformity: PBS consistently withdraws support for queer programming. (In 2005, *Postcards from Buster*, a television programme showcasing 'diversity' for children with a bunny called Buster Baxter, produced an episode called 'Sugartime' about harvesting maple sugar in Vermont, in a family with two mommies. Education secretary Margaret Spellings protested in a letter outlining her views on what educational television means to her [and will therefore mean for US policy]: 'Many parents would not want their young children exposed to the life-styles portrayed in this episode' (Gaffney 2006). PBS immediately pulled their funding for the series.)

In this climate, what the transition to digital television will mean is: more, faster. What the media activist sector *does* understand is that media studies need to step up, and queer media studies even more so, to shape a critical media practice. It's happening on TV already: I close with a long citation from Gamson on several years of talk television that offers the kind of diversity I like:

> [The last few years have seen shows on] lipstick lesbians, gay teens, gay cops, lesbian cops, cross-dressing hookers, transsexual call girls, gay and lesbian gang members, straight go-go dancers pretending to be gay, people who want their relatives to stop cross-dressing, lesbian and gay comedians, gay people in love with straight ones, women who love gay men, same-sex marriage, drag queen makeovers, drag kings, same-sex sexual harassment, homophobia, lesbian mothers, gay twins, gay beauty pageants, transsexual beauty pageants, people who are fired for not being gay, gay men reuniting with their high school sweethearts, bisexual teens, bisexual couples, bisexuals in general, gays in the military, same-sex crushes, hermaphrodites, boys who want to be girls, female-to-male transsexuals, male-to-female transsexuals and their boyfriends, and gay talk shows – just to mention a few.
>
> (Gamson 1998: 5)

Gamson confesses that watching these chokes him up: for queer people, 'whose life experience is so heavily tilted towards invisibility ..., daytime TV talk shows are a big shot of visibility and media accreditation. It looks, for a moment, like you own this place'. In that moment, something happens, even if we don't own the place. Not by a long shot.

Notes

1. The title of J.A. Yelling's book dates 'the' enclosure movement from the fifteenth century to the nineteenth: *Common Field and Enclosure in England, 1450–1850* (1977). Analyses of the 'new enclosure' movements include Michael Hardt and Antonio Negri's *Empire* (2000) but also the Retort Collective's more recent *Afflicted Powers* (2005).
2. Edward Klinenberg condenses the history of struggles over control of American media in his recent book, *Fighting for Air* (2008).
3. I treat *The L Word* at greater length in Villarejo (2007).
4. I develop this argument at much greater length in my forthcoming book, *Ethereal Queer: Television, Historicity, Desire*.
5. All of this information is available online at www.mediainfocenter.com. You can find the top 25 African-American television markets, alongside data on cable penetration, ownership, media content, and virtually every facet of media industries. Ranking, compilation, and presentation are never innocent activities, however, but there is some agreement on basic data to do with total revenue (compiled from advertising, spot advertising, and cable advertising data) and ownership.

References

Adorno, T. (1954), 'How to Look at Television', *Quarterly of Film, Radio and Television* 8(3): 213–35.

Agamben, G. (2000), *Means Without End: Notes on Politics*, trans. V. Binetti and C. Casarino, Minneapolis, MN: University of Minnesota Press.

Benton Foundation. Online: http://www.benton.org [accessed 28 January 2008].

Caldwell, J.T. (2008), *Production Culture: Industrial Reflexivity and Critical Practice in Film and Television*, Durham, NC: Duke University Press.

Edelman, L. (2004), *No Future: Queer Theory and the Death Drive*, Durham, NC: Duke University Press.

Freeman, E. (ed.) (2007), *Queer Temporalities, GLQ: A Journal of Lesbian and Gay Studies*, 13: 2–3.

Gaffney, D. (2006), 'Censured PBS Bunny Returns, Briefly', *The New York Times*, 18 December. Online: http://query.nytimes.com/gst/fullpage.html?res=9803E4DC 1331F93BA25751C1A9609C8B63&sec=&spon=&pagewanted=all [accessed 25 May 2008].

Gamson, J. (1998), *Freaks Talk Back: Tabloid Talk Shows and Sexual Nonconformity*, Chicago, IL: University of Chicago Press.

Hardt, M. and Negri, A. (2000), *Empire*, Cambridge, MA: Harvard University Press.

Heidegger, M. (1982), *The Question Concerning Technology and Other Essays*, New York: Harper Perrenial.

Keller, J. and Strayner, L. (2006), 'Introduction' in J. Keller and L. Strayner (eds) *The New Queer Aesthetic on Television: Essays on Recent Programming*, Jefferson, NC: McFarland, 1–8.

Klinenberg, E. (2008), *Fighting for Air: The Battle for Control of American Media*, New York: Holt Paperbacks.

Lim, B. (forthcoming), *Translating Time: Cinema, The Fantastic, and Temporal Critique*, Durham, NC: Duke University Press.

Lockett, A. (2002), 'Cultural Studies and Television' in T. Miller (ed.) *Television Studies*, London: BFI.

Lotz, A. (2007), 'If It's Not TV, What Is It?' in S. Banet-Weiser, C. Chris, and A. Freitas (eds) *Cable Visions: Television Beyond Broadcasting*, New York: New York University Press, 85–102.

McChesney, R.W. (1997), *Corporate Media and the Threat to Democracy*, New York: Seven Stories Press.

Media Information Center. Online: http://www.mediainfocenter.com [accessed 23 January 2008].

Miller, M. (2006), 'Masculinity and Male Intimacy in Nineties Sitcoms: *Seinfeld* and the Ironic Dismissal' in J. R. Keller and L. Stratyner (eds) *The New Queer Aesthetic on Television: Essays on Recent Programming*, Jefferson, NC: McFarland, 147–59.

Miller, T. (2002), 'Introduction' in T. Miller (ed.) *Television Studies*, London: BFI.

—— (2007), 'Bank Tellers and Flag Wavers: Cable News in the United States' in S. Banet-Weiser, C. Chris, and A. Freitas (eds) *Cable Visions: Television Beyond Broadcasting*, New York: New York University Press, 284–301.

Morley, D. (1986), *Family Television: Cultural Power and Domestic Leisure*, London: Comedia Publishing Group.

Polan, D. (2007), 'Cable Watching: HBO, *The Sopranos*, and Discourses of Distinction' in S. Banet-Weiser, C. Chris, and A. Freitas (eds) *Cable Visions: Television Beyond Broadcasting*, New York: New York University Press, 261–83.

Radway, J. (1984), *Reading the Romance: Women, Patriarchy, and Popular Literature*, Chapel Hill, NC: University of North Carolina Press.

Retort Collective (2005), *Afflicted Powers: Capital and Spectacle in a New Age of War*, London: Verso.

Rickels, L. (1991), *The Case of California*, Baltimore, MD: The Johns Hopkins University Press.

Rosen, P. (2001), *Change Mummified: Cinema, Historicity, Theory*, Minneapolis, MN: University of Minnesota Press.

Steigler, B. (1998), *Technics and Time, 1: The Fault of Epimetheus*, trans. R. Beardsworth and G. Collins, Stanford, CA: Stanford University Press.

Villarejo, A. (2007), 'Materiality, Pedagogy, and the Limits of Queer Visibility' in G. E. Haggerty and M. McGarry (eds) *A Companion to Lesbian, Gay, Bisexual, Transgender and Queer Studies*, Oxford: Blackwell, 389–403.

Williams, R. (1974), *Television: Technology and Cultural Form*, New York: Schocken Books.

Writers Guild of America. Strike FAQ. Online: http://www.wga.com/subpage_member.aspx?id=2686 [accessed 27 January 2008].

Yelling, J.A. (1977), *Common Field and Enclosure in England, 1450–1850*, Hamden, CT: Archon Books.

Chapter 3

Towards queer television theory

Bigger pictures sans the sweet queer-after

Michele Aaron

The aim of this chapter is to scrutinise the relationship between 'queer' and 'TV', not just between sexual dissidence, say, and popular culture but, more importantly, between this specific critical position and this specific media experience. In doing so I will map the various avenues that queer television theory might, and in some cases has begun to, take. Though influenced by work within TV studies and on debates on sexual citizenship within sociology and queer cultural commentary, this cartographic move will be informed both by queer film theory and by understandings of contemporary film cultures.[1] These are, for me, inevitable springboards for the argument to follow which moves the psychodynamics of spectatorship into the home during a time of media convergence. They also, I hope, prove highly productive in not only contextualising but also politicising the subject.

Three avenues arise immediately. The first, the 'queer and now', involves the critical exploration of contemporary texts that are deemed queer either in terms of the sexuality of their creators or audience, or through a 'gender-play' suggestiveness of their content. Though much work on 'queer TV' takes this route, it is often under-theorised and de-contextualised (favouring instead the quick fix of either gay–lib correctness or subcultural celebration). I would argue instead that these television texts must be located both in terms of the development of lesbian and gay cultural production in the AIDS era and, especially, in terms of the era's evolving definition or rather redefinition of queer. New Queer Cinema, with which queer TV has more than just creative talent in common, will provide obvious critical and cultural signposts for this discussion.

The second avenue, what I would like to call the 'sweet queer-after', similarly attends to the queerness of television makers and viewers but does so as a retroactive or, as some have called it, an archaeological project (Sullivan 2003). It represents a rereading and reclaiming of classical television texts: a retrospective queering of TV history. There has not been the same kind of independent tradition within the annals of television production as exists within film history. It remains more important than ever, therefore, to square this oft-romanticised recovery of a queerer past with the recuperative, nay neo-liberal, impulse of the mainstream in its appropriation of lesbian and gay issues. Though I will not be taking this avenue here and journeying into TV history, the latter emphasis on the ideological implications of mainstreaming, and on resisting romanticism, is a major theme in this discussion.

The third avenue, the realm of 'queer re:', of queer in relation to, questions the queerness of the medium – of the technology, and of viewing – itself. What do queer TV texts, indeed what does queer theory, reveal about viewers' experience of television? How does this experience reflect or impact upon the broader socio-political climate? How does sofa spectatorship, with its incumbent issues of visual pleasure (exacerbated by various recent shifts in the culture of viewing), sit astride the normative processes of everyday life? It is this third avenue that, I believe, presents the greatest challenge and is most needful of attention. It, in combination with the other two (for these must not be seen as totally discrete categories within queer television scholarship), affords a politicised evaluation of the productivity of applying queer to television, for it incorporates what I see as the essential frameworks to its discussion: questions of agency and interpretation; of fantasy and the family sphere; and both the libidinal and neo-liberal implications of, among other things, media convergence.

Fundamental to the approach in this chapter is an emphasis upon a critical definition of queer that complicates rather than assumes its association with homo-sexuality; that sees queer as a critical intervention, cultural product, and political strategy rather than simply as marking some highpoint of gay or even straight liber-ation. It can be no other way: as liberating as it might be to revel only in previously unseen images, or to distract oneself weighing up the ultimate conservatism of individual programmes or characters, one cannot omit or forget queer's heritage or what Richard Dyer (2002) points to as the 'old queer', for there is so much at stake in the ascription 'queer'. After all, this ascription resonates within a long history of the (homo)phobic policing of gender and sexuality and its repressive, if not violent or deadly, repercussions, as well as the development of gay culture in the West. The New Queer, then, is not merely an umbrella term for all that is, positively, not straight, or narrow. It is an oppositional stance intimately bound to an anti-normative trajectory and emerging from the activist politics of the AIDS era and its impact on social practices and cultural production. And it carries this legacy with it. It remains haunted by the (homo)phobic past, recent and otherwise, and the old queer which fuelled both its generation and its radicalism. Queer cannot throw off its nasty history nor should it: for it is its nasty history that keeps it on its toes, keeps it daring, dancing, and not only astute to the nastiness of the present, but capable of undermining it.

The queer and now

I want to begin by evaluating so-called queer TV, not for the authenticity or equal ops. of the queer moments of specific programmes, nor for its relation to a history of the treatment of homosexuality on television, but through a rigorous contextualisation of these shows within the contemporary sociopolitical scene. For me, here, this means situating queer TV against both the sociohistorical events and conditions that gave rise to queer activism and art in the first place, and within what could be called the New Queer Culture. By this I mean the mainstream embrace of a certain kind of queerness as a departure from the radical intent of queer texts, in particular those of the so-called New Queer Cinema.

Before applying some of the characteristics of these texts to television, it is important to note that there have been some key initial points made on this subject. As Ron Becker argued in 1998 and continues to in his book, *Gay TV and Straight America* (2006), gay television in the 1990s was about the commercialisation of queerness, an exploitation of it for economic ends, as a 'programming trend' (1998: 389). And as Anna McCarthy so persuasively points out in her discussion of *Queer Eye for the Straight Guy* in the 2005 *GLQ* dossier on queer TV, the so-called queer TV of current times represents, above all else, the neo-liberalist agenda of contemporary American politics. For her, it is not only that '*Queer Eye*'s performance of queerness ... is the theft of queer cultural capital in the name of marketing' (McCarthy 2005: 100), so that this trend is indicative of a form of commercial exploitation, but that 'these shows are anxiously liberal in their affirmative messages about gay people' (97). Indeed, she suggests, shows like *Queer Eye* '[teach] domesticity and care of the self to facilitate heterosexual coupling' (98). In other words, queerness has been appropriated by television for political as well as economic gain.

According to critics, one of the things that connected the disparate group of New Queer films was their 'insouciance', an air of defiance amidst their more popular pleasures that underpinned their sociocritical oppositionality and, hence, their queer status (Hoberman 1992; Rich 1992). This defiance operated on various aesthetic, narratival, and contextual levels, and was enacted through a set of characteristics that distilled the films' radical aspirations (Aaron 2004a). The play-off between the radical and the popular haunted the evolution of New Queer Cinema, and its theorisation, but also, I would like to suggest, underlies the queer narratives, like *The L Word* (first aired 2004) and *Six Feet Under* (first aired 2001), that have come in its wake.

In previous work I have talked about Showtime's hit series *The L Word* and its relationship to New Queer Cinema (Aaron 2006). Centred on a set of lesbian characters, their relationships and their community, and targeting that same community, as well as some of its best friends (by which I am referring to the straight male audience for 'lesbian' sex), the series seemed to provide an explicitly queer text in terms of subject matter and production history. The show was certainly in dialogue, albeit a glossy one, with the activism, sexual confidence, and visual prowess associated with New Queer Cinema. It also clearly benefited from the mainstream market potential that New Queer Cinema opened up.

Here, however, I want to move away from what, despite its relative success, is niche programming and consider, instead, a far bigger concern and far more mainstream product. Our attention will turn then to the multi-award winning Home Box Office (HBO) series *Six Feet Under*. Like Showtime, HBO is a subscription channel whose programmes tend to be far more sexually daring than those of the major networks in the US. But despite their common connection to the more sensational or taboo, the channels' ratings operate in different leagues. Where *The L Word* in its opening season would garner 'four times the network's usual prime-time audience' and Showtime would smash all its previous records with an audience of 1.23 million for the series finale of *Dexter* in 2007, *Six Feet Under*, though its ratings would slip over the years, had a weekly audience of five million during its opening season (Becker 2007; Hibberd 2004; Rice 2001).

These figures represent the domestic US market and it is important to note that both shows enjoy/ed international, that is, export success. But again, taking the UK as an example, the first season of *The L Word* would air on the cable channel Living TV, while *Six Feet Under*, in contrast, was broadcast on the terrestrial Channel 4.

Development of *The L Word*'s fan base has followed, if not epitomised or even defined, a very queer TV trajectory. Burnt DVDs of episodes would be passed on, contraband-like, from those who had cable to those who did not (this was, frequently, a move from straight men to lesbian friends). With the development of its online fan sites and communities – as well as the launch of the social networking site, OurChart.com, by some of the show's key players – a transnational, interactive, second life was created for the programme, in which plotlines are discussed, members of the cast are interviewed, merchandise is sold, but more importantly, through this, the actual airing of the show becomes just one way in which it is experienced, or bought into, by a queer audience.

While this evidences well how television and the home function as an alternative site and circuit of queer culture, it also suggests a fourth avenue for queer television theory. This fourth avenue I am inclined to call 'the extraterrestrial' in that its remit is this queer community and discourse generated by but existing beyond the analogue. This discourse is forged via other media (satellite, cable, the internet) and while it is linked to the television programme from which it originates, it also operates independently of it. Significantly, *Six Feet Under* does not work in this way, though other mainstream hits that are also not instantly identified as queer TV, like *Buffy the Vampire Slayer* and *Xena: Warrior Princess*, set the precedent for this kind of extraterrestrial queer status. Thus television texts can become queer through their queer audience and their queer audience practices, not as a retroactive appropriation but rather as a concurrent extratextual activity.[2]

Like *The L Word*, *Six Feet Under* has an out gay creator: Alan Ball. And like *The L Word* it gains a certain New Queer pedigree, not just in its timing but by drawing upon some of the directors associated with the film movement's success, such as Rose Troche, Mary Harron, and Michael Cuesta.[3] While *Six Feet Under* has a gay male character at the heart of its narrative, David, played by Michael C. Hall, it is an ensemble piece. Though David will provide the main focus for some of the gay-themed plots (e.g. on homophobia; gay adoption; bisexuality), such issues are not attached to him alone. Instead, the broader concerns of prejudice, of social conformity, of family, circulate freely in the narrative and are attached to a wider community of characters. On several levels the show is invested in the undoing of normative assumptions in what could be read as a distinctly queer way. It challenges both homosexual and heterosexual assumption. It is not the gay character who suffers from sex addiction but Brenda (Rachel Griffiths), and it is not the young gay man who will die before his time but Nate (Peter Krause). *Six Feet Under* complicates rather than concretises cultural norms: this isn't the same as defiance or radicalism for that matter – to raise questions, is, after all, a common liberal ploy – but it warrants further investigation and, therefore, comparison to New Queer Cinema.

The New Queer Cinema films were defiant in that they gave voice not simply to lesbians and gays but to the concerns of the more marginalised subgroups amongst them, thereby defying conventions of popular or acceptable subjects. *Six Feet Under*, set in a funeral home and focusing upon a family of funeral directors, immediately stakes its claim to the taboo subject of death. Rather than operating as a typically spectacular or punitive, but always (dis)engaging, end point, as is the common pop-cultural usage of death, each episode is, instead, prefaced by a to-death sequence: the unfolding of the, often banal, pre-corpse moments of the Fishers' latest 'incoming'. What is more, as Rob Turnock points out, 'each episode's narrative concerns the journey of the body from death to its disposal', and in doing so opens up a liminal space in which the characters journey or are transformed in some way too (Turnock 2005: 39).

Not only does the show defy death's conventional treatment, and its bildungsro-man applications, but its status as sanitised and sealed off from the rest of society. It declares this metonymically in its title, as Avi Shoshana and Elly Teman point out, for 'the phrase "six feet under" relates to the traditional European folk belief that the dead should be buried at a sufficient distance beneath the ground so that as [sic] to separate them from the living, lest the former harm or haunt the latter' (2006: 558). In *Six Feet Under* the dead do return to haunt, taunt and instruct the Fishers, often guiding them through that episode's emotional challenges: David will converse with the recently deceased who sits watching him embalm.

Where New Queer Cinema's defiance of death was rooted in its AIDS activist origins, *Six Feet Under*'s success has been linked to the post-9/11 cultural climate, or 'Americanitis', more than 'post-AIDS' rage or melancholy.[4] That said, Robert Deam Tobin rightly argues that the show's representation of death seems to be in dialogue with 'the rhetoric of AIDS' (2005: 85). Death in the show is the providence of all rather than the pathology of some, particularly the homosexual. However, *Six Feet Under* lacks the political zeal of other AIDS narratives and, I would add, especially of those associated with New Queer Cinema.

In *Six Feet Under*'s inevitable references to religion and religious practice, its rep-resentation of gay Christians provides an extremely rare representation of a marginal community. But the show deals with a range of other controversial issues – sex addiction; adultery; intergenerational relationships; schizophrenia – and it tends not towards the simple sensationalism, or judgementalism, that often accompanies said topics, especially within television series and especially television series that deal with causes of death (and I am thinking of the conservatism of the extremely popular *CSI* franchise in particular). Rather, *Six Feet Under* renders death and other difficult human conditions extraordinarily everyday even in their most graphic expression.

The programme's dalliance with taboo is immediately evident, as is this dualistic aesthetic of over- and understatement, of the reverential and the irreverent. In the pilot episode, we are introduced to our key characters, the Fisher family: Ruth (Frances Conroy) and Nathaniel (Richard Jenkins) and their children, David, the middle child who co-runs the business, Claire (Lauren Ambrose), the youngest who is still at school, and Nate, the oldest, who has flown home for the Christmas holidays, having fled the family fold several years earlier. Nate's exposition involves him fucking a stranger in a maintenance closet in the airport and teenage Claire's sees her taking crack.

And in case we haven't yet caught on to the show's daring, or its relationship to convention, it is amidst these activities that the siblings learn of their father's death. Nathaniel Fisher had been driving his new hearse to the airport to collect his eldest, and while lighting a cigarette (having just told his wife he has stopped smoking) is involved in a fatal collision with a city bus. While the pilot episode establishes that taboo-trashing is the terrain of the series, there is something more complicated, more dualistic or multilayered going on too. And it is going on, aptly, on various registers. As Peter Kaye argues of Nathaniel's death in these opening scenes, in his analysis of sound in *Six Feet Under*:

> There are several examples of cognitive dissonance here that ironically comment on what we are seeing. It is contemporary times but the song [that is playing] is old; it is a Christmas tune but we are in snowless, sunny southern California. Another emotional frisson occurs when the sweet song plays on over the image of the bus colliding with the hearse and killing Nathaniel.
>
> (Kaye 2005: 200)

Might such irony or multilayering be called camp, or even queer, or perhaps both? The emphasis on surface, on the dead in deadpan, and on camp un-hooked from homosexuality – so marvellously rendered in the funeral trade ads punctuating the pilot episode, and the musical numbers studding series one – connects to the 'queer camp' that Glyn Davis has associated with New Queer Cinema. Though talking about characters' delivery rather than texts' general register, the qualities he distinguishes are nevertheless telling. Davis writes: 'Whereas the delivery of the camp gay characters of mainstream cinema is usually shrieking, effeminate, and waiting for laughter, that of queer camp characters is "fake", deadpan, redundant' (2004: 60).

Camp, (sexual) recklessness, perversity, and even death, are effectively detached from 'gay' in the show's reckoning with stereotype: it is Claire's boyfriend, Gabe (Eric Balfour), who has a penchant for having his toes sucked, Brenda who picks up strangers, all the key characters who slip into the song and dance, and absolutely everyman who ends up on the slab in the Fishers' basement. Straights, *Six Feet Under* seems to say, are just as likely to defy sociosexual norms as gays, if not more. But, rather than there being a complete levelling of lifestyle choices, a pervasive anti-normativity, David does seem to come off best, indeed as virtually normal. It is he, after all, who is introduced as the dutiful, suit-wearing son. It is he who strives towards the American dream of the nuclear family: 'marrying' his long-term partner, Keith (Mathew St. Patrick), and raising a family.[5] Indeed, the contrast between David and Nate is heightened by the very different closets that they occupy in the pilot episode. Though, as Dana Heller argues, David is queer in his 'cultural awareness' and 'evolving critical stance' (2005: 80), his characterisation smacks of neo-liberalism, of a tolerance-oriented, rather than radical, recovery of rights.

Aside from its defiance of positive imagery (in its celebration of, albeit minor, mischief: think Ruth on ecstasy), of televisual convention (in its opening, to-death sequences, and general cinematicism) and even of death, *Six Feet Under* makes taboo palatable to a mass audience. It makes the quirky and the edgy accessible and entertaining. It turns dissonance, and even dissidence, into 'quality' television. In this way, it epitomises the mainstreaming, and de-politicisation, of 'queer', the popular appropriation of racier subjects that characterises our post-naughty nineties, post-New Queer Cinema, New Queer Culture. It also very much characterises the development of HBO which, in this same period, could 'dare to be different and push itself into new and often controversial television territory precisely because it is part of a vast economic conglomerate diverse enough to speculate and wait for a return on its investment' (Akass and McCabe 2005: 8).

There is something wonderfully anarchic about *Six Feet Under*, evident from the first; not just the pilot episode but, more than this, from the title sequence of the pilot episode. A single black crow flies across a cloudless blue sky. The camera tilts down to reveal a lone tree on a grassy hill and then tracks back to foreground a man's and woman's clasped hands separating. The show's celebration of dissolution, of the macabre, of American Gothic refracted for a postmodern audience, is boldly stated. Like the title itself, the sequence's final graphic outlining of the box buried under the soil, an architectural ruling in of what lurks beneath, is indicative of *Six Feet Under*'s relationship to what is normally obscured. But as I have suggested, this is partial. The more radical, the queerer, implications of its self-consciously contrived performances – the crow in the credit sequence has actually been blacked-up, and the American idyll depended on transplanting that perfect tree to its new setting[6]– remained to be seen.

Queer re:

The very notion of queer television, of conjoining such seemingly incompatible terms, might seem irreverent in itself. After all, TV inhabits the domestic sphere, the realm of the everyday, 'through embracing its common denominators— precisely the terrain against which queer agitates' (Aaron 2006: 36). What is more, its range of narratives frequently follow 'normative developmental narratives of sexuality' (McCarthy 2001: 599), which promote (heterosexual) romantic coupling and commitment invariably in the form of marriage and reproduction, and as such, seem instinctively anti-queer. However, as has already been indicated, the normativeness of such narratives can be contested, queerly contested even, by programmes like *Six Feet Under*. But it is to this sense of the sheer incompatibility of television and queerness that I want to turn, and to open up several points of queer contact and potential between the medium and its theorisation.

I have previously argued of cinema that there is something inherently queer about the spectatorial experience, that is, inherently oppositional in terms of its lines of desire (Aaron 2004b: 187). Visual pleasure, in other words, engages our desire for, or to be, on-screen characters counter to our 'normal' sexual orientation: we often fall for the leading lady's beauty, or align ourselves with the male hero, even though we are ourselves straight women, for example. Even Laura Mulvey's (1988) offer of a transvestite gaze hardly shields the spectator from, albeit a temporary, sexualised transgression.

While watching demands rather than just inviting non-normative practices of identification and objectification, New Queer Cinema and post-New Queer Cinema mainstream film exploits the freedom, or at least frisson, that such practices afford. But how might this extend to television? What kind of viewing practice does TV elicit? Does a gaze or a glance or a look convey how it can be loaded with desire as well as distractedness, can portend empathy as well as atrophy? What happens when the spectatorship of films shifts from the cinema to the sofa, and more 'classical' understandings of visual pleasure enter the home to merge with the 'flow' of family viewing? Or when television programmes are watched on the PC monitor as well as the TV screen? Or when television itself becomes just one site within the screen-based proliferation of queer discourse in a show's extraterrestrial life? In other words, how has media convergence impacted upon the domestic space and home viewing – rather than just the industry – and how are our understandings of the former's and latter's normative practices and pleasures to be adapted?

This opens or rather reopens the issue of applying the discussion of the psycho-dynamics of desire, to television. Sandy Flitterman-Lewis (1992) has argued for the huge differences in psychoanalytical terms between film and television that render the latter utterly outside of certain unconscious desires. In other words, those regressive fantasies of developmental processes, like the mirror stage or castration anxiety, which underpinned the seminal work from 1970s cine-psychoanalysis, would seem to hold no relevance for understanding television or the psyche of its viewer. And yet this seems highly unlikely.

Developments in TV screen-sizes and 'Home Cinema' speakers and projectors, combined with the massive growth in the DVD market and movies-on-demand through cable TV channels, suggest a replication of the cinema experience in the living room, but, more importantly here, point to how the 'dream-like' space of the cinema – its triggering of those frequently sexualised, regressive fantasies – is recreated in the home. But besides and before this, television has always been situated within the dramas of everyday life and the lived psychodynamics of the family.

The television must be reconsidered, therefore, for its potential influence on subject formation. Does it not provide potent images of idealised egos both in the framing and valuation of its 'celebrities', that is, in terms of its content, but also through their reception: how family members, dressed down and 'vegged out' in front of the box, admire them? Might a baby not catch its first reflection in the large screen of the living room's TV, so that the mirror stage becomes oddly terrestrialised? Doesn't children's television offer a first interface for interpellation, for the first summoning of the child's socialised, rather than simply familial, identity? And isn't it the case that parents enter the living room invariably during the only on-screen sex the teenager has witnessed throughout his or her viewing, thereby enacting some (not so) weird reversal of the primal scene?

While Flitterman-Lewis drew a clear division between the two media, she certainly didn't close off the domestic setting or television viewing to fantasy scenarios. Indeed, her articulation of how television affords 'numerous partial identifications' and a liberation of desire where '[v]oyeuristic pleasure is not bound to a single object, but circulates in a constant exchange' (1992: 219), has obvious queer potential. And this potential is not to be limited to those occasions when (size and sound enhanced-) television actually screens film or even quality TV or even queer(ed) quality TV. Indeed, in its emphasis upon sex and surveillance, upon various spectacles of subjugation and of titillation, it is the ever-expanding genre of reality TV that evidences the most consistent play of voyeuristic and narcissistic pleasures.

Rather than seeing queerness in the form of the text or the form of the viewer, can we locate it instead within the act and psychodynamics of viewing? (And, given how queerness in its radical, oppositional formation defies the essentialism of being attached to an object, but resides instead in a dynamic, in a desire, in an economy, is this not the most appropriate location for it?) The sense of a psychically invested or politicised dynamic to viewing has been implied by many, within, for example, what John Hartley (2004: 528) called the DIY citizenship of television, or as Robert Stam put it, its 'fictive we' (1983: 39), or what Karen Lury more recently termed its 'fantasy of community' (2005: 184).

And what about the distracted viewer's lack of commitment, his or her unfixity or, dare I call it, promiscuity? Hartley, writing in 2004, ran with the metaphor of romance to describe the relationship between the small screen and the viewer (and this certainly makes sense in terms of its need to ensnare and keep him/her). Back in 1999, in their audience study for the British Film Institute called *TV Living*, David Gauntlett and Annette Hill noted the common trope of seduction in how their respondents described their viewing patterns; that they 'reported feelings of guilt, like adulterers, when they had allowed TV to seduce them into watching more than they had intended' (1999: 288).

Where cinema requires a monogamous relationship between screen and spectator, television with its often more distracted, channel hopping, glancing, grazing viewer would seem to depend upon a non-monogamy of viewing. This non-monogamy, I'm suggesting, is potentially queer, though this is not to associate it with promiscuity. It must be stressed, and this is crucial, that I am not rendering queer untrue, only unconstrained, and in doing so bringing into relief the normative logic that it offsets.

It is unsurprising, perhaps, that the freedoms that technological changes have afforded are providing rich terrain for queer theorists of the media. Elsewhere in this collection, Jaap Kooijman likens zapping to cruising, in an attempt to challenge the normativeness of TV. That said, the impact of technology on viewing practices has been seen by some as negligible. Indeed, Nicholas Abercrombie, writing on television and society in 1996, put it thus (and please note the language): 'There is no serious evidence that zapping and grazing are particularly common, although every viewer may well perform these unnatural acts from time to time' (1996: 184–5).

In pointing to, in challenging, the normative logic of television viewing, indeed of television criticism, what gets thrown into relief are the assumed norms, the banalities, and even the harmlessness of home life. This is not to say that television has not been scrutinised for its ideological intent already. TV was, after all, the main choice for the radical reconsideration of the agency of the cultural consumer by the Birmingham School.

But the politics of television viewing lies not only in the distinction of difference (that audiences are diverse in terms of class, race, gender, etc.); they lie, I want to suggest, in the demystification of the home as haven, as homogenised, private space of (de-sexualised) hetero-romance. Queering this space requires us to emphasise the by now familiar question mark over the nuclear family. There is plenty of evidence to suggest the change in the demography of family life: the rise of the single parent, the advent of the alternative family, and also the cult of the single homeowner. But more than this, it requires us to acknowledge that families are often, typically even, dysfunctional and that this plays out through the everyday collision or suppression of wills on the home front. It requires us to place television into just that kind of dynamic of social and psychic interaction that was so much earlier demanded of film.

A first stop then is to recognise the relationship between sexuality and television, not in terms of programming – this has already been explored, and very successfully, by Jane Arthurs (2004) – but in terms of politicising and sexualising the space of viewing. Again, though I would want to get away from the emphasis on sexuality, from seeing sexuality and sexuality only as representing queerness, it is normative-ness and queerness' most useful or obvious vehicle. It is important to note, then, the domestic space's dual and often conflicted identity in terms of its sexualisation. It is the site of the conventionality of the nuclear family, of sanctioned versions of sexual expression and interpersonal relationships. It is also frequently the location of an individual's first sexual experiences: in terms of consensual acts – and the sofa has special resonance here – but, of course, of non-consensual acts too.

A second crucial point about sofa spectatorship and sex is that the expansion of sofa spectatorship – the growth of home viewing – dovetailed with the sexualisation of spectatorship. Sofa spectatorship, therefore, represents the move into the home, that is the privatisation of the perverse pleasures of viewing. With this assertion, I am responding to Linda Ruth Williams' work on the direct-to-video erotic thriller

(2005) in which she argued that the rapid development of the home-viewing market corresponded exactly to the explosion of this specific genre. It also depended upon two major technological advances during the same period: the birth of the world wide web in 1991, whose sexual potential 'was manifest from the start', and of the VCR, which meant 'you could watch whatever you wanted, whenever you wanted with whoever you wanted, in privacy' (Williams 2005: 7). And, as Robert C. Allen has noted, 'the VCR became the primary vehicle in the US for legally distributing hardcore pornographic films in the 1980s' (2004: 14) and 'made possible a form of low-tech "pay-TV" that was difficult if not impossible to police by government authorities' (15). With the shifts in viewing practices and in the 'nature' of private/home entertainment, '[t]he spectator could now control the erotic image (via the rental market, and the remote control), and own the image (via the retail market)' (Aaron 2007: 82).

That retail market has become ever larger and ever more significant. Of course, it also becomes an alternative exhibition circuit for queer production. While the home operates as an increasingly important site for lesbian and gay culture and of new possibilities of community, it must be noted that the television screen has always held a special role for lesbians and gays, quite probably providing the individual's first encounter with lesbian and gay imagery. With the advent of multi-television/screen homes, the ease of access would have been much aided. At the same time, I am reminded of Thomas Austin's important study of young men's reception of Basic Instinct (1992), in which he notes how, for example, the 'kudos', 'social disapproval' and 'embarrassment of watching sex scenes in public' affected their viewing (Austin 1999: 158). If they felt uncomfortable in the cinema, how comfortable could they feel at home? And so it is crucial to note how peer and family pressure and moral imperatives, as well as multi-screen homes, shape viewing and viewing patterns.

While much has been written about the impact of gender on viewing patterns in the household, very little so far has been written on the impact of sexuality on viewing patterns. We are not yet at the point where audience research has been carried out on the television practices of families with lesbian and gay members, whether as children or as parents, or of other cohabiting combinations: of students, of friends, etc, who may include non-heterosexual, even queer members. That said, audience research is not the key concern here. What I have preferred to dig up are the politicised practices, often unobtrusive, frequently unconscious, that underlie our engagement with culture and with each other. Television provides a fascinating focus for this, situated as it so commonly is within the first closet that is the home and amidst the family, the ultimate frontier for unpicking the normative processes of everyday life.

Notes

1. This cartography is indebted to, and moves on from, Alexander Doty's mapping of the development of queerness in mass culture in his introduction to *Making Things Perfectly Queer* (1993).

2. I am grateful to my PhD student Rosalind Hanmer and her work on 'Xena's Queer Discourse' for getting me thinking about this extratextual queer realm.
3. Troche directed the seminal lesbian film of the New Queer Cinema wave, *Go Fish* (1994), and is one of the main writer/directors for *The L Word*. Mary Harron directed *American Psycho* (2000) and Michael Cuesta directed *L. I. E.* (2001). Cuesta has gone on to make *Dexter*, with Michael C. Hall as a serial killer, which I'd like to suggest is the queerest of current TV projects.
4. See Sayeau (2005). What is more, Nate's illness and premature death is drawn from Ball's family history.
5. Though *Six Feet Under* was commended for its dealings with race, the naturalisation of homosexuality has been seen to compromise the visibilising of Keith and David's interracial relationship: see Foster (2005: 101).
6. Such *Six Feet Under* trivia can be found at various online sites on the show, such as www.imdb.com or Wikipedia, or within the commentary on the DVD.

References

Aaron, M. (2004a), 'New Queer Cinema: An Introduction' in M. Aaron (ed.) *New Queer Cinema: A Critical Reader*, Edinburgh: Edinburgh University Press, 3–14.

—— (2004b), 'The New Queer Spectator' in M. Aaron (ed.) *New Queer Cinema: A Critical Reader*, Edinburgh: Edinburgh University Press, 187–200.

—— (2006), 'New Queer Cable: *The L Word*, the Small Screen and the Bigger Picture' in K. Akass and J. McCabe (eds) *Reading* The L Word: *Outing Contemporary Television*, London: I. B. Tauris, 33–42.

—— (2007), *Spectatorship: The Power of Looking On*, London: Wallflower.

Abercrombie, N. (1996), *Television and Society*, Cambridge: Polity.

Akass, K. and McCabe, J. (2005), 'Introduction: "Why do people have to die?" "To make contemporary television drama important, I guess"' in K. Akass and J. McCabe (eds) *Reading* Six Feet Under: *TV to Die For*, London: I. B. Tauris, 1–16.

Allen, R.C. (2004), 'Frequently Asked Questions: A General Introduction to the Reader' in R.C. Allen and A. Hill (eds) *The Television Studies Reader*, London and New York: Routledge, 1–24.

Arthurs, J. (2004), *Television and Sexuality: Regulation and the Politics of Taste*, Maidenhead: Open University Press.

Austin, T. (1999), 'Desperate to See It: Straight Men Watching *Basic Instinct*' in M. Stokes and R. Maltby (eds) *Identifying Hollywood's Audiences: Cultural Identity and the Movies*, London: BFI, 147–61.

Becker, A. (2007), 'Showtime Series Break Ratings Records', *Broadcasting and Cable*, 20 November. Online: http://www.broadcastingcable.com/article/CA6504536.html [accessed 25 May 2008].

Becker, R. (2004 [1998]), 'Prime-Time TV in the Gay Nineties: Network Television, Quality Audiences, and Gay Politics' in R.C. Allen and A. Hill (eds) *The Television Studies Reader*, London and New York: Routledge, 389–403.

—— (2006), *Gay TV and Straight America*, Chapel Hill, NC: Rutgers University Press.

Davis, G. (2004), 'Camp and Queer and the New Queer Director' in M. Aaron (ed.) *New Queer Cinema: A Critical Reader*, Edinburgh: Edinburgh University Press, 53–67.

Doty, A. (1993), *Making Things Perfectly Queer: Interpreting Mass Culture*, Minneapolis, MN: University of Minnesota Press.

Dyer, R. (2002), *The Culture of Queers*, London and New York: Routledge.

Flitterman-Lewis, S. (1992), 'Psychoanalysis, Film and Television' in R.C. Allen (ed.) *Channels of Discourse, Reassembled*, 2nd edn, Chapel Hill, NC: University of North Carolina Press, 203–46.

Foster, G.M. (2005), 'Desire and the "Big Black Sex Cop": Race and the Politics of Sexual Intimacy in HBO's *Six Feet Under*' in R. Keller and L. Stratyner (eds) *The New Queer Aesthetic on Television: Essays on Recent Programming*, Jefferson, NC: McFarland, 99–112.

Gauntlett, D. and Hill, A. (1999), *TV Living: Television, Culture, and Everyday Life*, London: Routledge.

Hartley, J. (2004), 'Democratainment' in R.C. Allen and A. Hill (eds) *The Television Studies Reader*, London: Routledge, 524–32.

Heller, D. (2005), 'Buried Lives: Gothic Democracy in *Six Feet Under*' in K. Akass and J. McCabe (eds) *Reading* Six Feet Under: *TV to Die For*, London: I. B. Tauris, 71–84.

Hibberd, J. (2004), 'It's Showtime for Pay TV Net; Splashy "L Word" Could Bring Channel out of Shadows', *TelevisionWeek*, 9 February.

Hoberman, J. (1992), 'Out and Inner Mongolia', *Premiere*, 31 October.

Kaye, P. (2005), 'I'm Dead, Wow, Cool: The Music of *Six Feet Under*' in K. Akass and J. McCabe (eds) *Reading* Six Feet Under: *TV to Die For*, London: I. B. Tauris, 192–206.

Lury, K. (2005), *Interpreting Television*, London: Hodder Arnold.

McCarthy, A. (2001), '*Ellen*: Making Queer Television History', *GLQ: A Journal of Lesbian and Gay Studies*, 7(4): 593–620.

—— (2005), 'Crab People from the Center of the Earth', *GLQ: A Journal of Lesbian and Gay Studies*, 11(1): 97–100.

Mulvey, L. (1988), 'Afterthoughts on "Visual Pleasure and Narrative Cinema" inspired by *Duel in the Sun*' in L. Mulvey (ed.), *Visual and Other Pleasures*, Basingstoke: Macmillan, 29–38.

Rice, L. (2001), 'Death Grips', *Entertainment Weekly*. Online: http://www.ew.com/ew/article/0,,170643,00.html [accessed 5 January 2008].

Rich, B.R. (1992), 'New Queer Cinema', *Sight and Sound*, 2(5): 30–3.

Sayeau, A. (2005), 'Americanitis: Self-help and the American Dream in *Six Feet Under*' in K. Akass and J. McCabe (eds) *Reading* Six Feet Under: *TV to Die For*, London: I.B. Tauris, 94–106.

Shoshana, A. and Teman, E. (2006), 'Coming Out of the Coffin: Life-Self and Death-Self in *Six Feet Under*', *Symbolic Interaction*, November, 29(4): 557–76.

Stam, R. (1983), 'Television News and Its Spectator' in E.A. Kaplan (ed.) *Regarding Television: Critical Approaches – An Anthology*, Frederick, MD: University Publications of America, 27–38.

Sullivan, N. (2003), *A Critical Introduction to Queer Theory*, Edinburgh: Edinburgh University Press.

Tobin, R.D. (2005), 'Politics, Tragedy and *Six Feet Under*: Camp Aesthetics and Strategies of Gay Mourning in Post-AIDS America' in K. Akass and J. McCabe (eds) *Reading* Six Feet Under: *TV to Die For*, London: I.B. Tauris, 85–93.

Turnock, R. (2005), 'Death, Liminality and Transformation in *Sex Feet Under*' in K. Akass and J. McCabe (eds) *Reading* Six Feet Under: *TV to Die For*, London: I. B. Tauris, 39–49.

Williams, L.R. (2005), *The Erotic Thriller in Contemporary Cinema*, Edinburgh: Edinburgh University Press.

Part II

Histories and genres

Chapter 4

One queen and his screen
Lesbian and gay television

Andy Medhurst

A 2008 preamble

When the editors of this book contacted me to say they wanted to include 'One Queen and His Screen', I was simultaneously flattered and alarmed; flattered because it was considered interesting enough to be worth unearthing and reprinting, but alarmed because it is not a piece written with a standard academic voice or swathed in the usual methodological accoutrements. It has, for example, no footnotes, and makes only the slightest, glancing references to other writers who have tackled this topic, so compared with some other pieces in this book, it could well look flimsy, whimsical and distressingly deficient in theoretical muscle. Yet I don't want to apologise for how it was written, since it was originally commissioned for a book aimed not at an academic audience, but at a wider public interested in the social and cultural history of non-heterosexual life in Britain. As such, it sat in that book alongside a batch of similar overview pieces surveying lesbian and/or gay perspectives on other cultural fields (film, literature, theatre, fashion), a range of autobiographical accounts that considered the personal journeys of individuals (both celebrities and non-celebrities) and a small and only slightly poisonous bouquet of political polemics. Consequently, the tone used here deliberately minimised the usual academic trappings, and it would be disingenuous to deny the relief I felt in removing those manacles before squaring up to the keyboard. (There is a wider issue that could be debated here, if space permitted, namely the question of why so many working in what I fear I must in shorthand terms call the 'queer academy' remain so oddly, staunchly determined to make their writing as reader-unfriendly as possible.)

This chapter was written as a history – a brazenly selective one, undeniably, but nonetheless an attempt to trace some lines across the terrain of the cultural past. Years later, looked at in a different century, three things have happened to that history. First, the expansion (would it be too tacky to say 'explosion'?) of representations on television of non-heterosexual characters and themes has meant that writing a single chapter of this type is probably all but impossible today. I was pushing my luck writing this survey in the first half of the 1990s, as the essay itself acknowledges, but where could one start now? How could I find room for

Big Brother's predilection for camp men (and its almost phobic paucity of lesbians); John Paul's doe-eyed tribulations in *Hollyoaks* (if only he'd found solace with Justin, as he did inside my head …); the post-queer, pan-sexual perv-fest of *Torchwood*; and the flirtatious gay/straight buddy-shenanigans of Alan Carr and Justin Lee Collins? Would there be space to reflect on the conundrum that the two most plausibly gay men in *Will and Grace* are Grace and Karen, or to tease out the power-dynamics of the drag queen special editions of *The Weakest Link*, where the only woman we see, quizmistress Anne Robinson, is the most masculine person on screen?

The second, related development in how television history has skewed the history of television I quixotically tried to sketch is that in the face of this recently unleashed army of images, a curious historical amnesia has set in among some viewers. One sometimes feels that for many audiences, televised homosexuality only began with *Queer as Folk* (a series worshipped as holy writ by many, but stubbornly loathed by grumpy old me), before which there was nothing but an arid expanse of unacceptable stereotyping. If my chapter does nothing else, it may point out the limitations of that view, even if some of the names and titles I cite are baffling in their obscurity to some readers. (Dare I hope that bright young things will scamper off to Google for *Gems*?) Third, this history has in itself become a historical artefact, one link in the chain of how those of us living gay or queer lives (personally, I fluctuate) have tried to make sense of what the small screen has said to us, for us, despite us and about us. And yes, I know that 'small screen' might look anachronistic in an era of wide-screen high-definition plasma, and that any even half-reputable sexual–political academic should never use the word 'us' without a screeching flurry of disclaimers, but they are just two more of the reasons why I'm happy to stand by this essay, for all its flaws. It is a period piece, but I like to think that some of it may still resonate, even now.

– Andy Medhurst, 2008

ONE QUEEN AND HIS SCREEN

There are two stories that this chapter needs to tell. One is a story of industries, policies and institutions, while the other deals in a currency of dreams, hopes and feelings. This is as it should be, because television, more than any other cultural form, is where the public and the private merge and mesh. Simultaneously global and domestic, television is the medium that most envelops and informs our social lives while maintaining a direct hotline to the thoughts and fantasies that we hardly dare disclose even to ourselves. We watch collectively but we always watch alone – and it seems to me that lesbians and gay men have felt that tension with a particular intensity, developing our own devious, furious, poignant and scandalous strategies for negotiating its twists and turns.

We're fond of complaining that television either ignores us completely or gets us all wrong, but the grain of truth inside that bitter generalisation shouldn't be allowed to obscure the fact that there have nonetheless been thousands of images purporting to depict us, in every available genre and at all points of the schedule, from well-meaning liberal drama to crassly reductive sitcom, from *Kilroy* debates on lesbian motherhood to Hinge and Bracket appearing on the women's team in *Give Us a Clue*. To try and make sense of this dauntingly diverse output, to avoid producing nothing more than a shopping list of titles, I need to find a perspective, and so I want to relate the broader cultural history of these representations to another history which interests me even more: my own.

That sounds like a recipe for hopeless self-indulgence, but even the most shamelessly autobiographical account of television cannot avoid reflecting on the wider social and public characteristics of the medium. So while the story I want to tell is in some ways nothing more than that of 'One Queen and His Screen', its narrative will be informed by and integrated into the contexts within which my own viewing history must be located. I make no pretence of speaking for everybody, but isn't objectivity a heterosexual conspiracy anyway?

When I press the rewind button on my television recollections, it's never whole programmes that are conjured up, but moments and instants, snatched glances illicitly stored away for future reference. Friends I've talked to while writing this essay confirm this belief that what we learnt to cultivate in those benighted pre-video days were two specifically attuned senses: first a lightning-fast freeze-frame memory that glued key images into our minds, and second a keen nose for scenting out which programmes would be likely to deliver such treasures. Perhaps this was where we learnt to cruise, scavenging through the schedules, scouring and decoding the *Radio Times* for the slight but telling clue. Our quarry? Well, it would be comforting to report that we were seeking programmes that concerned themselves with responsible explorations of the homosexual world, but the truth is gloriously grubbier.

We were looking for men, men as naked as possible, fuel for our fantasies, sights and sounds that spoke to the feelings we probably hadn't yet learnt to articulate in any language that emanated from above the waistline. Whether it was two men kissing in a BBC2 dramatisation of Angus Wilson's *Late Call* or a documentary about the Liverpool team that revealed the truth beneath the football shorts, *The High Chaparral* or *Play for Today*, modern dance or rugby league, the ostensible content was irrelevant. I remember sitting through countless episodes of a particularly tedious 1970s naval drama series called *Warship* (that may not even be its correct title – such are the fickle filters of television memory) just for those moments when the sailors shed their uniforms and marched right off the screen and into my febrile queer imaginings.

Television's potential as an erotic resource was invaluable because it could be consumed, with due and daring surreptitiousness, in the unsuspecting midst of family life. No need to sneak off to forbidden films at the cinema or furtively visit a newsagent sufficiently distant from your usual high street; TV images were beamed straight into your expectant lap, provided your choice of viewing could be justified by an excuse plausible enough to fool the parents. Programmes directly concerned with gay matters were another issue entirely, which is why it's important to insist that television's relationship with its homosexual audiences should never be reduced to only those texts demarcated as being 'about homosexuality'. For the young queer at home, such programmes were off-limits, since to nominate them as part of the evening's entertainment would be far too risky, except of course as a handy opening gambit to pave the way for coming out. Those of us still to take that plunge (and without the benefit of a bedroom TV set) could only regard gay-themed shows as exotic, impossible temptations languishing in the listings.

Yet could they ever have lived up to their mystique? In the case most dear to my heart, the answer is one big screaming yes. Call it fate, or synchronicity, or just the ministering care of a good fairy watching over me, but the fact remains that the first evening I can recall my parents attending a family function without requiring me to accompany them was the evening that Thames TV first transmitted *The Naked Civil Servant*.

Dazed by this ridiculous stroke of luck, and conscious that they might return at any minute, I sat about six inches from the screen with one finger on the 'off' button, drinking in every second as if my life depended on it – which, of course, it did. Miraculously, the parental key wasn't turned in the lock until ten minutes after the film had ended, by which time I was sitting back amid my homework, the surface of fake studiousness stretched taut across the delirious cauldron of discovery beneath. No, *The Naked Civil Servant* did not 'turn me into' a homosexual (at 16, I had long been sure that I never had been or ever would be anything else), but its celebration of Quentin Crisp's unrepentant queenliness filled me with an elated, vertiginous sense of identification, belonging and defiant pride. His loneliness, lovelessness and the scorn and violence poured upon him were elements I either edited out or accepted as the price that lipsticked pioneers must pay. Although the film was set in the past, I had seen the future – and it minced.

It is, of course, the very exceptional status of that evening that made it such a swoon at the time and such a fond memory now. In the general run of events, all I could hope for was to cop the occasional eyeful of thigh and try not to wince too hard when the rest of the living room delightedly lapped up a homophobic joke spat out by some pig-ugly heterosexual comedian. This underlines the negative side of television's shared domestic context, since for every secret tingle I pilfered from the screen there were dozens more moments when thoughtless stereotypes reminded me of my isolation and vulnerability. These wounds hurt all the more because they were inflicted so routinely, part of that blithe, mundane, everyday arrogance through which heterosexual culture presumes its universality. Perhaps it is in such memories and in our consequent desire to spare others the pain we felt that the roots lie of the calls for 'positive images' that so regularly feature in discussions of representation.

These calls are deeply felt and well-intentioned. They demand that the media show some responsibility by providing supportive, balanced portrayals of minority groups, thereby catering for both the self-esteem of the group in question and the information and education of the wider public. One obvious way of facilitating this has been for politicised lesbians and gay men to become more involved in writing and producing for television. In 1979, an American gay writer called Len Richmond co-wrote a new British sitcom, *Agony*, in which the central heroine's best friends were a gay couple whose sexuality was an uncomplicated fact of life rather than any kind of 'issue'. This approach, Richmond hoped, would empower gay viewers and enlighten straight ones. He somewhat romantically speculated that 'some little gay boy in Scotland on a farm somewhere will see the show and realise that everyone who is gay isn't a neurotic weirdo' (*Evening Standard*, 9 March 1979).

The couple Richmond created, Rob and Michael, were certainly free of neuroses. They were admirably credible and impeccably respectable, white professional 30-something with non-effeminate facial hair yet non-macho table manners, rounded and likeable and unfussily tactile with each other, cracking gags about the ridiculousness of straight men, light-years ahead of the cardboard pansies which many other sitcoms wheeled on as one-joke disposables. They were positive images without a single shred of doubt, and at the time I was profoundly grateful for them, which is why I feel rather guilty for pointing out now that they seem really rather dull, their matey house-trained politeness crying out for an injection of flamboyance and scandal. They exemplify my fear that a 'positive image' means 'an image that won't upset heterosexuals'.

Rob and Michael, you see, were part of that breed of homosexual who 'just happens to be gay', a formula much admired and advocated by the proponents of positive images – let's have gay people doing ordinary things: going shopping, washing the car, boiling an egg, reading the papers; run-of-the-mill folk who just happen to be gay. This viewpoint would restrict homosexuality to a discourse of the bedroom, reducing it to nothing more than an occasionally deployed configuration of genitalia. It's a genial, liberal framework that sees sexuality as a relatively minor signifier of difference that shouldn't be overstressed – people are all the same, really – and the textual manifestations of this argument are those most likely to be awarded the label of 'positive image'. Close your eyes and he (because on British television the positive image is almost invariably male) will gradually materialise like someone beamed down in *Star Trek* – here he comes, taking shape, kind and caring, tasteful and tidy, not-at-all-camp and not-at-all-horny, he's Colin from *Eastenders* and he bores me beyond description.

There again, he wasn't written for me, because by the time *Eastenders* began (February 1985) I didn't need him. He was written for gay men's anxious parents and for A-level media studies teachers to show their students that there are some perfectly nice men who, hey, just happen to be gay. Despite my sarcasm, I'd never deny the importance of reaching those constituencies, nor the most vital group of all: those for whom Colin was created – the mid-1980s equivalents of Len Richmond's hypothesised Scots boy. The problem with Colins, however, is that their shoulder-to-cry-on sexlessness, their don't-frighten-the-horses ordinariness, is too frequently elevated into a paradigm towards which all homosexual representations should aspire. They have a value as a starting point, a focus for initial recognition and identification, but to be satisfied with them is to adopt a position of mewling gratitude which has no place in my conception of queerness. Blame my early exposure to Quentin Crisp.

The just-happen-to-be-gay version of homosexuality is also a coded plea for a particular televisual style, a pallid, cautious naturalism in which texts with points to make function as a kind of social work. Much of popular culture, however, depends on more vulgar and downmarket genres, where gently shaded psychological credibility is rejected in favour of schematic, polarised, unapologetically two-dimensional characterisations that allow audiences a more full-blooded involvement. After all, *The Terminator* would be a bit of a bore if we were asked to accept Arnold Schwarzenegger as a fully rounded sensitive individual who just happened to be a ruthless twenty-first century cyborg killing machine. Melodramas don't obey careful political agendas, they let us revel in excessively heightened emotional states. Any sober and rational account of Joan 'The Freak' Ferguson in *Prisoner: Cell Block H* would sorrowfully have to conclude that she was not a 'positive image' of lesbianism; but queer audiences rapturously took her to their hearts, her lying, cheating, sneering, fondling, gravel-voiced, hatchet-faced, up-yours bulldykery a bracing refusal of the condescensions of heterosexual tolerance.

The Freak's strength and impact reside precisely in her 'negativeness'; it was her loathsomeness that made her so queerly lovable. The bold, broad strokes of her villainy have not been matched in British soaps, where gay characters still tend to be the Bobby Ewings rather than the JRs. Before Colin brought tea, sympathy and the Filofax to Albert Square, there had been Gordon in *Brookside*, the vehicle for a thoughtful, if timid, coming-out narrative and predictably a member of the most middle-class household in the serial.

Even earlier, and often overlooked, two daytime ITV soaps had risked the inclusion of gay men. With its setting of a Covent Garden fashion house, *Gems* was almost duty bound to supply at least one temperamentally creative queen, and generously provided three (my favourite being Paul the petulant pattern-cutter). *Together*, based around a relatively well-to-do block of flats, was under no obvious obligation, so the presence of gay couple Pete and Trevor was a laudable step, particularly for 1980. Nonetheless, their living together was the subject of great debate among their neighbours, one concluding that she didn't mind 'because there weren't any kiddies living in the block'. Thirteen years later the 'kiddies' were deemed to be ready for a gay man taking up residence in their own most popular soap, with one storyline in the 1993 series of *Grange Hill* dealing with the repercussions of a teacher's homosexuality (inevitably, perhaps, he was the art teacher) becoming public knowledge all over the school. Given the age group of its target audience, *Grange Hill*'s decision to handle the story with a didactically liberal 'tolerance' slant was excusable – the problem is that when it comes to queers, all British soaps still tend to assume they're watched by surly teenagers in need of education.

Occasional plot lines aside, the British soap had been a lesbian-free zone until *Emmerdale* (of all unlikely candidates) took the plunge in the summer of 1993.

Encouragingly, the woman in question wasn't a specially imported exotic but an established member of the existing soap community. Of course, a small village in the Yorkshire Dales isn't exactly throbbing with lesbian nightlife, so Zoe the vet has had to venture into Leeds (*Emmerdale*'s preferred location for anything vaguely twentieth century) but at the time of writing she has met a lecturer from the university (note, yet again, that equation of queerness with the professional classes) and hands have been held. By the time this book is published heaven knows what might have happened down on the farm. *Brookside*, too, is reputedly limbering up for its first lesbian affair. It would be churlish to find too much fault with the gentle, gradual expansion of soap homosexualities, but perhaps they could risk a little less niceness.

For rare glimpses of lesbian explicitness, viewers have had to rely on other genres, particularly the literary adaptation. Mandy Merck's apt aphorism that if lesbianism didn't exist, art cinema would have to invent it, can equally be applied to 'art television'. Later-evening scheduling, minority channel location and the all-purpose cloak of cultural respectability have meant that programme makers can actually show lesbians between the sheets, provided it all originated between the covers of a book. In 1990, both the National Trust deviance of *Portrait of a Marriage* (where the lesbianism was not so much depicted as landscaped) and the spiky, spunky coming-of-age story of *Oranges Are Not the Only Fruit* benefited from this strategy, though in other ways they could hardly have been more different. More interesting, perhaps, than either was the achievement of Debbie Horsfield's extraordinary *Making Out*, a raucous, gutsy, moving comedy drama about a group of female friends working in a Manchester electronics factory. In its third series, one of the principal characters was seen not only at home but gleefully sharing a bath with her female lover; all this on BBC1, in a prime-time programme with a large and loyal popular following.

Television comedy is a notoriously contentious area, since humour seems particularly troubling to the guardians of political correctness, understandably so when one remembers all the times when jokes provided the neatest parcels in which to wrap homophobic abuse. When I and my student contemporaries used to gather together in the late 1970s for what in retrospect look like endearingly pompous discussions of 'gays and the media' we had one taken-for-granted benchmark starting point: comic stereotypes of camp, queeny men were A Bad Thing. There were two reasons for this – first, we were not like that (except of course after we'd finished our GaySoc meetings and went out to the bars to scream our tits off); and second, it gave straight people the wrong impression. Yet again, we were measuring our own culture with imported and inappropriate yardsticks, policing ourselves with the anxious wish not to offend.

One figure can be taken as emblematic of those arguments: Larry Grayson. A one-time drag act from the less glamorous reaches of the variety theatre circuit, Grayson achieved sudden, dizzying fame in the early 1970s with a stand-up comedy routine that basically consisted of fey innuendo, acrobatic eyebrows and the limpest of wrists. The more successful he became, however, the greater the fury of the gay political intelligentsia of the time. When he became host of the BBC's *Generation Game*, *Gay News* moved in for the kill, labelling this:

> the worst possible thing that could happen to gay rights on British television ... as far as we are concerned they do not come much lower than Larry Grayson ... He will earn many thousands of pounds at our expense. He will become a 'superstar' while he confuses and distresses our young teenage brothers.
>
> (*Gay News*, 143, 1978)

What was it about Grayson that prompted such a self-righteous tizzy? On one level, *Gay News* was making a useful point about the lack of range of available representations – if Grayson's persona was the only image of homosexuality given mass circulation, the picture created would undeniably be a distorted one – but underneath there is a more complex question of class. To *Gay News*, Grayson stood for an embarrassingly persistent tradition of working-class queer culture that refused to take its lead from the well-bred radicals of the 1960s (note the give-away use of the term 'brothers'). Beyond the campuses, camp thrived, the survival humour of the subculture. To look back at Grayson in full flow is to understand why – if straight audiences thought they were mocking his pitiful poofery, then more fool them; he was getting away with murder, hardly able to believe his luck, asserting the splendidness of not being normal by deploying the effrontery of effeminacy.

One of the most exciting aspects of the queer politics of the early 1990s has been its upsetting of historical applecarts, its insistence that the gay world did not begin in 1969, that there were older, richer, more diverse histories with which we could connect ourselves. The reclaiming of Grayson might be taken as one small symptomatic example of this. We have, I trust, now reached a stage where the importance of camp to gay male culture could be denied only by those sad folk who put 'no effems' in their personal ads; and that 1970s *Gay News* paranoia about queens now looks, with hindsight, like a brief defensive blip. Camp is one of the weapons we can use to make the world more amenable to our needs and perspectives; it's a language in which we're particularly and deliciously fluent, a notably witty example of its effectiveness being the way in which Channel 4's *Out* series spiced up an item comparing the laws pertaining to homosexuality in the countries that make up the European Community. A worthy topic, but potentially dry as dust, so *Out* turned it into a mock-up of the Eurovision Song Contest and (this being the little pink twist of camp that made all the difference) persuaded Katie Boyle herself to introduce it.

In many ways, the high-profile existence of *Out* was an indisputable landmark in the saga of television and homosexuality, yet it would be rash to imply that these pro-grammes received an unqualified welcome. Indeed, some of the most entrenched, curdled and bitter arguments I have ever had about television have centred on the merits or otherwise of particular items from that series, but this in itself is a healthy sign, an index of how *Out*'s lack of a party line, its irreverence and its glitziness and its argumentativeness and its anger, fed on and into the multiple homosexualities of recent years, demonstrating an increased confidence, a welcoming of diversity and a long overdue shedding of any need to 'justify' who and what we variously are. By contrast, the short-lived, London-only, graveyard-scheduled *Gay Life*, made by London Weekend Television in 1979, was still rooted in a model of explanation rather than celebration, stylistically unadventurous and ponderously even-handed. In other words, like any television programme, it was a text of its times, exciting and crucial by the sheer fact of its being there ('At last!' cried the cover headline of *Gay News* when the series began) but inevitably cramped and compromised. In the context of British broadcasting at that historical moment, how could it have been otherwise?

There are, of course, so many more titles to name and issues to explore – I haven't even mentioned Freddie from *Eldorado*, the lesbian and gay plots in *Casualty* or Channel 4's magical, perfectly pitched adaptation of *Tales of the City* – but the spectre of the shopping list looms large. It would be satisfying to find one final example, one sweeping rhetorical flourish, to encapsulate all the narrative strands and political tensions sketched so hurriedly above, but television isn't like that. Endlessly proliferating, it always resists definitive summary. Besides, audiences change even more rapidly than the programmes they consume: I've watched television as a secretive homosexual, a sanctimoniously right-on gay man, a screaming queen and now (just look at how they waste tax-payers' money) a queer academic, and the four of me are still fighting over the remote control – how could we ever agree on selecting a single representative image from all the thousands that we've seen? It's impossible, though the sight of Julian Clary (our wised-up, postmodern Larry Grayson) in all his take-no-prisoners, flagrant finery, descending the stairs to usher us into his *Sticky Moments* comes very, very, very close.

Chapter 5

'We're not all so obvious'

Masculinity and queer (in)visibility in American network television of the 1970s

Joe Wlodarz

While the era of 'relevant' television in American network TV has been widely praised (and closely analyzed) because of its engagement with issues of gender, race, and class identity in the tumultuous 1970s, less attention has been paid to the period's exploitation and examination of homosexuality.[1] On the heels of Stonewall and amidst the expanding gay liberation movement, network television in the 1970s also 'came out' to varying degrees and in unpredictable ways. Indeed, the emergence of denotatively gay and lesbian characters in the late 1960s and early 1970s marks a significant shift in what Lynne Joyrich (2001) has called the 'epistemology of the console.'[2] Although connotatively queer characters, such as Paul Lynde's Uncle Arthur on *Bewitched* (ABC, 1964–72), continued to inhabit the margins of the home screen, seventies television (and American media in general) often reveled in the epistemological promise of gay and lesbian visibility and open declarations of homosexual identity. Emblematic of this post-Stonewall moment, *Time* magazine's first cover story on homosexuality appeared in late 1969, proclaiming 'The Homosexual: Newly Visible, Newly Understood' (Foster 1969).

One of the earliest coming out scenes of the era occurs in a 1970 episode of *Medical Center* (CBS, 1969–76) that focuses on the outing of a successful gay scientist/physician, Dr. Ben Teverley (Paul Burke), through a smear campaign ('Undercurrent,' 23 September 1970). In a key scene, the doctor reveals his homosexuality to a female colleague who's romantically interested in him. As he informs her: 'I'm a homosexual ... I'm not one of the obvious kinds, and for that I'm thankful, but I'm not about to lead you to any altar.' This direct revelation intrigues because it's actually the second of *three* separate times that the doctor is forced to confess his homosexuality to other colleagues. His disavowal of the apparently feminine associations of 'obvious' homosexuality is clearly a position shared by the liberal humanist approach of the episode itself. In fact, his supervisor, who adamantly opposes the promotion of Teverley's research, blames his intolerance on a 'deviant ... limp-wristed son-in-law' who put the supervisor's daughter in analysis for over a year. But while Chad Everett's heroic Dr. Gannon confronts and denounces the supervisor's bigotry, the episode itself reveals a particular anxiousness about Teverley's own lack of 'obviousness.' For just as the episode's narrative exploits the enigma of Teverley's unreadable sexuality, his ambiguity nevertheless demands a seemingly endless series of conversations and confessions about homosexuality that work to resecure, however unsuccessfully, its definitional parameters in relation to more normative modes of gender and sexuality.

In a 2007 episode of Chicago Public Radio's *This American Life*, entitled 'What I Learned from Television,' gay sex columnist Dan Savage recalls the trauma he experienced as an adolescent watching 'swishy' gay stereotypes with his father on seventies TV programmes such as *Barney Miller* (ABC, 1975–82). He explains: 'when gays popped up on TV – something that inconveniently enough began to happen with greater and greater frequency just as I hit puberty – things got awkward. Here was this subject we were avoiding at all costs, and all of a sudden we were ambushed by the television set.' Knowing he was '*some* kind of fag,' but determined not to be the purse-carrying, poodle-owning queen that seemed to dominate the TV landscape, Savage turned away from the tube and 'made up [his] mind to be a different sort of homo.'

Had he been a more determined (or promiscuous) TV viewer in the seventies, though, Savage would likely have discovered several 'different sorts of homos' on the home screen. For the era of emergent gay visibility in American network television was also marked by a significant (if inconsistent) challenge to the long-standing 'sissy' stereotype. Indeed, a closer analysis of some of the groundbreaking but long-forgotten gay-themed episodes of the 1970s can help clarify the complex ways that male homosexuality was made visible (and invisible) in relation to traditional norms of masculinity during this key transitional period. The appearance of such images of masculine gay men on television is particularly revealing in light of the destabilization of white patriarchal norms that plays out in the late 1960s and 1970s in response to feminism, Black Power, the Vietnam War, and gay liberation.

Although lesbian images and 'queen' or 'sissy' figures have a similarly conflicted and controversial place in early seventies television, the tenuous visibility of masculine gay men proves especially disruptive. The masculine gay not only tests the presumed security of the homo/hetero binary, he also incites a complex interrogation of masculinity and male sociality. And while he seems to uphold certain myths of masculinity and fantasies of patriarchal prowess, his homosexuality remains unassimilable to the traditions and norms of hegemonic manhood. Furthermore, the patriarchal conflation of aggressive sexual desire with masculinity significantly keeps the masculine gay man sexualized, even in the presumed comfort zone of network TV. What matters most, though, is that the basic *invisibility* of the masculine gay – the fact that we can't tell he's gay until he tells us – functions in many of these seventies programmes to make hegemonic masculinity and heterosexuality *more* visible. In fact, the coming out of the masculine gay often tells us more about norms of gender and sexuality than about gay culture, gay masculinity, or gay sex. He denaturalizes masculinity and heterosexuality at the very moment that he seems to normalize homosexuality.

Two recurrent figures in such episodes best represent the troubled (and troubling) place of male homosexuality in seventies television: the masculine, adult gay jock and the ambiguously gay adolescent boy, who is also commonly positioned in relation to athletics. Tensions, contradictions, and conflicts between gender and sexuality are typically worked through *on the bodies* of these two recurring types, and the sports context paradoxically fuels the disruptive presence of these queer figures. Indeed, the sports world provided a major locus of queer visibility in the 1970s as Patricia Nell Warren's novel, *The Front Runner*, about gay, Olympic-level runners, became a best seller in 1974. One year later, NFL running back David Kopay caused a sensation when he became the first professional team-sport athlete to come out. Olympic decathlete Tom Waddell joined his male lover in the 'Couples' section of *People* magazine in 1976, and tennis player Renee Richards brought transsexual issues back to the mainstream media when she was denied entrance to the women's field of the 1976 US Open. Unlike such publicly 'out' figures, though, network television of the seventies assigns the adult gay jock a particularly *elusive* visibility; indeed, he often functions as the site and sign of the instability of hegemonic masculinity itself.

Potentially gay adolescents are similarly posited as figures of crisis in seventies television because there is increasing uncertainty about the outcome of their developmental trajectory. For the destabilizing potential of the masculine gay jock – in relation to dominant notions of gender and sexuality – is only enhanced by the broader interrogation of patriarchal manhood that takes place in the context of seventies America. As such, ambiguously gay adolescents often appear in TV texts ostensibly concerned less with sexuality per se than with the ever-shifting parameters of manhood itself. For example, a 1971 episode of ABC's *Room 222*, aptly entitled 'What is a Man?' (3 December 1971), explores the harassment of an artistic teenage boy, Howard (Frederick Herrick), by his high school classmates. Although the programme never clarifies Howard's sexuality, it does stage an incisive critique of the intolerance (and repressed homoeroticism) of high school jock culture and traditional notions of male sociality.

Throughout the seventies, teens like Howard find their televisual development ironically 'arrested,' not in a Freudian sense, but rather through the inability of network television and American culture to effectively predict, script, or even imagine a stable endpoint to their development. Seventies television thus posits male adolescence in general *as queer* in a variety of ways that not only manifest the instability of dominant masculinity itself but that also confound teleological, and heteronormative, developmental trajectories.[3] Given such ambiguities, though, and the fact that both figures are often sexualized, 'out' gay jocks and potentially gay adolescent boys are typically kept apart. This enforced separation attempts both to contain their mutually disruptive presence and to impede any potential intergenerational alliances, affinities, or desires. In the few instances when these figures do encounter and engage with one another in seventies TV (*The Bold Ones*, *Marcus Welby*) their relations are notably marked by hostility, panic, exploitation, and even violence.

Such textual and ideological obstacles foreground the representational stakes of male homosexuality during this period. They also reveal the crucial role that network television played – for better and for worse – in expanding gay and lesbian visibility during the 1970s. Indeed, the reemergence of many forgotten, censored, or archived queer televisual moments on DVD in recent years serves as an important instance of *re-visibility* that fosters new perspectives on both the current state and the history of queer media imagery.[4] This access helps complicate the reductive dismissal of early gay images on television as simply primitive, negative, one-dimensional, homophobic, or desexualized. It also enables a more wide-ranging appreciation and negotiation of the uniquely queer flow of gay representation in seventies network television.

Most scholarly work on seventies television and gay media visibility has been critical of the fact that gay characters during this era are limited to 'one-off' appearances and developed only within the limited parameters of the individual episode (Capsuto 2000; Gross 2001; McCarthy 2001; Tropiano 2002; Walters 2003). Although seriality as a narrative mode significantly expanded in seventies prime time television, Billy Crystal's Jodie on *Soap* (ABC, 1977–81) is the only notable gay character with an extended serial presence during the decade, and his ever-shifting relationship to homosexuality (and gay identity) over the run of the show both confirmed and confounded conventional notions of gay visibility.[5] Thus, while recognizing the historical significance of the limited serial presence of gays and lesbians – as well as the unpredictable nature of serial TV in general – it remains necessary to find alternative ways of framing, evaluating, and negotiating the disparate queer content in seventies television.

What's fascinating about gay representations in seventies television is the way that these images change, fluctuate, shift, *and* contradict one another over the course of the decade, particularly in relation to key cultural and political events (gay liberation, the APA decision, Anita Bryant, the Briggs Initiative, etc.). Looking across these diverse texts for what I will call a *cross-textual seriality* engages with the rapidly transforming nature of gay visibility during this period and connects and associates 'one-off' gay/queer characters from the variety of narratives, contexts, and programmes that circulate in seventies network television. Seriality in this sense addresses the developmental narrative of queer representation during this period. While this seriality occurs unpredictably, inconsistently, and often incoherently *outside* of the specific parameters of individual texts in seventies television, a fragmented narrative is illustrated piece by piece in the series of representations shown to us. These representations were not developed in a single (or singular) context due to the cultural, political, and industrial limitations of American network television, but it is nonetheless revealing to explore the connections between these disparate visions and what they reveal to us about sexuality in mainstream media.

This concept of cross-textual seriality could indeed be applied to patterns of development found in the representation of minority images in a wide variety of media and historical contexts – i.e. Vito Russo's *The Celluloid Closet* (1987). What's important about the approach here is that network television of the 1970s provides *the* crucial site for exploring the emergence, expansion, and development of denotative gay imagery in mainstream American media. As such, an unusually wide variety of critical publics – including gay audiences, gay media activists, the mainstream press, right wing fundamentalist groups, and other minority groups – traced, tracked, and commented upon the wide variety of gay images *across* the rapidly transforming televisual landscape of the 1970s.

Furthermore, homosexuality as a theme/topic was (and still is) used as a sign of American network TV's own development during this period. 1972's landmark made-for-TV movie, *That Certain Summer* (ABC, 1 November 1972), notably inspired a wide variety of critical commentary in the mainstream press on the relationship of this unique representation of a mature, middle class, masculine gay couple to television's own emerging 'maturity.' Anticipating the premiere, the *Chicago Tribune* promised that 'television is going to grow up a little this Wednesday night,' while the *Los Angeles Times* suggested that *That Certain Summer* 'represents a landmark in the emergence of television as a dramatic medium' (Champlin 1972; Kramer 1972). Perhaps most revealingly, *New York Times* TV critic John J. O'Connor, one of the decade's most frequent and insightful critics of gay TV representation, framed the successes of *Summer* in relation to the development of gay TV images from the mincing queen to the macho gay football player from *All in the Family*'s first season (O'Connor 1972).

Such cross-textual approaches are not simply a response to the complex process of televisual flow, they also mimic gay reception practices of the period. In an era of limited, if expanding, visibility in the mainstream media, gay audiences and critics would similarly jump from show to show, series to series, to watch the many one-off gay-themed episodes of the period. This more promiscuous gay viewership typically trumped individual series fidelity and thus continually recast the TV landscape as set by the networks and advertisers. More significantly, though, the prominence and variance of gay images in network television and the networks' insistence on returning to homosexuality as a central narrative issue also worked to serialize homosexuality – and sexuality in general – in increasingly unpredictable ways. By late 1979, in one of many overviews of gay TV representations of the decade, Gay Media Task Force representative Newton Dieter acknowledged that in spite of all the efforts of gay media activists there remained no clear 'pattern of progress' in images of gays on television (Taylor 1979).

Examining gay representation in seventies TV through this lens of cross-textual seriality thus foregrounds alternative, plural narratives of gender and sexual identity that challenge both the episodic marginalization of homosexuality *and* a potentially restrictive narrative of ideal, positive, or mature gay images. Thus, while on one hand this approach helps counter TV's tendency to simply arrest the development of potentially gay teens, it also retains the unpredictability, messiness, even negativity, of gay images during this period. Indeed, a cross-textual seriality that runs throughout the televisual landscape helps reveal an array of gay images that are less coherently or cohesively constructed, strategized, or premeditated. This potential opens up, rather than shuts down, a variety of queer associations, identifications, desires, narratives, and histories on and through television during this important transitional moment in American culture.

Activism, visibility, and masculinity

The representational slippages that play out in relation to gay male visibility in seventies television have a complicated relationship to media activism of the period. Gay visibility in early seventies television was accompanied by a surge in gay media activism. Groups such as the Gay Activists Alliance, the National Gay Task Force, the Gay Media Task Force, and numerous city-based affiliates participated in disruptive protests (or 'zaps') of major media stations/programmes and, eventually, became consultants and script advisors for gay-themed network programming (Alwood 1996: 101–55; Capsuto 2000: 59–114). Later in the decade, the Religious Right (Donald Wildmon, Jerry Falwell, Anita Bryant, etc.) also began to play an increasingly important role in limiting and recoding gay representation on network TV (Capsuto 2000: 115–44). The goals of the gay activists, in line with the politics of gay liberation, were primarily tied to a civil-rights based *minoritizing* strategy, which Anna McCarthy has, more recently, called an 'analogical approach to identity politics' (2001: 607).[6] Like African Americans, gay men and lesbians at this time required ostensibly stable, positive, normal, identifiable representations of themselves on screen to counter years of misrepresentation.

Such a strategy was reinforced to some degree by the American Psychological Association's early 1974 revision of the Diagnostic and Statistical Manual that removed (and thus depathologized) homosexuality from its listed mental illnesses. Similarly, the gradual transition from protest-based activist zaps to script consultation and negotiation with the networks did indeed work to 'uplift' gay images over the course of the decade. Such negotiations also made mainstream audiences more aware of both representational stereotypes *and* alternative possibilities via their coverage and debate in the popular press. In a late 1973 article in the *Los Angeles Times*, entitled 'Gays Lobby for a New Media Image,' Gregg Kilday explained the key complaints/requests of the National Gay Task Force's recent '8 point statement' on gay TV representation in relation to a series of gay images on TV from the late 1960s to the present day (Kilday 1973). A few months later, John J. O'Connor in the *New York Times* provided a detailed analysis of the input and effects of the Gay Media Task Force's reworking of the script for a graphic *Police Story* episode ('The Ripper,' NBC, 12 February 1974) about a killer of homosexual men (O'Connor 1974a).

Many mainstream critics (both pro- and anti-gay) resisted these strategic consultations because of their tendency to reduce the variability of televisual representations.[7] Despite their concerns, negative images hardly disappeared in the seventies, and, perhaps more importantly, television's complex relationship to structures of the closet continually resisted the reining in of gay images in network TV. In line with Eve Sedgwick's discussion of the minoritizing and universalizing modes of conceiving of and representing homosexuality, seventies television traffics in both modes rather extensively, presenting gay men as a distinct group of people *and* suggesting that 'sexual desire is an unpredictably powerful solvent of stable identities' (Sedgwick 1990: 85).

The key figure in seventies television that fully embodies both tendencies is not the conventional sissy or queen character, but instead the masculine gay man. This figure emerges from the shadows in some of the earliest programmes dealing with homosexuality on network television (*NYPD*, *Medical Center*) and remains both important and prominent throughout the decade. Many of the more liberal gay-themed episodes of the 1970s (*All in the Family*, *Medical Center*, *Alice*) work to normalize images of gay men by aligning them with masculine traditions and professions (athletes, cops, doctors, lawyers). Still, there remains in these episodes and in other more phobic programmes (*The Bold Ones*, *Marcus Welby*, *Dan August*) an anxiety about the various ways that the traditionally masculine gay man – typically a jock – impacts on gender, sexual, and social identity in general. As a result, we see a complex play between gay visibility and invisibility in these episodes that confounds the epistemological certainty conventionally associated with 'out' gay characters. Such figures also inevitably cast an interrogative light on hegemonic masculinity *and* heterosexuality; once gay men come out on prime time TV, straight men have to as well. And by the mid-to-late seventies, there is a wide variety of gay soldiers, gay cops, gay construction workers, gay jocks, and other traditionally masculine types on prime time programming. What we see in such representations, particularly in the image of the gay jock, is a universalizing approach that inadvertently functions to queer patriarchal norms and institutions, especially sports.

This tenuous, and disruptive, gay visibility is further enhanced by the stock TV genres and formats of the era. Medical dramas, law and order programmes, and sitcoms all necessarily anchor gay images in the context of traditional social institutions (and plot templates) that exist to contain modes of social disorder and deviance. As such, these genres oftentimes work to police the boundaries of sexuality, and yet their formal, narrative, and ideological conventions are also tested by the disruptive power of queer difference. Many of the earliest representations of homosexuality on network television in the gay liberation era position gay men as an oppressed minority, as victims of individual and institutional bigotry. For example, both 1967 episode of *NYPD* (ABC, 1967–9), 'Shakedown,' and the aforementioned 1970 episode of *Medical Center* focus on gay men as victims of blackmail and/or smear campaigns. They hint at the importance *and* difficulty of coming out as well as plead for liberal tolerance. They also break new ground by presenting their gay male characters as conventionally masculine.

In the 'Shakedown' episode of *NYPD* (5 September 1967), James Broderick plays Gaffer, a closeted gay construction worker – and blackmail target – described by *Variety* at the time as one of the '*virile* third sexers' (quoted in Tropiano 2002: 60, my emphasis).[8] The programme also introduces Charles Spad (John Harkins), an out gay businessman, similarly represented against type, who resists the detectives' request for 'insider' information on gay blackmail targets by exposing their own hypocrisy on sexual matters. In a remarkable speech for a 1967 television show, he directly critiques the 'moralistic … straighter-than-thou … body politic' who 'do their own secret things and call it having a little fun,' but consistently classify what others do as 'perversion.' This mirror held up to the straight male detectives (and mainstream society) by Spad is an element that recurs in other programmes featuring masculine gay men throughout the decade, but the 'unreadability' of such figures is also handled in more anxious ways in early seventies TV.

A 1970 episode of *Dan August* (ABC, 1970–1), 'Dead Witness to a Killing' (28 January 1971), takes a somewhat different tack as the ambitions of a closeted politician, Arthur Coleman, (Laurence Luckinbill from *The Boys in the Band*) lead him to murder his sister and his gay lover Norman Sayles (Martin Sheen). Coleman's confession is especially revealing: as he tries to connect his murderous actions to his victimized status he simultaneously breaks down and weeps uncontrollably in an as-yet-unseen effeminate manner. His confession, his 'coming out,' establishes him as both killer and victim. It also marks a shift from an ostensibly invisible, normative masculinity to a visibly deviant identity anchored by gender inversion. Male homosexuality can indeed be *seen* here, but it's primarily visible as either a physical abnormality – Sheen's Sayles has a bleeding ulcer – or as a gender inversion (Coleman's confession). The casting of hypermasculine Burt Reynolds as Dan August also works to enhance the association of Sheen and Luckinbill with a less vigorous manhood, and their presentation here suggests that the 'truth' of homosexuality will eventually manifest itself on and through the body. But even as the conclusion of *Dan August* struggles to contain homosexuality through a marked visibility, much of the episode exploits the dramatic potential of unreadable sexual identity.[9] 'Dead Witness to a Killing' also features one of the earliest prime time treks inside a gay bar and one of the rare *black* gay men – the bar's owner – in seventies TV. As the conventionally masculine owner informs August: 'we're not all so obvious, you know.' The space of the gay bar here both licenses and fuels the ethnographic impulse of seventies TV. It provides a context that anchors gay visibility – even as the bartender complicates the typical (or presumed) whiteness of homosexuality – at a moment in which gay identity is particularly elusive.

The gay jock

Dan August and *Medical Center* negotiate the potential unreadability of the masculine gay man in different but equally revealing ways, but the figure that most clearly embodies the representational crises incited by the issue of gay visibility on network television is unquestionably the gay jock. The earliest, and perhaps most memorable, example of this character type appears in a groundbreaking first season episode of the most influential 'relevant' programme of the entire decade, Norman Lear's *All in the Family* (CBS, 1971–9). The 'Judging Books by Covers' (9 February 1971) episode establishes a common sitcom trope of 'mistaken identity' in which the unreadability of a queer character incites a variety of homoerotic (and homophobic) responses.[10] Here Archie (Carroll O'Connor) incorrectly assumes a thin, well-dressed, effeminate man is gay, and he makes a number of derogatory remarks about his apparent sexuality. Later, at the local pub, a bartender tells Mike (Rob Reiner) that Archie's burly, masculine, ex-pro football player buddy, Steve (Philip Carey), is actually gay. Adopting a variety of fey gestures, without ever mentioning the word homosexual, the bartender says he's OK with Steve because he doesn't 'camp it up.' Mike inevitably outs Steve, and Archie berates Mike for 'smearing the name of a great linebacker ... a man, a *real* man.'

After watching a boxing match and complimenting Steve on his 'big mitts,' his 'size,' and his 'strength,' Archie challenges him to an arm wrestling match. As Steve quickly overpowers him, Archie pleasurably moans: 'Oh geez, oh beautiful; boy, what an arm.' He then laments the new generation's disrespect for the 'old institutions,' the 'things that separate the sexes,' namely 'sports, sportsmanship, guts, and guns,' in a direct conflation of sex, gender, and sexuality. Finally, in another heated bout of arm wrestling, Archie, hesitantly and indirectly ('I can't even say it'), asks Steve about Mike's accusation. Steve's defiant affirmation ('He's right!'), in close-up, is followed by Archie's continued disbelief, even as Steve suggests that the 'privacy' of the 'bachelor' life that Archie associates with him may indeed have other connotations. With a sharp punch to Archie's shoulder, Steve exits the bar and the series. Still, Archie's disbelief persists: 'Well, if that's the punch of a fruit ...' Then, as the camera zooms in to his face, the unsettling effects of that very possibility begin to register.

As Eve Sedgwick notes, 'the double-edged potential for injury in the scene of gay coming out ... results partly from the fact that the erotic identity of the person who receives the disclosure is apt also to be implicated in, hence perturbed by it' (1990: 81). Thus, Archie's appreciation of Steve's body and strength, and the erotic dimension of the arm wrestling, work not only to trouble stereotypical norms of gay male sexuality but also to implicate male homosociality, especially sports and physical games, in those same systems of desire.

A similar scenario plays out in the premiere episode 'Alice Gets a Pass' (29 September 1976) of the first season of *Alice* (CBS, 1976–85). In 1976, just months after NFL running back David Kopay's coming out makes national head-lines, the gay jock plot is used to *introduce* a new sitcom, foregrounding both the proliferation and importance of homosexuality to network TV at the time. In this episode, Mel's (Vic Tayback) college room-mate, Jack Newhouse (Denny Miller), an ex-pro quarterback, returns to town and causes a stir when he stifles Alice's (Linda Lavin) romantic advances on a date by coming out to her. At the diner the following day, Alice's co-worker Flo (Polly Holliday) uses a series of football metaphors to inquire about the presumably heterosexual romantic entanglements of the previous evening. When Alice finally reveals the truth ('Jack's gay'), Flo's skepticism leads Alice to repeat the revelation two additional times. Still uncon-vinced, Flo chuckles, and with her quick, clipped delivery and heavy Southern accent, she explains to Alice the ridiculousness of this declaration:

'Alice, Jack Newhouse is a *football player*, honey. He's big and strong. Any woman would die to take that hunk-a-candy home. Why he spends half his life surrounded by big, *virile* men, in locker rooms, in showers. Being tackled by other football players ...
[Flo pauses, her delivery slows with her realization, the camera zooms in]

Jumpin' up and down and huggin' each other …
[A longer pause, a closer shot, even slower delivery]
Pattin' each others' *butts* …
[After an even longer pause, Flo returns to her rapid fire delivery]
If that don't beat all, Jack Newhouse gay!'

What's amusing (and revealing) about this particular moment is Flo's transition from assuming that sports – and their associated male rituals – guarantee heterosexuality to assuming that they guarantee homosexuality. The joke is that the truth lies somewhere in-between, but in the context of the seventies sitcom, that very truth must also remain a joke. The remainder of the episode focuses on Alice's newfound anxiety about a fishing trip her 12-year-old son has been planning to take with Jack and Mel. Although Tommy (Philip Mckeon) isn't necessarily coded as sexually ambiguous, and Jack eventually persuades Alice to let Tommy go, the episode nevertheless introduces the possibility that some unspoken indiscretion did indeed take place on the trip. After keeping his mom in a panicked suspense, Tommy eventually reveals that Jack and Mel let him drink half a can of beer, and, as Alice finally relaxes, she tells Tommy that Jack is a homosexual. Tommy admits to being surprised, but only because he 'thought you could always tell.' Thus, even as the episode defuses the social (and sexual) threat of the masculine gay jock, it exploits the disruptive potential of this figure until the very end. In the programme's closing line, Mel denies the possibility of Jack's homosexuality by insisting: 'If Jack Newhouse is gay, I'm gay!'

A double-edged quality thus persists in relation to the gay jock tied to his elusive visibility and to the queer associations he incites. Such transgressive potential seems also to mandate the exclusion of the gay male jock from more traditionally developmental, serialized narratives. Indeed, as Stephen Tropiano (2002: 238) suggests, recurring gay characters in seventies sitcoms are typically coded as more feminine than masculine.[11] The drag queen character Beverly (Lori Shannon), for example, makes three appearances, before being killed off, on *All in the Family* between 1975 and 1977. And while *Soap*'s Jodie isn't consistently posited as a queen, he is generally associated with effeminacy, particularly in the first season when he considers a sex change in order to maintain his relationship with Dennis, a closeted *football player* (Bob Seagren).[12] The larger ideological assumption here is that masculinity mandates sexual desire in ways that gender inversion cannot. So while the gay jock might seem to be a figure of gay normalization, he retains a destabilizing potential because he insistently sexualizes his encounters with other men. Although *Alice*, and sitcoms in general, use humour to alleviate this tension, dramatic programmes of the era often reveal a more pronounced anxiety (even paranoia) about the wider social (and symbolic) effects of such figures.

In a notorious 1976 essay, syndicated columnist Nicholas von Hoffman – no friend to gay activism in the 1970s – lambasted the Bicentennial year as 'The Year of the Gay' (von Hoffman 1976).[13] Enacting a particularly anxious form of cross-textual seriality, von Hoffman warned that 'the gays are swarming' on television: 'you can hardly dial around on prime time without clicking on to some actor explaining to a disappointed, would-be girlfriend that he's gay.' More than any other figure, it was the macho gay footballer that most disturbed (and enticed?) the columnist. Referencing the *Alice* episode, von Hoffman dwelt on the 'big, hairy, courageous ... ex-football quarterback' and his 'large, hirsute' figure. Later in the article, he asked whether 'a new stereotype [was] being born' and presented a fantasy scenario in which NBC news would be given over to a 'hairy-chested linebacker' and called 'Gay News.' As von Hoffman's hair-obsessed rant suggests, the gay footballer remained an important (if complex) figure of gay visibility through-out seventies television, and his cross-textual presence (and threat) were hardly contained by the potential limitations of his one-off TV appearances.

'Teetering on the brink': queer adolescents

Gay liberation and increased gay visibility incited a homosexual panic and paranoia in seventies American culture that often played out through the figure of the vul-nerable, impressionable child. And in line with Anita Bryant's notorious 1977 'Save Our Children' campaign to rescind anti-discrimination rights for homosexuals in Florida's Dade county, the 'child' in such panic-laden narratives was a conflation of actual children with post-pubescent adolescents. In 1970, in its first front page acknowledgment of gay liberation, the *New York Times* 'balanced' coverage of the gay liberation movement with one psychiatrist's lament about the movement's potential effects. As he noted, 'It's possible that this movement could consolidate the illness in some people, especially among young people who are teetering on the brink' (quoted in Alwood 1996: 103). Although seventies television adapts and expands the 1950s *Tea and Sympathy* model of ambiguous adolescent sexuality for an age of gay visibility, it nevertheless stages its troubled teens in remarkably sim-ilar ways. These 'confused' and 'vulnerable' boys are often uncertain about their manhood; like Howard in *Room 222*, their alterity is also marked through an associ-ation with less conventionally masculine interests and hobbies (theatre, art, baking, etc.).[14] And yet, many of them are competent sportsmen, and their social and sexual struggles remain figured in relation to athletics.

Some of these troubled teens suffer because they have gay fathers (*That Certain Summer, The Bold Ones*), others are exploited by substitute father figures (*Marcus Welby, MD*). There is no singular mode of representing male adolescence in sev-enties TV. Some programmes naturalize the gender and sexual ambiguity of the teenage years, while others viciously attempt to police the boundaries (and bodies) of these boys. Indeed, Anita Bryant's anxieties (and phobias) play out much earlier in television's dramatization of teenage trauma. The decade-long debates about the effects of media violence and sexuality on TV along with the failed institution of the 'family hour' in 1975 only served to fuel the fires of Bryant's late-seventies cam-paign. And even after the APA's 1974 revision, associations of homosexuality with illness and contagion persisted, especially in relation to impressionable, ostensibly 'innocent' youth.[15] The adolescent has, in fact, long been used in a variety of media forms as a way to negotiate and work through the ambiguities and uncertainties of sexuality in general.

What the many approaches to male adolescence across seventies television share, though, is a strident resistance to the declaration of a gay identity. Ambiguously gay teens simply *never* come out at this time, but this doesn't necessarily shut down their queer potential. For in strenuously avoiding coming out scenes, the shows fall back on a more fluid, uncertain, and unpredictable presentation of adolescent sexuality that's based on both gender liminality and/or romantic 'crushes' and thus can be read as even *more* queer than a simple coming out scene. A coded form of coming out is ubiquitous, though, in the numerous *confession* scenes that force adolescent boys to tell us what they're feeling, experiencing, and desiring (within limits). If these programmes can't exactly show us the sexual turmoil of these figures, they can't stop talking about it. Still, the frequent confessional scenes do little more than keep the troubled teen in his ambiguous state; they function as confessions, but somehow resist disciplining codification. They clarify nothing, and therein lies their resistant potential. For while these characters appear time and time again across the televisual landscape in the 1970s, their narratives remain unresolved. Their sexual identities are indeterminate, and the formal and narrative strategies used to engage such figures only end up enhancing their ambiguity.

In a first season episode of the inner-city high school basketball drama, *The White Shadow* (CBS, 1978–81), 16-year-old Ray Collins (Peter Horton) is transferred to Carver High after rumours spread at his elite high school about his sexuality 'Just One of the Boys' (27 January 1979). A talented basketball player, Collins is initially set apart from his team-mates by his class status and his whiteness, but when the coach (and later his team-mates) learns about the rumours, he becomes both a target of homophobic harassment and a key symbolic threat. The expansive gender trouble incited by Collins is actually cued in the episode's opening scene in which Coach Reeves (Ken Howard) subs for the home-economics teacher in a floral apron with pink trim. On his first day at Carver, Collins comes into the classroom late and tells Reeves he's taking home-ec because he 'likes to bake' and he has 'a lot of eclectic interests.' When the subject of basketball comes up, Collins is surprised to learn that Reeves is the coach. Reeves responds defensively – 'Do I look like the home-ec teacher?' – before Collins slyly notes: 'The apron fits.'

Later, in a homoerotic shower scene with his new team-mates, Collins is kidded about his aggressive, rugby-like, 'hands on' approach to practice. This practice style becomes a source of anxiety, though, once Coach Reeves learns about Collins's past. Wincing every time Collins hand checks a team-mate or gives another a friendly pat on the ass, Reeves eventually stops practices and accuses Collins of 'trying to dance' with his team-mates. The combination of Collins's ambiguous sexuality with his physical prowess not only forces Reeves to look at his sport, his athletes, and their physical contact in an entirely new (and, for him, disturbing) way, it also implicates Reeves himself in these very disruptions.

Collins quits the team after his team-mates learn about the rumours, and Coach Reeves eventually corners him in the gym and asks about his past. Although he denies having been with another guy, Collins remains ambiguous about his sexuality. Then, in a remarkable scene, he begins to cry as he confesses to a serious crush on a charismatic male friend from his former high school. Coach Reeves frames his questioning here as a defense of Collins's individual rights, but the directness with which he confronts young Collins is indicative of his own desire to rein in the trouble caused by Collins's queerness. Significantly, though, the confession scene fails to satisfy that particular desire. Collins is ultimately encouraged to return to his former high school by the African American Vice Principal (Joan Pringle), but the question and crisis of his sexual identity are significantly unresolved.

The heteronormative developmental narrative, commonly used to contain the queerness of youth, is itself consistently troubled in seventies television, particularly in relation to TV's ambiguously gay teens. This destabilized endpoint – the fact that we simply can't guarantee that these boys will grow up 'normal' – fosters an increased anxiety about these very figures and their narratives. Indeed, the widespread challenges to dominant patriarchal myths and norms in seventies American culture both *incite* the troubled teens and *inhibit* any clear resolution of their conflicts of identity and desire. For not only do 'bad' father figures and criminal or monstrous patriarchs abound in seventies American culture – from Nixon and Kissinger to *Chinatown*'s Noah Cross and *Dallas*'s J.R. Ewing – but the broader interrogation (and indictment) of hegemonic masculinity also impedes a clear path to 'real' manhood. Indeed, the question posed in early 1971 by *Room 222* – 'What is a Man?' – seems just as appropriate and unanswerable for Collins in 1979.

Television thus repeatedly uses these adolescent boys to address (and possibly work through) broader social crises in gender and sexual identity. TV keeps these teens in a state of narrative and representational ambiguity, but this state also suggests a broader cultural uncertainty about both adolescent sexuality and potentially stabilizing myths of futurity amidst the economic, political, and social crises of the 1970s. In his discussion of the 'sad young man' – a clear precursor to the adolescent boys of seventies TV – Richard Dyer suggests that there is typically a notion of '*finite* uncertainty' to the developmental trajectory of this figure. In other words, there is an understanding that the uncertainty and ambiguity of the figure will come to an eventual end (Dyer 1993: 88). Significantly, though, the ambiguously gay teens in seventies TV remain in a state of *perpetual* uncertainty tied to both the televisual form and to the destabilization of patriarchal notions of gender, sexuality, and identity in seventies America. As noted, part of the motivation (however unconscious) for the 'arrested' presentation of the ambiguously gay adolescent in seventies television is a desire to inhibit potential interactions between the teen and the adult, typically masculine, gay man of seventies culture. Consequently, *Alice*'s Jack and *All in the Family*'s Steve present potential 'endpoints' for the ambiguity of *The White Shadow*'s Collins that only cross-textual seriality can effectively entertain.

In her recent analysis of seventies television, Elana Levine suggests that TV of the period typically presents sex and the sexual revolution as 'a grave danger to youth' (2007: 12). Focusing on made-for-TV movies of the 1970s, she notes a combination of 'the titillating and the cautionary, the exploitative and the educational,' aspects that are only heightened by the mid-1970s moral panic about the sexuality of youth' (105). Such representational tensions and anxieties play out in revealing ways in the rare gay-themed narratives in seventies TV that *do* bring together the troubled teen with the conventionally masculine gay man (or jock). Here, father/son conflicts are used to block clear similarities between the masculine gay man and the confused adolescent. These programmes instead suggest that the queerness of the father (or father figure) is the primary *cause* of the adolescent boy's problems. Overall, the programmes work overtime to try and retain a traditional developmental narrative for the adolescent boy by demonizing the deviant developmental endpoint for the ambiguously gay teen: the gay man. They try, but fail, to renarrativize male adolescence in more conventional terms, but the excessiveness of the disruption that is marked by the presence of the masculine gay male (and the deviant father) suggests just how troubled seventies network television and American culture were by this queer potential in American youth.

Two key medical drama episodes, 'Discovery at 14' (5 March 1972), a 1972 episode of *The Bold Ones: The New Doctors* (NBC, 1969–73) and 'The Outrage' (8 October 1974), a controversial and widely protested 1974 episode of *Marcus Welby, MD* (ABC, 1969–76) exemplify such representational conflicts. Jason Jacobs notes that the explicit discussion of traditionally taboo social subjects in the seventies medical drama involved, among other things, 'a desire to map social anxieties onto the body' (Jacobs 2003: 7). He explains: 'in these shows, the body was not only a site for the application of benevolent medical science, but also a physical canvas for the display of the consequences of the transgression of morality and mores' (7).

Exposing the anxious undercurrent of most representations of potentially gay adolescents in the 1970s, both *The Bold Ones* and *Marcus Welby* stage the interaction of the impressionable teen and the gay male adult as *bodily* violations. 'Discovery at 14' is arguably more subtle in its depiction of this particular physical trauma, in part because it presents an actual father/son narrative, but what's interesting here is the way that it mirrors the moral panic fueling the molestation episode of *Welby*. Young Ron Howard plays Corey Merlino, a shy, sensitive, tennis play-ing teen who signals the episode's primary enigma by mysteriously bleeding in the opening sequence. Corey's 'passive manner' and his *internal* trauma – we later learn he has a bleeding duodenal ulcer – are initially contrasted with the more conventionally masculine, sports-related *external* injuries of his brother. As the show repeatedly insists, Corey's problem is a psychological one that man-ifests itself physically through the bleeding ulcer. The episode repeatedly uses discourses of 'the closet' to frame Corey's illness, but it ultimately posits Corey's gay father, Jack (Robert Hogan), also a tennis player, as its causal scapegoat. Indeed, Corey's ulcer is ostensibly the result of an internalized homosexual panic incited by the mere visibility of his gay father. Although his mother and his grandfather repeatedly deny and disavow his gay father, Corey inadvertently stumbles upon a gay revelry at his father's apartment, featuring, as Jack puts it, a number of

'obvious' types. Yet another gay jock in seventies TV, Jack may not be as obvious as his friends, but as suggested by the episode's own voyeuristic peek inside
a shadowy, cruisy gay bar, he's clearly guilty by association. In fact, Dr. Fallon's
(Jane Wyman) cautious exploration of the space of the gay bar serves to mirror (while safely displacing) Corey's own traumatic 'discovery' of queer difference
and desire.

Jack appears just once in the entire episode – far removed from Corey's impressionable gaze – when Dr. Fallon tracks him down after a tennis match. Here he
confesses the truth about himself and about Corey's surprise visit. The episode
ultimately disavows the crisis of both gay male visibility and paternity, though, by
insisting that Corey's interest in tennis doesn't necessarily mean that he's a chip
off the old block. But even as it insists on homosexuality as a choice rather than
a genetic legacy, 'Discovery at 14' also refuses to bring father and son together
again. By the end of the programme, Corey's recovery is signaled by his successful
return to the tennis court, but his father is literally (and necessarily) nowhere to be
seen.

'The Outrage' episode of *Marcus Welby, MD* literalizes the specifically erotic
panic that pervades 'Discovery at 14' through the depiction of the molestation
of a 14-year-old boy by his science teacher on a camping trip. As was thoroughly reported in the media at the time, the National Gay Task Force unleashed
a widespread campaign against the *Marcus Welby* episode that led to local ABC affiliates pulling the episode as well as a variety of changes in the script itself. In spite of
the insistence of one expert in the episode that 'there's nothing homosexual about
this … it's a case of violent child molestation,' gay activists and even mainstream
critics were well aware that the conflation of homosexual and child molester would
nevertheless persist. While late 1974 was likely too early for the residual effects of
the APA decision to be felt in the representational practices of network television,
the proliferation of gay and lesbian villains/predators at this time nevertheless reads
as a form of backlash.[16]

The episode begins as Ted (Sean Kelly) awakens in his bedroom surrounded
by a wide variety of sports-related photos, figures, and equipment. As he (and the
camera) scan the various images of professional athletes that decorate the walls of
the room, his gaze finally rests on a pile of rumpled clothes and a pair of muddy
shoes, ostensibly his outfit from the night before. After getting out of bed, he
moves to the mirror above his dresser, takes some aspirin, and stares at his heavily
bruised, nearly naked body. Given the fact that this episode was widely publicized
and controversial before its airing, this opening intrigues because of the ways that
it conflates the more normalized physical abuse of sports with the potential horrors
of sexual assault. After Ted leaves for school, the opening segment concludes with
a scene of Ted's mother, Marian (Marla Adams), pulling back his bedsheets and
recoiling in horror. Quickly calling Dr. Welby (Robert Young) in a panicked
state, she declares: 'there's something terribly wrong with Ted – he's *bleeding!*'

This apparently horrific combination of beds, boys, and blood suggests the trouble with adolescent male bodies and desires in the mid-1970s. After all, it's not

adolescent *boys* who are conventionally traumatized by their bleeding bodies – just ask Carrie. We later learn, in unusually graphic detail for a medical programme of this era, that Ted is suffering from acute peritonitis due to 'internal injuries related to [a] forceful assault.' As Welby explains in a particularly charged (and coded) statement: 'We're going to have to go in and repair the damage.' Such attempts to 'repair the damage' done through the actual (or potential) encounter of the adolescent boy with the masculine gay adult proliferate throughout this period. Seventies television incessantly tries to heal the wounds of hegemonic masculinity through figures like the vulnerable adolescent boy, but these traumatized bodies (and minds) nevertheless persist. While obviously serving as a coded figure of the trauma of gay sex for straight men, the bleeding adolescent boys in these programmes are also indicative of a more metaphoric 'bleeding' that's tied to their transgression of sexual, social, and corporeal boundaries.

Although 'The Outrage' traffics in particularly offensive and reactionary modes of representation by scapegoating the triumvirate of the single mother, absent father, and predatory homosexual, it also implicates dominant masculinity through its positioning of the science teacher as a visibly similar father figure who takes physical activities between man and boy too far. The tenuous realm of athletics and physical culture are again referenced in the episode through the camping incident and the science teacher's defensive response to Marian when she asks him about Ted's injuries. As he insists: 'I was disappointed in Ted. He wasn't ready to rough it out there.' Furthermore, the science teacher's only onscreen interaction with Ted takes place in a school locker room. Closing a caged door as he enters the locker room, Mr. Swanson (Edward Winter) calls the boy 'Teddy,' looms over him in the frame, and repeatedly places his hand on Ted's shoulder. Then, standing ominously behind Ted in a close 2-shot, Swanson criticizes him in a more authoritative manner for not being 'a man.'

Even though the episode attempts to identify and police a queer threat (however coded and disavowed), it can't help but also suggest that 'daddies' of any variety might be equally dangerous. Ted's actual father, George (Edward Power), not only admits that he was a 'bad father,' he also violates Ted in more psychological ways after the attack. Assailing his already wounded son, he demands: 'how could you let it happen? Isn't there something you could have done?' Ted's trauma, and the homosexual associations of it, thus dangerously reflects back on the father himself. And although Dr. Welby concludes the episode by affirming Ted's bravery and masculinity in the aftermath of the incident – 'you acted like a man' – the damage has clearly been done. Indeed, 'The Outrage' indirectly exposes a more widespread cultural anxiety in the wake of gay liberation that suggests there is actually no 'safe space' in seventies American television or culture to work through (or revel in) the instability of male adolescence.

And yet, such cultural anxieties need not completely restrict the queer potential of network television in the 1970s. For while the episodic, 'one-off' approach to gay–themed subjects in seventies television typically works to bracket off (and shield) the ambiguously gay teen from the masculine gay man (or gay jock), these figures can also be conceived of together and in relation to one another through cross-textual seriality. Indeed, the presence of the masculine gay male in network television further complicates the heteronormative developmental trajectory of the adolescent boy by indirectly queering normative masculinity *and* by suggesting that sexual desire itself remains invisible and unknowable even in adulthood. A cross-textual approach can even further foreground alternative developmental narratives for the ambiguously gay teen that need not shut down the queer potential of the adolescent experience nor simply posit adult gay sexuality as a stable, predictable state. After all, these boys may indeed grow up to be Archie's buddy Steve, Edith's drag queen friend Beverly, *Soap*'s Jodie, Starsky, or Hutch. And in this conflicted and controversial period of nascent gay visibility, such variability suggests the richness, rather than limitations, of queer imagery *across* network television and mainstream media of the 1970s.

Acknowledgement

Thanks to Lucas Hilderbrand, Allison McCracken, Albert Snell, Glyn Davis and Gary Needham for their helpful editorial suggestions and comments. Special thanks to Stephen Tropiano for generously supplying me with copies of the hard-to-find episodes.

Notes

1. In her insightful discussion of the class, gender, racial, and aesthetic associations of the widely circulated discourses of 'quality' and 'relevance' in 1970s television, Kirsten Marthe Lentz (2000) inadvertently writes homosexuality out of existence. She notes how quality television of the MTM variety was associated with feminism, a middle class aesthetic, and self-reflexivity, while the relevant TV of Norman Lear was typically aligned with racial politics, liveness, authenticity/realism, and a working class aesthetic. Homosexuality, though, straddles both the categories of quality and relevance in a variety of often conflicting and contradictory ways in seventies television. That said, the typical alignment of relevance with racial politics and authenticity suggests one reason why gay issues are seldom discussed in relation to 'relevant' television just as it indirectly exposes the construction of homosexuality (with a few exceptions) *as white* in seventies TV. For more on the shift to relevant television, see Gitlin (2000).
2. Television never does (and likely never *can*) come out completely, though, since the closet continues to anchor formal, visual, narrative, and thematic modes of making meaning in mainstream television, and these modes are influenced by the representation of sexuality itself (Joyrich 2001: 448–50).
3. In their anthology on 'the queerness of children,' Steven Bruhm and Natasha Hurley note that childhood sexuality is typically policed through heteronormative narratives of temporality that contain 'child queerness into a story that will not *be*, but will only *have been*' on the path to heterosexual maturity (2004: xviii–xix). And although adolescents should definitely not be confused with 'children,' that very conflation fuels much of the moral panic in seventies culture and the presumed relationship of homosexuality to pedophilia, child abuse, and 'recruitment' scenarios.

4. No doubt fueled by the seventies nostalgia of Generation X, full season sets of popular TV programmes from the era have proliferated since the emergence of the DVD format in 1997. Season-long collections of *Police Woman*, *All in the Family*, *Soap*, *Barney Miller*, *The White Shadow*, *The Streets of San Francisco*, *WKRP in Cincinnati*, *Three's Company*, *The Mary Tyler Moore Show*, *Mary Hartman*, *Maude*, *Sanford and Son*, *The Rockford Files*, and many others have enabled and enhanced this reassessment of queer imagery in 1970s TV.

5. An argument could be made for Lance Loud as a gay serial figure in the reality TV pioneer *An American Family*, but the limited number of episodes, the public broadcasting forum, and the documentary based mode posit the series as an anomaly in seventies TV. ABC's *The Corner Bar* (1972–1973), Norman Lear's *Hot L Baltimore* (ABC, 1975) and ABC's *The Nancy Walker Show* (1976) were three other short-lived programmes in the decade with serial queer characters.

6. Of course, the analogical mode of queer identity politics is also persistently complicated by the universalizing mode in the conception of homosexuality. For if everyone's potentially gay, then the black civil rights parallel must be reconfigured in some way. This returns us to the complex issue of visibility (televisual or otherwise) in the period of gay liberation.

7. By late 1974, John J. O'Connor began to change his tune somewhat: 'But in attempting to replace the old and frequently abusive stereotypes of homosexuals with only "positive" non-abusive stereotypes ... the homosexual groups are veering toward an unreality of their own. That unreality is as objectionable as any other' (O'Connor 1974b). In 1977, Anita Bryant expressed her own disdain for the revamped TV landscape: 'What concerns me is that by caving to the small but vocal (number of) homosexual activists, those who sponsor American television and other forms of entertainment will give the impression that this sick segment of society represents society on a much broader basis than it does in reality' (quoted in Clarke 1977).

8. Tropiano notes, though, that the *Variety* review quickly qualified this observation by insisting that Broderick 'shaded the rugged construction worker with just enough of that fey quality to make the point' (quoted in Tropiano 2002: 60). Actually, though, in the episode, Broderick reveals none of the ambiguous 'fey' qualities that the *Variety* reviewer suggests; instead, the reviewer himself seems driven to impose readable codes on a figure whom the episode insistently presents in conventionally masculine terms.

9. Along these lines, the *queen* figure continues to play a prominent role throughout seventies TV as the object of both ridicule and liberal tolerance. More specifically, drag queens and transgender figures typically function as murderous deviants (*The Streets of San Francisco*, ABC, 'Mask of Death,' 3 October 1974; *Police Woman*, NBC, 'Night of the Full Moon,' 28 December 1976; *Vega$*, ABC, 'The Man Who Was Twice,' 12 March 1980) or humorous, supportive, and at times revealingly critical characters (*All in the Family*, 'Archie the Hero,' CBS, 29 September 1975; *Starsky and Hutch*, ABC, 'Death in a Different Place,' 15 October 1977). Although the queen can (and does) function in disruptive ways in seventies television, the queen also transitions more clearly from connotation to denotation in various programmes; as such, the queen doesn't initially trouble the epistemological structures and goals of network television as clearly as the masculine gay male and the troubled adolescent in this particular context.

10. Steven Capsuto notes that this particular format would remain the norm from 1971 to 1976. It includes the following elements: 'a series regular learns

a longtime friend is gay; the gay man or lesbian is single, attractive, and "straight-acting"; if male he is an ex-football player; there is no mention of other gay people with whom the character is friendly; the script teaches: "you can't spot a gay person just by looking"; it preaches tolerance, if not acceptance; the gay character and the series regular are on good terms by the end; despite their long friendship, the gay character never appears again' (Capsuto 2000: 71).

11. 'While the gay male characters who appear on single episodes of shows like *All in the Family* and *Alice* are overtly masculine, regular or recurring characters are typically more feminine than masculine – a strategy by producers to insure they pose no "threat"' (Tropiano 2002: 238).

12. Many of these gay jock figures in seventies television were actually played by presumably straight professional athletes. Bob Seagren was a gold medalist in Olympic pole vault and Denny Miller – *Alice*'s Jack – was a UCLA basketball star. This fact only enhances the broader critique of the programmes because it extends the interrogation of heterosexual manhood and homosociality to real world athletics.

13. von Hoffman was more direct in the *Rocky Mountain News* version of the article in which he called 1976 'the year of the fag' (Alwood 1996: 153).

14. The ambiguously gay teen of seventies TV is clearly a descendant of the 'sad young man' figure that has long partially defined gay identity in a variety of media forms. As Richard Dyer explains: 'The sad young man is especially strongly marked in terms of transition, not only by virtue of age but also by virtue of the notion of moving between normal and queer worlds, always caught at the moment of exploration and discovery' (Dyer 1993: 87).

15. Eve Kosofsky Sedgwick has also argued that the depathologization of adult homosexuality by the APA may have only exacerbated the cultural and psychiatric focus on proto-gay children/adolescents and 'deviant' or 'dysmorphic' gender identity (Sedgwick 1993: 154–64).

16. In fact, the fall season of 1974 also saw the airing of the other most widely protested and controversial episode of the entire decade, the 'lesbian killers' episode of *Police Woman* entitled 'Flowers of Evil.' *TV Guide* called the episode 'the single most homophobic show to date' (quoted in Alwood 1996: 150); and as Steven Capsuto notes, 'every sexual minority character in a network drama that fall was a violent criminal' (2000: 107).

References

Alwood, E. (1996) *Straight News: Gays, Lesbians, and the News Media*, New York: Columbia University Press.

Bruhm, S. and Hurley, N. (eds) (2004) *Curiouser: On the Queerness of Children*, Minneapolis, MN: University of Minnesota Press.

Capsuto, S. (2000) *Alternate Channels: The Uncensored Story of Gay and Lesbian Images on Radio and Television, 1930s–the Present*, New York: Ballantine Publishing.

Champlin, C. (1972) 'Homosexuality Faced in "Certain Summer,"' *Los Angeles Times*, 1 November, F16.

Clarke, J. (1977) 'Gay Rights Dispute Stop Bryant's Show,' *Washington Post*, 25 February, B1.

Dyer, R. (1993) *The Matter of Images: Essays on Representation*, London: Routledge.

Foster, R. (1969) 'The Homosexual: Newly Visible, Newly Understood,' *Time*, 31 October, 56–67.

Gitlin, T. (2000) *Inside Prime Time*, 2nd edn, Berkeley, CA: University of California Press.

Gross, L. (2001) *Up from Invisibility: Lesbians, Gay Men, and the Media in America*, New York: Columbia University Press.

Jacobs, J. (2003) *Body Trauma TV: The New Hospital Dramas*, London: BFI.

Joyrich, L. (2001) 'Epistemology of the Console,' *Critical Inquiry* 27: 439–67.

Kilday, G. (1973) 'Gays Lobby for a New Media Image,' *Los Angeles Times*, 10 December, D1.

Kramer, C. (1972) '"That Certain Summer": Dad is a Little Different,' *Chicago Tribune*, 29 October, W1.

Lentz, K.M. (2000) '*Quality* versus *Relevance*: Feminism, Race, and the Politics of the Sign in 1970s Television,' *Camera Obscura* 43(15): 1, 45–93.

Levine, E. (2007) *Wallowing in Sex: The New Sexual Culture of 1970s American Television*, Durham, NC: Duke University Press.

McCarthy, A. (2001) '*Ellen*: Making Queer Television History,' *GLQ: A Journal of Lesbian and Gay Studies*, 7(4): 593–620.

O'Connor, J.J. (1972) 'That Certain Subject is Here,' *New York Times*, 29 October, D21.

—— (1974a) 'TV: Expert Advisers,' *New York Times*, 14 February, 83.

—— (1974b) 'Pressure Groups Are Increasingly Putting the Heat on TV,' *New York Times*, 6 October, 139.

Russo, V. (1987) *The Celluloid Closet: Homosexuality in the Movies*, 2nd edn, New York: Harper & Row.

Sedgwick, E.K. (1990) *Epistemology of the Closet*, Berkeley, CA: University of California Press.

—— (1993) *Tendencies*, Durham, NC: Duke University Press.

Taylor, C. (1979) 'Television and Gays: Out of the Video Closet?' *Los Angeles Times*, 9 December, N3.

Tropiano, S. (2002) *The Prime Time Closet: A History of Gays and Lesbians on TV*, New York: Applause.

Von Hoffman, N. (1976) 'And Now, The Year of the Gay: A Commentary,' *The Washington Post*, 15 October, B1.

Walters, S.D. (2003) *All the Rage: The Story of Gay Visibility in America*, Chicago, IL: University of Chicago Press.

Warren, P. N. (1974) *The Front Runner*, New York: William Morrow.

Chapter 6

'Something for everyone'

Lesbian and gay 'magazine' programming on British television, 1980–2000

Gregory Woods

The penultimate decade of the twentieth century was a troubled and demoralising time for lesbians and gay men in Britain. The start of the AIDS epidemic coincided with, and was exacerbated by, the fact that an energetically ideological, Conservative government was in power, led by Margaret Thatcher from 1979 to 1990 and then by John Major from 1990 to 1997. The Thatcherite moral project was characterised by a coercive return to 'Victorian values' alongside an incompatible assertion of the freedom of the individual from interference by the state. While the 1970s had promised so much in the way of 'gay liberation' – to use the expression of the time – such aspirations had not been met with much significant institutional reform by the time of the Thatcherite political backlash of the early 1980s. The AIDS epidemic developed, from 1982, in an unsympathetically judgemental atmosphere, led by government and enthusiastically fomented by a hostile, right-wing press.

In many respects, the low point of the 1980s came with the enactment of the Local Government Act 1988. The part of the Act that came to be known by the convenient epithet 'Section 28' prohibited the so-called 'promotion' of homosexuality by local authorities in England and Wales. By a clever sleight-of-hand, homophobic groups and individuals – including the right-wing press – successfully manipulated perceptions of the new law to the extent of making it appear to apply to the education system, which it did not. As a consequence, the compliant school-teaching profession in general took the law as sanctioning active neglect of gay pupils and the avoidance of gay topics wherever they arose, both within and beyond the classroom. Even if no prosecutions were ever brought under the Section – which was repealed by the Labour government of Tony Blair in 2003 – its cultural presence exacted a heavy cost in atmospheric terms.

The setbacks of the time were met by grass-roots responses shaped by the successes of the 1970s gay liberationist political and community activities: the founding of the Terrence Higgins Trust in 1982 was a prominent example, as were a number of spectacular demonstrations against Section 28. Moreover, by the turn of the 1980s, gay print media were sufficiently well developed to be able to respond to AIDS when the time came, with information more reliable than the straight media seemed either willing or able to provide. Out of these circumstances emerged a sense of gay 'community' more united, through solidarity in crisis, than had actually ever been the case in the 1970s. It seems to have been around this notion of a cohesive audience in search of further affirmation that gay television series of the 1980s and 1990s were tentatively developed. However, the actual birth of British gay television slightly pre-dated the worst excesses of Thatcherism and the onset of AIDS.

The front-page headline on issue 184 (7–20 February 1980) of Britain's then national gay and lesbian newspaper *Gay News* said 'GAY TV!' with, in a starburst to one side: 'AT LAST'. The implication was, of course, that something to be thought of as gay television was about to arrive, and that it had been a long time coming. For all that it was announced with such fanfare, the story itself did not appear until page 14, the paper's leader page. Here, the headline was: 'Londoners prepare for gay TV'. The programme in question, a series called *Gay Life*, came from the newly established Minorities Unit at London Weekend Television (LWT); it was about to be screened, but in the London region only.

The producer of *Gay Life*, Michael Attwell, himself a gay man, described this moment as 'a landmark in gay history in Britain', adding that 'One could claim that it is the first time in the world that a major national TV company has given a whole series to gays'. The production team consisted of nine people, only three of them gay. Little wonder, then, that they had been faced from the start with what would come to be seen as a perennial problem about the divided audiences for gay broadcasting (and film and literature and music...): 'All the team agree that in a sense they are trying to ride two horses – putting forward the gay viewpoint and relating to non-gay people' (quoted in Coen 1980).

The first *Gay Life* programme was broadcast by LWT on Sunday 11 February 1980, at 11.30 at night. The next issue of *Gay News* carried a television review by John Russell Taylor under the headline 'Making a start' (Taylor 1980). This piece is worth re-reading now, since it raises certain basic, but crucial, issues that would keep cropping up in relation to gay television programmes for the next two decades. To begin with, Taylor reports that he has been 'amazed... at the amount of outright hostility' he has 'heard voiced on all sides by gays about the very idea of such a programme'. The general tenor of the objection was along the lines that 'It would be better not to have such a programme if it's going to show...'. The two particular examples Taylor raises are men in drag and men in leather. He quotes representative arguments about drag queens: 'Drags give the gay community a bad name; everybody knows that drag isn't a specifically gay phenomenon anyway, and this is just confirming the usual erroneous impression the straight world has'. And about the leather/SM scene: 'Everybody thinks we're all sadistic maniac killers anyway: wait till they see all the denizens of the Coleherne [the leather pub in Earls Court, London] with their whips and chains'. If one were to follow this line of thinking, Taylor says, an acceptably well-behaved programme could only show 'your basic stolid, responsible, respectable gays who lead as ordinary, boring lives as everybody else'. In the letter pages of *Gay News*, as in general gay conversation, the same argument raged annually over Gay Pride marches, especially since what little television news coverage these ever attracted always focused on images of men in drag or leather (or both). Here was the problem: because they had never represented it except in brief moments of scandalous news, the straight media tended to treat gayness as extraordinary, and therefore had to seek out vivid representatives of it in order to confirm their own pre-constructed version of it.

Given the expense of broadcasting, and its collective nature, the concept of 'gay TV' generates a series of problems for the broadcaster. While an item of 'gay literature' – a novel, let us say – might be written by a gay author and read by a gay reader, might be about a gay theme and might even be published by a gay publisher, thereby allowing for an apparent integrity of shared identity or experience across the processes of production and reception, the collective nature of broadcasting, like that of film, obviates any such definitional clarity or symbolic unity centred on the sexual identity of those who generate it. Moreover, one would think that gay television was television for a gay audience, but programmes about homosexuality often give the impression of being intended for non-gay spectators, either to inform or to scandalise them. The reason for this is obvious. In both broadcasting and publishing, commercial realities militate against products that are aimed solely at an interested minority. Even given the dutifully egalitarian ideals of public service broadcasting, the mainstream offers more reliable returns. Where ratings matter, so do majorities.

Of course, even this argument I am conducting, shallow as it is, depends on a theoretical model of fixed and divided sexualities. It depends on our knowing, or professing to know, who or what a gay viewer is, and how s/he differs from a straight one. Our culture has become fixedly used to discussing such matters as if bisexuality had never existed, or as if we still could not bring ourselves to believe in our own hypothesis of a range of polymorphous, plural queernesses.

Continuing his review of the first *Gay Life*, John Russell Taylor asks the obvious questions about its intended audience:

> To an extent, it is important whom exactly this programme is intended for. Is it meant as a painless introduction to the gay world and its ways for uncomprehending straights? Or is it meant mainly to preach to the converted, those who want to see something about themselves, for themselves, on television (like, say, broadcasts in Welsh)? I suppose the answer is, a bit of both. And therein may lie the major danger.

He means that such programmes may sacrifice singularity of purpose by adopting divided aims. Indeed, his own argument then acts out, apparently unwittingly, the kind of confusion that might be generated by indecisiveness about audiences. Commenting on an item about the exclusion of lesbians and gay men from the Civil Service for 'security risk' reasons, Taylor argues that 'it probably should not have come so early in the series. First of all, establish some kind of norm, and then you can feel free to deviate a bit from it, to go into special cases'. He supposes that because 'many straight viewers' might not be aware that certain matters 'hardly affect your friendly neighbourhood gay at all' they might be misled into thinking them typical. Taking the topic as a narrow one about national security, rather than a broad one about access to employment, he appears to have missed the fact that the latter was, indeed, likely to affect gay people in many walks of life. He comes to a conclusion that somewhat coincides with those of the objectors from whom he was distancing himself at the start of his review: 'it would be fairer to start with something more humdrum and everyday, and make it fascinating, as all the best documentaries do anyway, simply by the quality of the observation'.

The brief flurry of debate around this early programme raises a number of significant questions that would continue to confront programme makers. In a sense, they are always rhetorical questions, since they cannot be satisfied with a single answer. In the first place, who is gay? Then, is gayness normative or radical/subversive? Is it mundane or 'fabulous'? Is it respectable or sleazy? Does the content of television aimed at gay viewers have to be 'gay'; and, if so, what does that involve? And finally, even more problematical, does television aimed at gay viewers have to be aimed also at non-gay viewers? (And, if so, which is the more important audience? The smaller or the larger? If gay people are a minority, does gay television always have to be aimed at straight viewers, the supposed majority? Or can one assume, after all, that the viewers of a programme flagged up as gay will be mostly gay, and therefore allow the content to target them as its *majority* audience?)

It is clear that the very format of some early gay programmes constituted an attempt to solve such conundrums – or, perhaps, to gloss over them. By compiling 'magazines', capacious miscellanies that covered many different topics for many different types of people, broadcasters might eventually give the impression of having covered everything for everyone. In fact, however, only a narrow range of possible ways of being gay, or types of gay people, were actually represented in any given series. For instance, Colin Richardson has given detailed attention to Channel 4's *Out on Tuesday*, which ran for two series in 1989 and 1990 respectively, before a move to Wednesday and a name-change to *Out* for two more series in 1991 and 1992. (The programme was then cancelled, but briefly resurrected in 1994.) Although made by Abseil Productions, a company named after the spectacular coup by a small group of lesbian women, who abseiled into a working session of the House of Lords in 1988 to demonstrate against Section 28 of the Local Government Act, *Out* was not a campaigning programme. Richardson notes that it included items on 'lesbian yuppies with six-figure salaries, opera queens, the society magazine *Tatler* and lesbian and gay members of the Conservative Party', thereby in his view 'reinforcing the hoary old stereotype that homosexuality is a middle-class affectation'. It had no place for 'lesbian pimps, prostitutes or strippers, nor for rent boys, escorts or masseurs. Here men didn't go cruising at dead of night on windswept heaths or commons, nor did they look for sex in public toilets' – at least until the very last episode, when, presumably, the makers had nothing to lose (Richardson 1995: 233).[1]

Over the next few years, a number of compromise attempts were made to supply varied gay viewing for one-off whole evenings, rather than for the long haul of a whole series. Only after monitoring the progress of the commercial Channel 4's

Out on Tuesday in its first two series did the public-service BBC decide to risk dipping its toe into the maelstrom of gay programming. On Saturday 16 November 1991, in celebration of the twenty-first anniversary of the birth of the Gay Liberation Movement in the UK, they screened more than five hours of programmes about lesbians and gay men. From 8.30 in the evening to 1.40 the following morning, they dedicated the BBC2 schedule to what they called *Saturday Night Out* but what they plainly hoped would persuade significant numbers of lesbians and gay men to spend an unaccustomed Saturday night *in*. Despite the tone of its title, the evening actually provided a high proportion of quite serious programmes, rather than just a weekend-appropriate wave of light entertainment. True, it did begin relatively lightly, with fifty minutes of *The Gay Rock 'n' Roll Years*, a year-by-year compilation of songs and sound-bites, with no connective commentary, spanning the period from 1954. The musical clips were general rather than gay, providing a pretext for visual clips that offered a gay history from the setting up of the Wolfenden committee onwards.[2] Coverage was broad but inevitably superficial; the tone was lively, even if essentially nostalgic.

After a ten-minute item in which Bea Campbell interviewed outspoken, homophobic journalists Gary Bushell, Auberon Waugh and Peter McKay – an intelligent interviewer probing articulate interviewees, but much too briefly to pin down the topic – a twenty-minute programme with the predictable title *To Be or Not to Be* scrutinised the myth of the theatre as a gay-friendly space. This was followed by the centrepiece of the evening, at 9.50, a screening of Jack Gold's 1975 biopic about Quentin Crisp, *The Naked Civil Servant*, with a brief postscript on *Quentin Crisp Today*. A flurry of other short items before midnight included a fifteen-minute documentary on the Isle of Man's resistance to homosexual law reform; a monologue by Neil Bartlett, *That's What Friends Are For*, responding to his father's question about his gayness, 'Won't you be lonely?'; and a rather fatuous, factless documentary, fronted by the lesbian comedian Huffty, on lesbianism and tennis.

At five past midnight came the evening's most serious item, a twenty-minute programme called *Futures*, speculatively examining issues likely to impinge on and influence the future development of sexuality. Speakers included Maureen Duffy, Stuart Hall, Jeffrey Weeks, the geneticist Mary Jennings and Neil Wallace, a writer. Duffy raised anxieties about genetic manipulation to eliminate homosexuality; Weeks, too, spoke of a 'legitimate suspicion of science', given how sexology had defined homosexuals as sick. Although these and other matters, including globalisation and the rise of religious fundamentalism, were presented in bite-sized chunks over a constant background of music, this proved to be one of the most resonantly intelligent segments of any of the series I have been examining. It ended with Hall's resounding words: 'I think the position of women will never be the same again; I think the position of sexuality will never be the same again'. Viewers could choose for themselves whether this sounded thrilling or depressing. The evening drew to a late conclusion with *Some of My Best Friends*, fifteen minutes of interviews with black film makers Isaac Julien, Isiling Mack-Nataf, Marlon Riggs and Shakila Maan, followed by a screening of Riggs' hour-long film *Tongues Untied*.

Further experiments in gay programming – if not of whole evenings, of substantial chunks of them – would follow. The series *Dyke TV* would take over Channel 4's airwaves late at night – one such evening in 1996 began at 11.25 pm and ended after 4.00 am, with three hours and twenty minutes of special programmes, made by various production companies, followed by a one-and-a-half-hour screening of the 1931 film *Mata Hari*, starring Greta Garbo and Ramon Novarro – allowing the individual viewer who was not an insomniac to video up to five hours of continuous programming (assuming we can include the old movie among the lesbian items), in order to replay them on a later evening at a more convenient time.

Gaytime TV, which had its first season in 1996 and its last in 1999, was the BBC's most sustained provision of gay programming. Although various changes were made during this period, the basic format remained the same. Made by the production company Planet 24, it was an upbeat, not to say frivolous, magazine programme aiming to celebrate the positive aspects of lesbian and gay lives, mixing entertainment and information, but with a distinct bias in favour of the former. Presented in front of a live audience, with one lesbian presenter (comedian Rhona Cameron) and one gay (comedy writer Bert Tyler-Moore for one season, and then pop singer Richard Fairbrass), this was a show rather than a mere programme. Coming after *Newsnight*, the BBC's flagship news and current affairs programme late on a Thursday evening, *Gaytime TV* seemed to turn resolutely away from the seriousness of both its immediate neighbour and the tendency of previous gay programmes.

Each 45-minute programme in the first series in 1996 aired a variation on the same basic elements: brief documentaries on aspects of gay life (generally around six or seven minutes long), the interviewing of a studio guest, a series of items on gay icons (three minutes), a light-hearted guide to some aspect of gay life by one of the presenters and a closing song, supposedly a torch song, from a studio guest. The effects of this format were both positive and negative. Cumulatively, each series covered an impressively broad range of topics relevant to the lives of many of its viewers, and yet each individual programme could seem predictable: even if you were surprised by a single item, you knew that within just a few minutes the programme would revert to its customary rut. If you were looking for serious stuff, you got entertainment; if you were looking for entertainment, you got serious stuff – and all in frustratingly short bursts. Yet that, surely, is how a magazine programme always works.

The two titles that come most readily to mind when one thinks of British magazine programmes on television are *Nationwide* (1969–83) and *Pebble Mill at One* (1973–86), both on BBC1. The former, which went out after the main early evening news on all weekdays, combined serious current affairs coverage with lighter entertainment and consumer affairs. Its political coverage included analysis, interviews and discussions. The hub of the programme was based in the BBC studios at Lime Grove in London, but, true to its title, the main emphasis of *Nationwide* was on the bringing together of the regions. During the first twenty minutes of the programme, viewers in each region were given their own local news and sports coverage, broadcast from regional studios; and those satellite studios remained, as it were, on call for the rest of the programme, so that any item could be finessed with a range of regional inputs.

Pebble Mill at One was broadcast from the airy foyer of the BBC's Pebble Mill studios in Birmingham. Starting at 1.00 on weekday afternoons, the programme delivered forty-five minutes of informal talk, light current affairs (mainly regional), cookery and music. Its highly successful blend of information and entertainment seemed to be aimed mainly at housewives. (Students and the unemployed were their circumstantial bed-mates.) Cynics claimed it was mainly watched by mothers and toddlers who were waiting for the children's programmes that followed it at 1.45. It aimed to relax mothers who had been working all morning, and to calm their kids.

What immediately strikes one about these two programmes as possible models for *Gaytime TV* is that both tended to have an audience distracted by, among other things, a mealtime. Like proper magazines, which are not produced to be read systematically from cover to cover, these were programmes to be dipped into and wandered out of; they were cooked and eaten in front of. Some members of the family would arrive home from work or school during *Nationwide* – and it was, indeed, always presented as a programme for the family, to be watched collectively rather than alone. It was interruptible, yet it sought always to bring people's attention back to the screen in the corner of the room. It may have been the last of the major BBC programmes that held families together on a regular basis. Viewing conditions would later be irrevocably changed by TV sets in individual bedrooms, microwave meals and, of course, more recently, satellite, cable and internet access.

But *Gaytime TV* was a late evening programme. If watched when broadcast, rather than subsequently on video, it was likely to be the last thing most of its viewers watched before bedtime, especially if they had to go to work on the Friday morning. Most evening meals will have been taken long before the rolling of the opening credits. It was too late for housework or most other comparable distractions. At most, it would be accompanied by an alcoholic drink of some kind – or a calmative mug of cocoa. My point is that, unlike its two hugely successful precursors, *Gaytime TV* is likely to have been watched right through, by an undistracted audience. And this will have worked both in its favour and against it.

Any gay programme that has a chat-show element must rely on the willingness of good guests to appear under the 'gay' title. Reporting on the creation of *Gay Life* back in 1980, Harry Coen pointed out that 'it hasn't been easy for the *Gay Life* team to get results. Surprisingly, people from whom they had expected the most support have been the ones to let them down. Men and women whose names and even photographs appear regularly in *Gay News* have suddenly developed an insuperable shyness about appearing on telly' (Coen 1980). In terms of who gets invited to appear on such programmes, or who accepts such invitations, the consequences of this problem are far-reaching. They affect not only programme quality, but even the very definition of what might be considered interesting to a gay audience. There were times, especially by 1997, when this field of interest was being widened beyond the limits of plausibility, merely to accommodate some unlikely guest who had agreed to appear. Even camp itself, usually a resilient aesthetic, seemed threatened by such inclusiveness. Although one could see guests like the pop group Steps or the minor soap starlet Adam Rickitt on TV any night of the week, and they were therefore bringing nothing intrinsically special (short of coming out as gay themselves, which none of them did) to an appearance on *Gaytime TV*, the mere fact of such an appearance was grounds for – what? – admiration or gratitude, or some comparable response on the part of the gay audience, whether in the studio or at home. Certainly, such artistes' agents will have known this. An appearance on a gay programme would consolidate their gay fan-base and increase their album sales to gay consumers. Whether the gay audience got anything more out of the deal than that cringe or gratitude and the consequent, self-inflicted commercial exploitation is questionable.[3]

A different set of issues was raised by the programme makers' choices of not guests but people to be celebrated on a gay series. For instance, subjects of the 'Gay Icons' items in the 1997 season of *Gaytime TV* included the right-wing romantic novelist Dame Barbara Cartland, the singer and anorexia martyr Karen Carpenter, the Christian anti-pornography campaigner Mary Whitehouse, the Princess of Wales (Diana Windsor), the *Top of the Pops* female dance troupe Pan's People and the BBC television journalist and foreign correspondent Kate Adie – all female, but apparently none lesbian (even if the latter, Adie, would have made an excellent lesbian role model). Apart from the apparent initial premise that there is something intrinsically camp about being female, and unless a secret office exists somewhere for the sole purpose of number-crunching the statistics of gay approval, I can see little reason why one figure might get named as a gay icon and another might not. These light-hearted items were either entirely predictable or staggeringly unexpected. The standard Diana-worship of the piece on the Princess of Wales – 'Royal, glamorous, doomed' – was punctured only by the happy chance of a subsequent comment from the live studio guest, Quentin Crisp. Sceptical of a narrative that set Diana up as the victim of a haughty and unfeeling royal family, Crisp showed no sympathy for the supposed anguish of her marriage: 'She must have *known* the racket', he said sharply (and plausibly).

Because she had been adjudged a 'gay icon', the item on the pernicious Mary Whitehouse was inexcusably uncritical to the point of cretinism. This was the woman who, in the 1970s, was largely responsible for the demise of *Gay News*, which, at her behest, was successfully prosecuted under archaic laws against blasphemous libel. Inveigling the whole audience into its fatuous forgiveness of her career-long, obsessive targeting of gay culture, the voice-over said: 'You might hate us, Mary, but we *love* you'. Such abdication of political engagement conjures up further alarming and no more unlikely candidacies for iconicity: the Roman Catholic Church, perhaps, or National Socialism. The voice-over's coercive 'we', implicating the whole audience in its collaborative abjection, made for extremely uncomfortable viewing. To argue that the item was a camp joke does not excuse it. Call me naïve, but the very least I expect of a gay programme is that it not be anti-gay.[4]

Somewhat more intelligent and lively – if mainly because each programme lasted for half an hour rather than three minutes – was the four-part series *Celluloid Icons*, which Channel 4 screened on two evenings in 1996. The four candidates for iconic status were Jodie Foster, 'black divas', River Phoenix and the ITV soap opera *Coronation Street*. But even here, iconicity was left undefined and largely unexamined. In the last programme especially, viewers might have received the impression that iconic status was confirmed merely by the presence of a few gay fans of 'The Street'.

This returns me to the matter of broadcasters' having to cater to the sheer breadth of a 'gay audience'. The question that arises is, how effective was the magazine format in the case of *Gaytime TV*? Plainly, part of the point of the programme had been to offer as broad a variety of items as possible to catch the attention of a potential audience with extremely varied interests and tastes. On the principle that a minority programme should at least try to reach the majority of the minority in question, the aim appears to be that there should be 'something for everyone'. However, the studio audience, presumably meant to be a microcosm of something, never looked representative: as one reviewer pointed out, they seemed to be 'almost exclusively young, slim and fashionable' (Radcliffe 1996: 87); and their visibility became increasingly important because, from the second series onwards, they were moved from behind the camera to the centre of the studio floor, in the style of *Top of the Pops*.

Moreover, when one actually breaks down the contents of a series of *Gaytime TV*, this supposedly broad range of possible lesbian and gay interests served up for the audience boils down to something quite narrow. The reason for this is that, like many of the makers of programmes which are not intended for a gay audience but do refer to gay people, the makers of *Gaytime TV* seem to be stereotyping and essentialising who we are – sometimes in jest, but generally, and even perhaps unconsciously, in earnest. Yet they do not dare to recognise this explicitly. Suppose they were to acknowledge, for instance, that quite a large number of gay men do, indeed, go into hairdressing or interior decoration. The reason they do not is obvious: that is a stereotype, associated with effeminacy, which they are trying to gainsay. Yet, if the series is genuinely aimed at lesbians and gay men, why should they need to be going through the tedious motions of countering such stereotyping? Could they not take certain matters as being assumed and understood? Well, no, they cannot; and the reason is that, even on a programme supposedly aimed at a particular 'minority', they have to pander to the surveillance of the 'majority'. In other words, unsurprisingly, hetero-normative values still prevail in mass broadcasting, and therefore also in this show, albeit in their liberal, be-nice-to-gay-people manifestation.

It is worth noting that, even while a watered-down version of camp seems to be the prevailing ethos or style, rather old stereotypes of effeminacy in men are still being countered by the makers of *Gaytime TV* – as when a gay rugby team is paraded through the studio dressed in most of their kit (but presumably not in their boots, whose studs would scratch the dance floor) – but they are being replaced with other stereotypes, such as those decreeing that lesbians and gay men should never be ordinary. They always have to be – to use a word indiscriminately overused in gay circles – *fabulous*. So, just as Colin Richardson had to ask why there were no cottagers and whores in *Out*, we might identify another rank of absentees from *Gaytime TV*. Why do we never see any gay chartered accountants, or actuaries, or bird watchers, or mathematicians, or ...? There are several obvious reasons for this, perhaps the main one being that such people are perceived to be dull – not just televisually, but ontologically as well. If you were going to fill a programme with such folk, you might as well not have specifically gay programmes at all: for such occupations are like the professional equivalent of 'straight-acting', or even of 'straight' itself. Yet, in the scheme of things, is not the kind of homo we are supposed to be, in order to be considered fabulous, no less boring? Does a preoccupation with sequins in a man, or with motorbike parts in a woman, really make us interesting subjects?

How grateful programme makers must have been for the apparently infinite capaciousness of the concept of camp! You could identify any old dross as camp and it was suddenly sprinkled with gold dust. This must, at times, have saved a lot of effort and money. Any old film – especially if graced by an over-acting woman – could be screened; any bad singer – especially an over-acting woman – could be given a platform. Call it camp and it becomes acceptable entertainment for queers. (Camp works in much the same way as the gay icon in this respect.) Writing in the *Guardian* in 1995, Mark Simpson used *Gaytime TV* as evidence of the proposition that 'the gay sensibility isn't gay any more: straights ... seem to do it better'. Gay culture's very purchase on the camp aesthetic seemed to him to have been weakened, with the consequence that the broadcasters' reliance on it seemed increasingly desperate. He continued:

> Here the attempt to use camp – Dayglo sets and the arch look-my-cheek-has-my-tongue-in-it presentation of Bert Tyler-Moore and Rhona Cameron – to lighten the heavy burden of worthiness that curses community programming [...] and offer the audience a point of identification, merely piles on the agony. The presenters, the show and even homosexuality itself come across not so much as swell swishers at the forefront of mass culture as sorry victims of it.
>
> (Simpson 1996: 173–4)

Short of (say) gay liberationist politics – too much of a downer – or separate screenings of lesbian and gay pornography – too much of an upper – what glue but camp was ever going to unify a supposedly 'gay' audience? Indeed, what would ever define such an audience but its appreciation of camp? So, if camp itself should fail, what then remained of an audience for gay television?

There is no point in gay broadcasting that undermines the very concept of a gay audience – or is there? Given that, at least by 1998, a major cultural and political shift had been taking place (from gay into queer), *Gaytime TV* could have more aggressively pushed the notion of a more generalised queerness. Yet, from its titles onwards, even in its last series, the programme lagged behind the development of queer politics in the wake of the AIDS epidemic and the related agenda shift from sexual identities to sexual practices. But to have acknowledged this latter point might just take a programme maker in the direction of a programme like *Eurotrash*. And, in truth, despite being screened late at night, *Gaytime TV* never did treat sexual activities seriously. Indeed, it was pretty squeamish about sex altogether, to the extent that some of its few items about sexual practices really did come tonally close to the adolescent chortle of *Eurotrash*.[5]

Surveying the total output of *Gaytime TV* offers quite impressive results. Live studio guests included Jimmy Somerville, Scott Capurro, Ned Sherrin, Richard O'Brien, Liza Minnelli, Sandra Bernhard, Antony Sher, Stephen Twigg MP, Chastity Bono, pop impresario Tom Watkins, Alexander McQueen and Ian McKellen. The topics of serious documentary items included: the country's then (1996) only gay awareness training course for police officers; gay AIDS funerals; the age of consent; homophobic bullying in schools; gay rights in Hong Kong after the hand-over to China; male prostitution; Edmund White; Armistead Maupin; the 1999 nail-bombing of the Admiral Duncan;[6] the 'barebacking' resistance to safer sex; and Christian 'conversion' ministries. But in order to see such items the viewer had to sit through great stretches of blandness and banality, patronised into a stupor by a remorselessly upbeat and downmarket tone.

Looking back at these programmes from a distance, and especially at *Gaytime TV* as it declined into its later series, one perceives through their effortful cheerfulness an atmosphere of demoralisation. More than a decade of repressive Conservative policies and the AIDS epidemic seem to have taken their toll. There are signs that the subculture, which tended to speak of itself as a distinct and cohesive minority 'community', was beginning to realise that it had reached the limit of its capabilities as a force for change. In this context, the construction of gay programmes for gay viewers was starting to seem pointless. While the queer movement, born out of the AIDS movement through such organisations as ACT-UP and OutRage!, may have been applying freshly sceptical attitudes to minority discourses to revitalise not only gay/queer politics but also the aesthetics of the queer, programme makers must have been looking the other way. In the subsequent years, enough (if still few) programmes based around openly gay entertainers like Graham Norton, notwithstanding their obvious limitations, would demonstrate that the place for gay men and lesbians in British television was not likely to be in 'gay programming' after all, but in mainstream popular entertainment. If the consequence of this shift was to reduce the potentially disruptive dissonance of queerness to an amusing quirk, that very fact might have to be recognised as the price you pay for assimilation into mass culture.

Queerness has to be normalised if it is to be popular. Where it might become subversive, it must be shown to be compliant. Where it is perverse, it must be shown to be laughable. Wanting to be seen on television was always going to raise similar problems as wanting to be represented in parliament. Concessions would only be granted in response to subcultural compromise. What we always required of the mainstream was that it recognised *not everyone is not gay*. To an extent this has happened, in particular since the election of the Labour government in 1997, the equalisation of the age of consent in 2001 and the repeal of Section 28 in 2003. Magnificent though that was, it does not take the occasional explicitly gay drama like *Queer As Folk* to establish that times have changed for the better. It is when we see the occasional male–male or female–female couple on holiday programmes, quizzes, house-hunting programmes, make-over programmes, etc., that we know we have arrived. If we are disturbed by the sheer respectability, the ordinariness, the boringness and the conventionality of such appearances in mainstream programmes, well, that, too, is one of the prices we have to pay for representation. That is the unavoidable ambivalence of entryism – 'kinda subversive, kinda hegemonic', as Eve Kosofsky Sedgwick once pithily put it (Sedgwick 1993: 15). Assimilation was always going to exact a price.

Notes

1. Colin Richardson argues that *Out* was not, properly speaking, a magazine pro-gramme, on a number of grounds, including the facts that it had no studio audience, no common presenter across a whole series and was pre-recorded; also, many of its individual items were too long (Richardson 1995: 223, 225). On all these counts, by contrast, the later *Gaytime TV* would, indeed, qualify as a magazine.
2. The Wolfenden Committee, convened in 1954 to reassess national laws on prostitution, subsequently widened its remit to include male homosexuality and in 1957 recommended the decriminalisation of male homosexual acts between consenting adults. This reform was enacted – but only in England and Wales – in the Sexual Offences Act 1967.
3. The most awkward guest appearance was that of Andy Kane ('Handy Andy'), a married builder who had been appearing on the domestic make-over programme *Changing Rooms*. Introduced plausibly as 'an unlikely gay pin-up', Kane struggled through a completely pointless interview, in which Richard Fairbrass asked such questions as 'When did you first discover – maybe it was just today – that you were a gay pin-up of some kind?' and became so desperate when receiving a negative answer to 'Do you get much gay fan-mail?' that he asked it again. As an object lesson in barrel-scraping, this item must surely have few equals.
4. Another breath-taking moment of this sort occurred when Rhona Cameron, a supine interviewer at the best of times, allowed the narcissistic cultural com-mentator Camille Paglia to get away, unchallenged, with such remarks as: 'It is often the case that open homosexuality is a feature of a culture just before it collapses, okay, so we have to be careful'.
5. Made by the company Rapido TV, *Eurotrash* ran on Channel 4 for sixteen series, presented originally by the actor and comedian Antoine de Caunes and the couturier Jean-Paul Gaultier, but later by the former on his own. (Gaultier had

more important fish to *sauter*.) Based on the premise that non-Anglophone foreigners are irresistibly comical and peculiar, especially in the kinkiness of their sex lives – the production company's website (www.rapidotv.net) makes no bones about this point, openly boasting that '*Eurotrash* has become the nation's way of laughing at the madness of all things foreign!' – the programme managed to convey a certain amount of interesting information about European sexualities almost in spite of itself. Its main stock in trade was a liberal mix of nudists, big breasts, saucy sadomasochism, cross-dressing and bodily functions (with a particular emphasis on shit). Most of the participants were interviewed in their own European languages, but then dubbed into English with farcically discordant UK regional accents. Sex in this world view was relentlessly funny and still sniggerishly dirty. The main target audience appears to have been heterosexual boys in their teens and twenties. As the company website put it, 'It's the only sexy show on television that you can sit and laugh at with your girlfriend ... and your parents!' (This was clearly not addressed to young lesbians.)

6. On 30 April 1999, the Admiral Duncan, a gay pub in Soho, London, was nail-bombed by a right-wing fanatic who had already bombed two venues frequented by black and Asian Londoners. The bomb in the crowded gay pub killed three people and injured about seventy.

References

Coen, H. (1980), 'Londoners Prepare for Gay TV', *Gay News* 184(7–20 February): 14.

Radcliffe, M. (1996), 'A Gay Time in the East End', *Gay Times* (July): 86–7.

Richardson, C. (1995), 'TVOD: The Never-Bending Story' in P. Burston and C. Richardson (eds) *A Queer Romance: Lesbians, Gay Men and Popular Culture*, London and New York: Routledge, 216–48.

Sedgwick, E.K. (1993), 'Queer Performativity: Henry James's *The Art of the Novel*', *GLQ: A Journal of Lesbian and Gay Studies*, 1(1): 1–16.

Simpson, M. (1996), *It's a Queer World*, London: Vintage.

Taylor, J.R. (1980), 'Making a Start', *Gay News* 185(21 Feb–5 March): 25.

Chapter 7

Guy love

A queer straight masculinity for a post-closet era?

Ron Becker

> Our guy love
> That's all it is,
> Guy love
> He's mine, I'm his
> There's nothing gay about it in our eyes.
> You ask me about this thing we share -
> And he tenderly replies,
> 'It's guy love between two guys ...'
> JD and Turk, *Scrubs*
> ('My Musical,' 18 January 2007)

In the musical episode of the quirky NBC sitcom *Scrubs* (NBC, 2001–8), the highlight (at least for me) is 'Guy Love' – a duet between the show's main protagonist JD and his best friend and co-worker Turk.[1] The best friends' love song playfully acknowledges the queerness of their unconventionally close relationship. The two guys declare their commitment to each other ('You know I'll stick by you for the rest of my life') and admit the difficulty of facing society's disdain ('Though I'm proud to call you chocolate bear, the crowd will always talk and stare'). Wrapped in irony (e.g. the satirical use of the genre, the actors' overwrought performance styles, several 'not-in-a-gay-way' disclaimers), the scene enables viewers not to take this 'guy love between two guys' seriously. In this article, however, I will, because while 'Guy Love' may have been uniquely clever, it was not exceptional. Representations of queer straight masculinity could be seen throughout US television in the 2000s.[2]

'Guy Love' and other such queer moments present hegemonic masculinity in the process of being redefined. While it's a cliché to claim that masculinity is in crisis, it is hard to deny that assumptions about what men are (or should be) like have been destabilized by various, often interconnected sociohistorical forces. Second wave feminism, multiculturalism, 11 September, de-industrialization, computerization, and an ever-expanding consumerism, for example, have altered the terrain within which men live and hierarchical gendered relations operate. Media scholars work to understand the manifold connections between the representations of straight men on television and these changing contexts – between the objectified male bodies of Bod body spray ads and the logics of late-capitalist commercial media, or between the newly home-bound husbands and boyfriends of *Trading Spaces* (TLC, 2000–) and the distribution of domestic labour in an era of working women; between the nihilistic juveniles of *Jackass* (MTV, 2000–2) and the political benefits of irresponsibility for privileged white men, or between the beefy but bruised men of *The Ultimate Fighter* (Spike TV, 2005–) and the erosion of US manufacturing jobs (see Connell 2005; Gardiner 2002; Gardiner 2005; Kimmel 1995; Pfeil 1995; Savran 1998; Takacs 2005). Television, as these brief examples suggest, is a site where hegemonic masculinity gets negotiated, recuperated, and reimagined.

And what of JD and Turk's best friend love song? In this article, I connect the emergence of such queer *straight* guys to the emergence of openly *gay* guys on US television and to changes wrought by the gay rights movement. By challenging heterosexuality's taken-for-granted status as natural and morally superior, gays and lesbians have (perhaps only temporarily and certainly only partially) destabilized heteronormativity. In doing so, they have made it at least possible to envision alternative ways to think about straight masculinity and to organize (hetero)sexual identities, desires, and behaviours. Like the anxious exploration of straight-guy intimacy in 'Guy Love,' much of US television reveals a culture negotiating what it means to be a straight man in a gay-friendly world.

Hegemonic masculinity and gay rights

In his celebrated history of gay, New York during the first half of the twentieth century, George Chauncey describes a world where gender, sexual identity, and sexual behaviour were regulated quite differently than they currently are in US culture. As recently as the 1920s (and as late as the 1940s and 1950s in some African–American and working class communities) sexuality was still organized by a rigidly bifurcated Victorian gender ideology – a fact that was reflected in the various terms men who had sex with men used to describe themselves and others as ('fairy,' 'queer,' 'trade,' and 'gay'). Such labels were not interchangeable but rather mapped out discrete locations within a historically specific gender and class structure. The fairy, Chauncey asserts, 'was defined as much by his "woman-like" character or "effeminacy" as his solicitation of male sexual partners' (Chauncey 1994: 13). In contrast, the label 'trade' referred to often unmarried men living in sex-segregated immigrant communities who engaged 'in extensive sexual activity with other men' but who were not considered abnormal or homosexual and didn't risk 'stigmatization and the loss of their status as "normal men"' as long as they conformed to masculine gender norms – norms that included taking the active role in sexual encounters (13).

This taxonomy, however, would gradually and unevenly be replaced by a gay/straight binary that divided men not on the basis of their gender identity but rather on the basis of sexual object choice. By the 1950s, a new generation of mainly white, middle-class men had adopted the term 'gay' and 'a new, self-consciously "masculine" style' to distance themselves from the effeminacy of the fairy and to challenge the cultural equation of homosexuality with gender deviance (Chauncy 1994: 21). In doing so, they helped to reconfigure how masculinity and male sexuality was defined, regulated, and experienced. This newly hegemonic gay/straight binary reduced identity positions available to men. By the 1970s, most people considered any man (no matter how masculine) who had any kind of sex with men (no matter what role he played in the sexual encounter) to be gay. Thus, 'trade' virtually disappeared as a viable sexual identity in mainstream US culture. Chauncey, for example, recounts the complaints of older gay men about how difficult it became to find straight men willing to get a blowjob from a guy. For men who identify as straight, the idea of any sexual contact with another guy became taboo – a fact that likely altered many men's sexual activities and erotic imaginations.

Chauncey's history dovetails well with Eve Kosofsky Sedgwick's discussion of male homosexual panic. Sedgwick argues that changing concepts of sexuality (specifically the modern idea that people's sexual desires and behaviours are intrinsic parts of their psyches) has profoundly shaped how hegemonic masculinity has been regulated and experienced. Since the nineteenth century, Sedgwick asserts, Anglo–American men have found themselves in a double bind rooted in the fuzzy line between homo*sexuality* and homo*sociality*. On the one hand, with the psychiatric 'discovery' of 'the homosexual,' same-sex behavior became an utterly stigmatized perversity, socially prohibited and definitionally incompatible with the newly emerging construction of a heterosexual masculine identity. On the other hand, access to the benefits of patriarchal privilege required men to participate in a range of same-sex relationships (e.g. 'male friendship, mentorship, admiring identification, bureaucratic subordination, and heterosexual rivalry') that forced 'men into the arbitrarily mapped, self-contradictory, and anathema-riddled quicksands of the middle distance of male homosocial desire' (Sedgwick 1990: 186). The anxiety produced by men caught in the middle has been fueled even more by the uncertainty surrounding the nature of sexual identity – by the always closet-able nature of sexuality, by the prospect that some latent homosexual urges could suddenly emerge, and by the far too fine line between sexual desires and relational intimacy. For Sedgwick, male homosexual panic – a virulent homophobia directed both outward and inward – became a defining characteristic of an always insecure heterosexual masculinity and a coercive mechanism that has promoted careful conformity to hegemonic gender norms and in the process reinforces the gay/straight binary Chauncey describes.

Such historical and theoretical work refutes heteronormative assumptions about the immutability and innateness of both gender and sexuality by illustrating the varied permutations that can emerge from what Judith Butler calls the heterosexual matrix – a 'cultural grid of intelligibility through which bodies, genders, and desires are naturalized' (Butler 1990: 151). Our binary gender system and the regulation of sexual desires have been legitimated and coordinated by two *seemingly* self-evident assumptions: that human bodies unproblematically fall into one of two categories (male/female) and that those categories are the result of the biological imperative of sexual reproduction. Although claiming to merely describe human nature, this heteronormative ideology actually prescribes how we are to think about our bodies and organize our identities. In the process, it has worked to channel (or discipline) the vast diversity of human bodies, emotions, and libidinal energies into hierarchized binaries like male/female, masculine/feminine, heterosexual/homosexual, and sexually active/passive that undergird historically specific patriarchal and heterosexist social orders and privilege those who conform to 'normal' sex/gender/sexual identities.

Of course the invariable existence of 'deviants' belies the smooth inevitability of such constructions and illustrates the ways in which hegemonic alignments of sex, gender, desire, behaviour, and identity are always responding to the ultimately unruly diversity of people's lives as well as to the changeable material conditions of complex societies. As Annette Schlichter argues, the most valuable queer and feminist scholarship on gender and sexuality problematizes 'the representation of heteronormativity as a single monolithic position' (2004: 558). She encourages scholars to look for evidence of ways in which 'master narratives of heterosexual formations of gender, race, and sexuality' can be disrupted and points to cultural texts like transvestite comedian Eddy Izzard, images of alternative sexual communities on HBO's *Real Sex* (2000), the depiction of fag hags on *Will & Grace* (NBC, 1998–2006), and the popularity of *Bend Over Boyfriend* (a video guide for female-to-male anal sex) as fruitful case studies (560).

Television's queer straight guys certainly suggest that the relationship between hegemonic masculinity and (homo)sexuality is shifting. It would be surprising if it weren't, since LGBTQ political activism and cultural visibility has destabilized elements important to certain heteronormative configurations of gender, desire, and identity. First, by dismantling much of the power and appeal of the closet and by overturning anti-sodomy laws, gaining marriage rights, and enacting anti-discrimination legislation, the gay rights movement has eroded much of the social stigma associated with homosexuality. In the process, gay rights discourse has helped establish a widespread, if not dominant, construction of (homo)sexuality as genetically determined rather than a choice – a discourse that works in important ways to clarify and stabilize the relationship between gay and straight. If the taboo on homosexuality, the existence of the closet, and an uncertainty about the nature of sexuality have been central to the coercive force of male homosexual panic, such changes would likely alter the regulation of heterosexual masculinity (Becker 2006: 13–36).

Second, the gay liberation and civil rights movements have worked to denaturalize heterosexuality, in part, by helping to disarticulate sex from the biology of reproduction. LGBTQ politics (along with developments like the feminist movement, the legalization of birth control, advances in reproductive technology, and consumer culture) have advanced alternative ways to think about the purposes of erotic pleasure and have helped normalize a wide range of sexual practices like masturbation, pornography, premarital sex, casual sex, S&M, as well as homosexuality. Furthermore, gay rights rhetoric has tried to challenge heterosexuality's monopoly over law-of-nature claims by insisting that homosexual behaviour is both innate and a natural part of the human experience, arguing that forms of homosexuality have existed throughout time and in every culture. Such epistemological shifts undermine assumptions that support certain heteronormative alignments of sex, gender, desire, and behaviour.

Finally, I'd argue that gay male identity is being increasingly disarticulated from sex. While Chauncey traces the shift from a sexual regime based on gender status to one based on sexual object choice, recent forces are reconfiguring being gay as a cultural identity – one based on a lifestyle as much as on whom one has sex with. The AIDS crisis, for example, changed the role sex played in many gay men's lives and reorganized priorities within the gay community. And despite early homophobic press coverage of the epidemic that hypersexualized gay men, AIDS education efforts have created an orientation-neutral safe-sex discourse that has reframed how many people, both gay and straight, talk about sexual practices. Such shifts were furthered in the 1990s by an assimilationist political agenda that focused on issues like employment protection, marriage laws, and access to military service rather then sexual liberation. Such civil-rights debates also advanced a discourse that helped define gayness as a trait, like skin colour, rather than a set of sexual desires or behaviours (Becker 2006: 37–70). Meanwhile, commercial culture's images of gay men have tended to represent gay men as trendy consumers or straight women's best friends more than as men who have sex with other men. The commercialization of gay culture itself has often encouraged such constructions. As Fred Fejes asserts, 'In the past, "coming out" was chiefly about acknowledging long repressed sexual desires; today it is as much if not more about consumption and the creation of an acceptable masculine image'(2000: 115). And David Gilmore laments, 'We've shed our sexual identity for a social identity' (2005: 4).

This is where 'Guy Love' and television's queer straight men come in. But before I discuss them, I want to make a few comments about the presence of openly gay guys on TV. TV's most recent crop of gay guys not only reveals and reinforces the current shifting politics of sexuality, but they also serve as a prerequisite for the existence of their queer straight counterparts. Below, I argue that the representation of queer straight guys is dependent upon the presence of television's openly gay guys and upon what might be called post-closet TV narratives.

Come Out, Come Out …

Since the mid-1990s, gay men (and to a lesser extent lesbians) have become increasingly common on US television. Of course many critics have rightly exposed how circumscribed the images of gay life offered on television have been (see, for example, Battles and Hilton-Morrow 2002; Dow 2001; Joyrich 2001; Shugart 2001; Tropiano 2002; Walters 2001). The representation of gay characters has conformed to the demands of a commercial medium steeped in heterocentric genre formulas, supported by advertisers anxious to avoid controversy, filtered by network executives keen on reaching the most lucrative consumers, and targeted to the interests of mostly straight viewers who (although often interested in watching gay-themed programming) still demand stories that speak to their experiences (Becker 2006: 108–35). As a result, gay characters have only rarely upset the heterocentric, consumption-friendly flow of US television.

One of the most noticeable characteristics of much gay-inclusive programming has been the chaste existence of many gay characters – certainly an important factor in the growing cultural disarticulation of gayness from sex. Gays have often been token characters for whom sex or even romance are rarely options in the all-straight worlds in which they usually find themselves. CBS's reality series *Survivor* (CBS, 2000–) and *Big Brother* (CBS, 2000–) for example, often exploit the real or potential romances between their young attractive heterosexuals – an opportunity denied the one openly gay guy (it has almost always been a gay guy) that invariably gets cast. Even on Bravo's all-male *Boy Meets Boy* (2003), a dating reality show in which a gay man sought a romantic connection from among a house full of supposedly gay suitors, the carnal climate was structurally limited. In the series' key twist, some of the suitors were actually straight. In order to guard the secret premise, producers carefully controlled the kind of physical interaction the 'gay' guys could have (Bennett 2006). The real de-sexualization of gay men, I'd argue, takes place via their seamless incorporation into a number of typically sex-free genres like home makeover shows (TLC's *Trading Spaces*), real-estate shows (HGTV's *House Hunters*, 1999–), and occupational reality shows (Bravo's *Project Runway*, 2004–).

As important as *how* gay men have been represented is the seemingly unproblematic presence of openly gay men and gay male characters on TV. In the mid-1990s, the debate over whether gays should be seen on American television was a highly charged political issue. Since the late 1990s, however, gay men (and perhaps to a lesser extent lesbians) have been integrated into the landscape of US television with little fanfare and perhaps even less resistance. They have appeared in prime-time network series like *Brothers & Sisters* (ABC, 2006–), *Ugly Betty* (ABC, 2006–), *Desperate Housewives* (ABC, 2004–) and *America's Next Top Model* (UPN/CW 2003–) and in a vast array of cable series (from high-profile dramas like HBO's *Six Feet Under* (2001–5) and *The Wire* (2002–8) to low-profile, low-budget programming like HGTV's *Curb Appeal* (1999–) and Bravo's *Top Chef* (2006–). Meanwhile, many of the most gay-inclusive series of the 1990s (e.g. *Friends, Roseanne, ER, Spin City*) have become the syndicated mortar that holds television line-ups together. Also noteworthy is the fact that most of these gay men are openly gay; they are rarely caught up in the kind of closeted or coming out narrative that defined much of the gay-themed programming from previous eras. Being openly gay is often the starting point for their stories, not the end point. As a result, the presence of openly gay men on television has become virtually banal.

There are so many openly gay guys on television which enables the construction of a queer straight masculinity by supporting a liberal assumption that we have entered a 'post-gay' civil-rights era. First, from a perspective that equates cultural visibility with political progress, TV's openly gay guys indicate that for all practical purposes homophobia has seriously decreased and with it, gay men's need to be in the closet and liberal straight men's need to feel guilty about their heterosexual privilege. Second, TV's openly gay guys shore up confidence that the distinction between gay men and straight men is self-evident and stable – an anxious issue if one believes that homophobia (long a structuring principle of heterosexual masculinity) is politically regressive or simply passé. By way of a comforting slippage, the naïve, liberal belief that gay men *can* be out becomes the reassuring assumption that they *are* out. In other words, the banal ubiquity of television's openly gay guys supports the illusion of a post-closet world where all men who are gay are out, and any man who isn't out is obviously (and securely) straight – otherwise they'd be out.

For what might be called post-closet TV, gay men who are *not* out – who fail to identify with the label waiting for them, who refuse to accept the straight world's tolerance, who expose the gaping hole in this post-civil-rights logic – are a real problem. To maintain confidence in the clarity of the line between gay men and straight men, these closet cases must be helped out. Such was the case with much of the public discourse surrounding *Brokeback Mountain*, the 2005 film that tells the story of the homosexual relationship between two Wyoming ranch hands, Jack and Ennis. The movie puts Jack and especially Ennis within a closet constructed by the threat of homophobic violence and the exigencies of their geographic, economic, and historical contexts. Both are married, have children, and live as straight men; they never identify as 'gay.' Nevertheless, the film was consistently referred to as 'the gay cowboy movie' (a phrase perhaps most widely circulated via television's vast public relations juggernaut). This flippant moniker effortlessly provides the language that Jack seems to be struggling so hard to discover, that Ennis seems so anxious to avoid, and that a post-closet, liberal US culture seems to find self-evident and perhaps necessary (given the obsessive use of the phrase). Calling *Brokeback Mountain* a 'gay' cowboy movie outs Jack and Ennis in the public reception of the film in a way that they never are in the movie and, in the process, works to make the closet-ridden world of the film epistemologically safer for a post-closet era and for a queer straight masculinity.

Other narratives have been far more punishing in their treatment of closeted gay men – perhaps none more literally than a 2004 episode ('Double Exposure,' 24 January) on the CBS's crime drama *Hack* (2002–4).[3] The narrative begins when Jamie (a series regular) and his old college friend Wilson are bashed on the street by four masked men who hurl anti-gay slurs. When he enlists the help of Hack (a one-time cop now a justice-seeking cabbie looking for redemption from past mistakes), Jamie discovers that Wilson is gay and doesn't want to pursue the case for fear it will out him to his family. Determined not to let other gays get hurt, Hack and Jamie refuse to stop, even when faced with the threat of violence. Meanwhile, Wilson, afraid to go to a gay bar, takes the 'riskier' (in the logic of the episode) path of cruising a park at night where he is murdered. Hack eventually figures out that the murderer was not only one of the four masked bashers but also one of the beat cops who had been assigned to the original case. The key narrative twist, however, is that the beat cop (Boyle) is a closet case himself, driven to gay-bash and murder by his self-loathing.

Although gay killers have been a staple of mainstream film and TV narratives for decades, 'Double Exposure' reflects a post-closet variation. The episode, for example, works hard to emphasize that there is nothing wrong with being *openly gay*. When Jamie relates how he momentarily baulked when Wilson came out to him, Hack, the moral centre of the show, is clearly disappointed. Jamie, however, later redeems himself by risking his life to pursue the case and by delivering a eulogy at Wilson's funeral in which he castigates himself for not having wholeheartedly welcomed his friend out of the closet. Being a *closeted gay man*, however, is another thing. Wilson cowardly subverts the justice system, putting others at risk to keep his secret, only to get himself killed by cruising the park. Later, his fear of parental rejection is revealed to have been baseless; when his parents find out the truth after his death, they mourn the pain their son had experienced rather than express anger or shame over his gayness. Boyle, of course, is the real object lesson, as is made clear during the final confrontation when Hack pummels Boyle in an oddly long and one-sided fight. As Boyle crawls on the ground whimpering, Hack asks him, 'You beat up these guys to what – to prove that you're straight?' Thus, the closet becomes a violent place constructed by the pathetic and ultimately senseless fear of gay men rather than by the fear/hatred of homophobic straight men or by a heteronormative social order. Boyle's three accomplices, for example, are noticeably absent in the episode's final act, their motivation left unexplained and their anti-gay hate crimes left unpunished.

Black gay men who refuse to come out have become even more common and widely vilified targets for such post-closet narratives. On an episode of NBC's *Law & Order: SVU* ('Lowdown,' 6 April 2004), the murder of a white assistant DA leads the detectives and viewers into the 'shocking' world of life on the down low. When Jeff York's body is discovered, evidence initially suggests he was killed by a female prostitute. As the investigation unfolds, however, we learn that he was actually gay and was HIV-positive. When evidence leads detectives to suspect Andy Abbott, Jeff York's married, African–American colleague in the DA's office, they become suspicious of both his sexuality and his alibi. He claims to have been at a weekly poker game attended by other successful African–American men, but things don't quite add up. Det. Tutuola, a black detective in the precinct, believes the men 'are on the down low.' When his white colleagues look confused, he explains:

> Black men having sex with other men ... That's sex on the down low. They say it doesn't mean they're gay; it's just sex. They hang out, have a few drinks, pretend that what goes on downstairs isn't who they are. You grow up being black, you're supposed to be a man, become a father. Your church, your family, your friends – they all see being gay as a white man's perversion.

When Det. Benson points out that the epidemic of meth use in the gay community shows that white men have trouble with being gay too, he insists, 'It's different for black men. They go out, have sex with other men, then come home and have sex with their woman and pretend they're straight.'

The stakes involved increase when detectives learn that Andy Abbott is also HIV-positive and realize that his unsuspecting wife has likely been exposed. To make a solid case, though, Abbott's alibi must be exposed. Tutuola confronts DuShawn McGovern, a former pro-football player who was at the poker game. McGovern finally admits that the poker game did serve as down-low cover, that he and the other men in it were having sex with each other, and that they had lied to give Abbott an alibi. Despite this revelation, McGovern tells Tutuola, 'I am not gay. I have relationships with women and sex with men.' With what the narrative privileges as the commonsensical response, Tutuola replies, 'And I got news for you. That means you're gay.' When McGovern refuses to testify, however, the case is in jeopardy again. The only solution, it seems, is to get Abbott to confess. To do so, the DA and detectives break the law. They tell Abbott's wife that her husband is HIV-positive, and when she finds out that she is as well and realizes that a lengthy trial will only add to her family's troubled future, she pleads with her husband: 'I'm asking you Andy to be a man, and admit what you've done.' Eventually he confesses that he had been having sex with Jeff, but that Jeff had pushed him to leave his wife. 'I couldn't admit I'm gay,' he tells her, explaining why he got so angry and killed Jeff. By the end of this closet case, life on the down low is framed as self-delusion, leads to obstruction of justice, threatens the lives of innocent straight women, and ruins a family. Once again, we see that a man's need to stay in the closet leads him to kill, and the narrative resolution seems as invested in forcing Andy to acknowledge that he's gay as in forcing him to confess to the murder.[4]

These narratives support a liberal assumption that contemporary, white America has entered a post-closet era. Jack and Ennis's closeted lives can be read as history – as a peek into an unenlightened, closeted, pre-1990s world. Wilson's death and Boyle's self-hatred are tragic because they are unnecessary. And Andy Abbott's crime simultaneously exposes the corrosive effects of the closet and constructs it as a subcultural phenomenon of particular concern to Black America. These closet cases work in conjunction with television's seemingly ubiquitous openly gay men and the gay-friendly straight people who surround them to reconfirm a liberal notion that the closet is gone and the homophobia that constructed it is increasingly irrelevant.

Straight but not narrow

What happens to straight masculinity when the closet is *seemingly* dismantled? When gayness becomes a hip lifestyle as much as a set of sexual behaviours? And when the anxious uncertainty about the nature of sexuality is replaced by a liberal confidence in (or at least insistence upon) its stability? If the always closet-able nature of homosexuality and the fear of being called a fag has disciplined men to conform to specific gender and sexual identities, then the liberal belief that being gay is neither perverse nor contagious will very likely destabilize the configurations of sex, gender, and sexuality that have undergirded heteronormative masculinity. In television's queer straight men we see heterosexual men sometimes cautiously, sometimes uneasily, sometimes playfully, and sometimes ironically exploring and transgressing the boundaries of hegemonic masculinity long guarded by homosexual panic.

A 2002 episode of *Friends* ('The One with the Male Nanny,' 7 November) comically suggests the liberatory potential of queer straight masculinity. Throughout the episode, Ross has a problem: he isn't comfortable with Sandy, his baby's new nanny. Sandy (played by Freddie Prinze Jr.) is a professional childcare provider who believes that 'the most satisfying thing you can do with your life is take care of a child,' who is brought to tears by being 'welcomed into a new family,' and who makes his own moisturizing lotion. Rachel thinks he's perfect, but Ross thinks he's 'weird.' The source of Ross's discomfort seems to be Sandy's sexuality; he's straight – a fact we find out when Ross asks him if he's gay. That he's straight is clearly not the answer Ross expected or wanted to hear. (Later, when Sandy insists on a group hug, Ross insists 'You've gotta be at least bi'). The episode doesn't question Sandy's heterosexuality nor does it suggest (as one might expect) that Ross is jealous of a possible romance between Rachel and Sandy. Instead, laugh track cues and editing choices encourage the viewer to laugh at Ross's discomfort with Sandy's 'weird' straight masculinity. Eventually, Sandy's unorthodox gender behaviour is so troubling to Ross that he fires him. In the episode's final scene, he admits to Sandy: 'It's my issue … I'm just not that comfortable with a guy who's as [with hesitation] sensitive as you.' When Sandy asks why that is, the moment becomes a therapy session in which Ross uncovers the childhood roots of his gender anxiety.

Ross: Um, because of my father? … When I was growing up he was kind of a tough guy … I always got the feeling that I was too sensitive.

Sandy: That must have been hard.

Ross: It was hard. I remember I was in my bedroom playing with my dinosaurs … and my father walks in and says 'What are you doing with those things? What's wrong with you? Why aren't you outside playing like a real boy?'

Sandy: But you are a real boy.

Ross: (breaking into tears) I know I am. And when it's summer and it's hot why can't you wear a tank top?

Although safely wrapped in comic exaggeration, the episode presents the possibility of a straight masculinity no longer disciplined by homophobia. While Sandy remains blissfully unphased when Ross assumes he's gay, Ross's insistence on a specific configuration of gender and sexuality is framed as bigoted, laughable, and in the final scene somewhat pathetic.

Sandy wasn't the only straight man on US television redefining what straight masculinity might look like in a gay-friendly, post-closet world. Every straight guy on *Queer Eye for the Straight Guy* (2003–7), for example, puts his lifestyle in the hands of five gay men who ostensibly transform him for the better by schooling him on the principles of fashion, interior design, and skin care. The success of the Bravo series in the summer of 2003 helped fuel the metrosexual moment in US pop culture as pundits announced the discovery of a supposedly new breed of urban or urban-minded straight man – one who seemed to embrace the consumer habits and cultural tastes of his gay counterparts. By claiming it was now acceptable for straight men to enjoy the Pottery Barn, of course, *Queer Eye* and the discourse of metrosexuality primarily freed straight men to become more active consumers – hardly liberating, but a change in heteronormative constructions of straight masculinity nevertheless.[5] Series like *Boy Meets Boy* and *Gay, Straight, or Taken* (Lifetime, 2007) as well as one-off episodes of shows like *Miss Match* (NBC, 2003) and *Sex and the City* (HBO, 1994-2004) featured openly metrosexual men and explored what happens when the cultural norms that had long helped define the boundary between gay and straight men weaken.

Another mark of TV's queer straight guys seems to be their ability to openly love other straight men. Ostensibly freed from a homophobia that has long made homosocial relations a tricky business, the post-closet liberal straight guy now seems emotionally liberated. In this regard, *Scrubs'* JD may be among TV's queerest straight guys. He is openly desperate to forge a close and acknowledged bond with his mentor, Dr. Cox (even in the face of Cox's verbally abusive resistance that usually involves impugning JD's masculinity). And his relationship with Turk (his room-mate, co-worker, and best friend since college) is the deepest and most important in his life. The unusually close nature of their friendship is fodder for narrative development throughout the series. They share numerous inside jokes and have endearing pet names for each other. And even when they are involved with women, JD and Turk's status as a couple remains secure. Consequently, when the series produced a quirky musical episode, it seemed natural that it would contain a love duet between the two guys.

On the ABC drama *Boston Legal* (ABC 2004–), Denny (William Shatner) and Alan (James Spader) form a similarly close straight-guy couple. As lawyers in the same firm, Denny and Alan are colleagues but over the course of the series they become much more – a fact narratively underscored by the series' convention of ending each episode with the ritual of the two men sharing a quiet moment and a cigar. They also share each other's bed. Denny first spends the night to help Alan deal with night terrors, but their 'sleepovers' (as they refer to them) become a common part of their friendship. The queer nature of their relationship gets fully acknowledged in an episode in which Denny becomes jealous when Alan develops a close working relationship with another lawyer ('On the Ledge,' 6 November 2006). The emotional climax of the plotline serves as a dramatic counterpart to the musical comedy of 'Guy Love.'

Denny: Don't talk to me.
Alan: It's not like I went fishing with him.

Denny: And don't make fun of me. I don't know whether you know this, not many men take the time every day to have a cigar, a glass of scotch, to talk to their best friend. That's not something most men have.

Alan: No, it isn't.

Denny: What I give to you, what … what I share … I do with no one else. I like to think what you give to me, you do with nobody else. Now that … that may sound silly to you. But here's what I think is silly: the idea that jealousy or fidelity is reserved for romance. I always suspected that there was a connection between you and THAT man. That you got something you didn't get from me.

Alan: I probably do. But gosh, what I get from you, Denny … People walk around today calling everyone their 'best friend.' The term doesn't have any real meaning anymore. Mere acquaintances are lavished with hugs and kisses upon a second or, at most, third meeting. Birthday cards get passed around offices, so everybody can scribble a snippet of sentimentality for a colleague they've barely met. And everyone just 'loves' everyone. As a result, when you tell somebody you love them today, it isn't much heard. I love you, Denny. YOU are my best friend. I can't imagine going through life without you as my best friend. I'm not gonna kiss you, however.

Denny: I don't want you on my balcony – on any balcony – alone with that man.

Alan: Okay.

Like many David E. Kelley series, *Boston Legal* is known for its quirky excesses, including Shatner and Spader's over-the-top acting styles. This scene, however, is done 'straight;' the production doesn't cheat the intimacy of the dialogue. Without a playful tone or ironic winking, this declaration of guy love offers a decidedly queer take on male bonding.

Predictably, such queer straight men make sure to distinguish their guy love from gay love. Alan jokes that he 'hadn't gone fishing with him' (a reference to *Brokeback Mountain*) and clarifies that he isn't 'gonna kiss' Denny; JD and Turk's duet repeatedly references (in order to distance their guy love from) anal sex. Yet these moments of homosociality aren't established in any simple homophobic opposition to homosexuality – through a shared exploitation of women or cooperative violence against fags, for example. Instead, I'd argue, gay love helps give meaning to this guy love by being amiably acknowledged, even as it is being disavowed.

A casual exchange on NBC's *Today* show offers an example of this dynamic. On Matt Lauer's tenth anniversary as the show's co-host (5 January 2007), Bryant Gumbel, his predecessor, made a surprise visit. Along with co-host Meredith Vieira, Lauer and Gumbel warmly reminisce about their long friendship. Gumbel lavishes praise on Lauer's success, and Lauer speaks about how much Gumbel's support as a mentor and friend meant. Toward the end of the segment, the producers run a montage of photographs featuring the two men over the years reflecting a long, warm relationship. When the camera cuts back, Lauer and Gumbel are teary-eyed and speechless. Amid the highly emotional moment, Vieira playfully observes that the photographs had a *Brokeback Mountain* quality to them. (Some of the photographs included photographic conventions typically associated with romantic couples, such as one in which the men sit side by side on a golf bench bathed in the glow of a setting sun.) Everyone in the studio laughs. Although the tension is cut, the men continue to express their feelings for each other until the segment concludes; notably, neither man gets particularly defensive. The comment, I'd argue, serves less to discipline the men's masculinity than to foreground the depth of their friendship. Certainly the joke helps mitigate the awkwardness of a moment that transgressed hegemonic gender norms. And certainly, as with jokes in general, Vieira's comment was open to multiple readings. (Some viewers may have taken the gay reference as a harsh rebuke.) But given the tone of the conversation before and after the joke, and given Vieira's, Gumbel's, and Lauer's cosmopolitan public personae, the gay reference could help viewers appreciate the significance of the men's relationship rather than punish it. Whether or not this interpretation is the preferred reading, it seems the most likely reading for liberal viewers who believe (or want to believe) they live in a post-closet world.

Although JD, Turk, and Alan draw a line they won't cross, TV's queer straight guys push us to consider just how differently the relationship between sex, gender, and sexuality could be configured both in cultural norms and lived experience.[6] Heteronormative constructions work to obscure the complexity of sexuality – the fact, for example, that there is no necessary correspondence between gay identity and the enjoyment of receptive anal sex. There are plenty of gay men who, for psychological and/or physiological reasons, have no interest in anal sex. At the same time, there are straight men whose psyches and/or bodies are built in such a way that anal stimulation is intensely pleasurable – a fact evidenced by the (hetero)sexual practice of pegging (i.e. women using fingers or dildos to anally stimulate their male partners). While heteronormativity stigmatizes such practices and pleasures, I wonder how different straight male sexuality might look in an actually realized post-closet culture where being gay is defined by one's cultural identity rather than one's sexual practice, where the line between gay and straight is assumed secure, and where one's masculinity is not defined by one's repudiation of homosexuality or haunted by the closet.

Could a queer straight masculinity ever develop down a path that would enable straight men to have sex with other men? Of course straight men already have sex with men (in prisons and the sex work/porn industries, dorm rooms, and military barracks). Such behaviour, however, remains stigmatized and marginal, and any admission of enjoying it draws one's sexual identity into question. I want to exploit TV's queer straight guys, using them as an opportunity to consider a post-closet future where expressions of same-sex desire or participation in same-sex practices might actually be compatible with mainstream constructions of straight masculinity. Feeling free to be emotionally intimate with men, after all, could just be the thin edge of the wedge of a radical reconfiguration of sex, gender, and sexuality.

Such a future is not as implausible at it may seem. Attitudes about erotic practices and intimate relations can shift dramatically, perhaps particularly so in our post-industrial culture where sexuality is increasingly integrated into a commercial economy, where erotic pleasures become ends-unto-themselves, and where the consensus about issues of sexual propriety has eroded (Attwood 2006). For a post-Clinton generation, for example, 'having sex' means having vaginal or anal intercourse; the rest is just 'messing around' – an alien concept for many who came of age in the safe-sex-obsessed early 1990s. Meanwhile internet sex tapes and reality-TV exhibitionism help redraw norms regarding the public/private nature of sexual practices and desires. And in an Abercrombie & Fitch era, eroticized images of male bodies are on offer to men and women, gay or straight. It would be surprising if such changes didn't alter how straight masculinity and sexuality was organized, at least in some way.

Just how might a queerer construction of straight masculinity look? Hints can be glimpsed both on the margins and in the mainstream of US culture. On the edgy HBO prison drama *Oz*, for example, homosexuality is integral to prison life, presented not only through various same-sex rape narratives but also through the development of an at-first-sexual-then-romantic relationship between Keller and Beecher (the narrative's representative of normative 'straight,' white, middle-class masculinity). As Joe Wlodarz (2005) argues, *Oz* offers viewers an image of male desire and sexuality that can potentially destabilize any easy equation between sexual identity and sexual behaviours and desires.

Houseguest Nick on *Big Brother 8* (US edition) offers a less graphic but more mainstream example of a sexually queer straight masculinity. The producers firmly establish Nick's credentials as a straight guy; he is a powerfully built, former professional football player who, after flirting with a number of women, settles into a typical reality-TV-style romance with Daniele. But he is also thoroughly comfortable with the gay guys in the house – so comfortable, in fact, that he playfully flirts with them too. Nick appears happy to be the object of women's and men's desires. He is also happy to express his own interests in other men. While chatting with straight housemates Dick and Zach about hunky celebrity Ryan Reynolds, he casually mentions that 'he's a good looking dude' and could definitely be on 'his top 5 list.' When Dick and Zach do a double take, he explains that he and his friends keep lists of guys they would do if they were gay. Top on his list is Mathew McConaughey. When Dick and Zach razz him, Nick clarifies 'I won't do anything with any guys unless they're on my top 5 list at that moment.' Although at times Nick's comments are clearly playful (e.g. when discussing Brad Pitt's position on the list with Daniele, he says 'Have you seen *Snatch* or *Fight Club* ... Wow!'), he never recants or gets defensive and matter-of-factly states in a confessional 'I'm not homophobic; I am comfortable in my own skin and in my own sexuality' (22 July 2007 episode).[7]

The notion that obviously straight men like Nick could find other guys hot and that, in fact, they could have a crush on a certain guy has found expression in an emerging idiom: 'being gay for' someone. The concept was the premise for a C-plotline on the hip NBC sitcom *30 Rock* when an otherwise heterosexual Frank suddenly realizes, in the middle of a staff meeting, that he's 'gay for' a hot, twenty-something coffee boy ('Cougars,' 29 November 2007). Predictably, his co-worker Lutz ridicules him for being gay ('You're gay ... You wanna kiss him.'). But like Nick, Frank is unphased by such taunts ('I do. I want to kiss him on the mouth and hold him.') When Lutz looks for back up for his homosexual-panic jeers, the others in the room leave him hanging as they go on about their business as though nothing weird had happened. 'Why isn't this any fun?' he asks in confusion and disappointment.

Conclusion

I want to end with a few caveats. First, I don't want to imply that images of queer straight guys like JD and Nick are ubiquitous or reflect a sea change in the representations of straight masculinity in US popular culture; they are not and do not. That most queer straight guys are found safely wrapped in comedic irony reveals a culture nervously processing its changing politics of gender and sexuality rather than one fully confident in a vision of some queer future. Furthermore, they are often segregated on shows like *Scrubs* and *30 Rock* – shows that use a variety of unconventional elements to appeal to the sensibilities of a specific demographic of 'hip' viewers. In this regard, TV's queer straight guys are imbricated in the cultural politics of distinction that both fuel and are fueled by post-network era narrowcasting. In other words, that queer straight guys can only be found on certain shows is likely part of their appeal to those viewers who imagine themselves in opposition to a homophobic or hegemonic politics of masculinity.

Second, I don't want to suggest that every example of straight men in seemingly queer contexts offers the same or in fact any alternative to traditional masculinity. Margot Miller, for example, comparing the ironic gay jokes in *Seinfeld* (NBC, 1989–98) to those in *Friends* (NBC, 1994–2004) argues that in certain situations, ironic humour can re-establish a character's heterosexuality rather than queer his masculinity. According to her, the proliferation of such jokes in the 1990s actually 'reflected a new hostility toward queerness in straight male characters' (Miller 2006: 148).[8] An infamous Snickers ad from the 2007 Super Bowl provides a clear example of a joke that seems designed to discipline rather than queer masculinity. Referencing *Lady and the Tramp*'s spaghetti scene, the ad features two auto mechanics eating from opposite ends of a candy bar until they end up lip-to-lip at which point they recoil and proceed to rip out their chest hair in an attempt to establish their masculinity. Snickers also set up a website where visitors could watch video of NFL players' disgusted reactions to the ad's inadvertent same-sex kiss. 'That ain't right,' one player states. Certainly, the campaign seems predicated upon the homosexual-panic assumption that guy love and straight masculinity are definitionally incompatible.

The Snickers campaign, however, underscores a third point – that much of the meaning of TV's queer guys rests in the varied readings made by viewers.

(This fact is particularly true of highly polysemic comedie representations.) Gay and gay-friendly viewers who don't think there's anything wrong with two guys kissing could laugh at the paranoid stupidity of the men's reactions.[9] Conversely, less gay-friendly viewers could read 'Guy Love' as a mockery of gay love or interpret Alan and Denny's love scene as a sign of their immoral characters.[10] And many viewers likely mix a range of responses, reflecting a deep ambivalence about the changing world in which they find themselves.

So what conclusions can we make about TV's queer straight guys? At my most provocative, I want to suggest that such images can help us imagine the possibility of a future in which being gay and straight are disarticulated from sex – in which a self-identified straight man could enjoy sex with other men and not have his straight identity ever be in question. I offer this argument not because I think such a future is inevitable (I doubt that it is even likely) nor that it would be free of heterosexism (I doubt it would be); instead, I offer it as a critical stance against the profound ambiguity and winking irony that marks so many of these texts. 'Guy Love' may be teasing us with its straight guy love duet, but we can take its joke seriously. TV's queer straight guys reveal a post-closet culture working through the fact that gender and sexual identity categories don't easily map onto the diversity of people's experiences and remind us that heteronormative alignments of sex, gender, behaviour, and desire are not natural or inevitable. The changing political and cultural position of gays and lesbians has destabilized many of the mechanisms that have undergirded a specific regime of sex and gender – in part, by undermining the homophobia that had regulated and legitimated the hegemonic masculinity at the heart of that regime.

How might such developments unfold? Perhaps more quickly than we may imagine. According to Chauncey, the hetero-homosexual binary that we now take for granted emerged over the course of just a few decades. But he also emphasizes that it emerged unevenly. Imbricated as they are within other social structures like class and race, the post-closet politics I describe and their impact on heteronormativity will as well. Post-closet TV narratives about openly gay and queerly straight guys suggest that hegemonic constructions of gender and sexuality intersect with structuring forces like class (e.g. the presentation of gay and metrosexual identity in consumerist terms in shows like *Queer Eye*), race (e.g. down-low narratives that present a Black America trapped in the politics of the closet), and geography (e.g. *Brokeback Mountain* and hip shows like *Scrubs* that imply openly gay guys and their queer straight counterparts can only be found in big cities). What will straight masculinity look like next season? Stay tuned to find out.

Author's note:

I would like to thank Glyn Davis, Jennifer Fuller, Hollis Griffin, Elana Levine, and Gary Needham for their feedback on this article.

Notes

1. There is evidence to suggest that the producers and/or NBC marketers thought so too. The night before 'My Musical' aired, actors Zack Braff and Donald Faisson performed the song on *Jimmy Kimmel Live*. It was also the first of two numbers NBC made available on youtube.com and was the only one featured as a free download on iTunes.

2. Nor, of course, are they limited to television. Justin Wyatt skillfully analyses how the 1996 film *Swingers*' depiction of the close friendships among a group of straight male friends 'blurs the boundaries between the homosocial and homosexual' (2001: 62). Wyatt argues that '*Swingers* demonstrates the cooptation of gay male friendship within a supposedly "straight" comedy, signaling that queerness can be accommodated openly within increasingly conventional media texts.' In linking *Swingers*' queer take on straight masculinity to 'the integration of gay male friendship into straight society' (61), Wyatt hints at the important connection between depictions of queer straight masculinity and the wider politics of sexuality (61). I hope to draw out that historical connection more explicitly. Wyatt's work also encourages us to consider the ways queer straight masculinity has been incorporated into films in the 2000s. Movies like *Blades of Glory* (2007) and *I Now Pronounce You Chuck and Larry* (2007) raise obvious questions about the depiction of straight masculinity in relation to homosexuality. Such movies are beyond the scope of this essay and, I suspect, would raise significantly different representational issues.

3. That Jack and Ennis can be treated sympathetically, rather than demonized, is enabled by the historical setting of the film.

4. Getting black men who have sex with men to come out was also a priority for Oprah who did an exposé on the problem of the down-low for the benefit of her female viewers. Oprah's hour long interview (16 April 2004) with J.L. King (author of *Life On The Down-Low: A Journey into the Lives of 'Straight' Black Men Who Sleep with Men*) reflected much of the same post-closet discourse. Oprah's gay-friendly credentials are impeccable; she had been integral to the Ellen coming-out moment, not only interviewing Ellen DeGeneres and Anne Heche on her show, but also playing Ellen Morgan's fictional therapist on the famous episode. During the down-low interview, Oprah stands in for her worried straight female audience's panic and confusion about black men's down-low evasion of gay identity. The discussion (which included not only Oprah and King but also black male safe-sex educators and numerous audience members) included various perspectives about the nature of sexual identity, including what might be considered very queer notions about the definitional distinctions among often-conflated concepts like sexual desire, sexual identity, sexual behaviour, racial identity, and romantic love. When Oprah is completely flabbergasted by what she thinks is the denial of these men who have sex with men, King tries to explain that there's a distinction: 'it's not about orientation, its about gratification.' Interestingly, Oprah eventually says she 'gets it,' but by the end of the discussion, the consensus (though certainly not uncontested) seems to be that these black men are really gay, that they are in denial, but that the culture of Black America and the stereotype of gays-as-white explains their closeted denial of their true sexuality. Unanimously agreed upon, however, is the fact that this down-low culture exposes straight women to AIDS and must be fought.

5. Despite all of the attention given to *Ellen* and *Will & Grace* in the popular press, *Queer Eye* must be the most discussed gay-themed programme in

academic literature. Some examples relevant to my discussion here: Becker (2006), 220–1; McCarthy (2005); Sender (2006); Westerfelhaus and Lacroix (2006).

6. Sociologist Robert Heasley offers a typology of 'queer masculinities of straight men' to help us better appreciate the various 'ways of being masculine outside hetero-normative constructions of masculinity' that currently exist (2005: 310, 315). His typology includes: straight sissy boys, social-justice straight-queers, elective straight-queers, committed straight queers, and males living in the shadow of masculinity. Although I agree with Heasley that such queer straight masculinities have been culturally marginalized by the hegemony of heteronormative masculinity, I also want us to consider whether such queer masculinities might not just operate in contrast to hegemonic masculinity but actually be in the process of altering it. And further, I wonder just how queer dominant definitions of straight masculinity could feasibly or theoretically get.

7. Edgy fictional accounts and mainstream reality-TV versions of queer straight masculinity's possible future come together in gay pornography like that found on the popular SeanCody.com – a site where 'average' guys allegedly discovered on the street or through the site itself are paid to do a solo video. Each video is accompanied by a description that gives some contextual info, including the guy's sexual orientation. Roughly half of the models are identified as gay – a detail that likely inspires confidence in the truth of the other half's straight identities (as do conversations with the models that often include references to girlfriends). Some of the models also appear in subsequent videos that (at least for the straight guys) tend to follow a standard line of progression – from getting and then giving a blowjob to being a top and then a bottom in anal sex. Although there is a long gay-for-pay porn tradition, SeanCody.com's amateur-video style establishes the 'reality' of the models and their sexual pleasures in ways that differ from the fictional narratives of porn films. The accompanying text and on-camera conversations also encourage the viewer to believe that many of the straight guys 'really' enjoy their experiences. That some of the guys seem nonplussed about certain activities, for example, can help verify the pleasure of those straight guys who appear to (and sometimes discuss) enjoying it. Like *Oz*, the site destabilizes the notion that sexual pleasures match up neatly with sexual identities – that just like some gay guys, certain straight guys physiologically enjoy the sensation of anal sex and others don't. Such a view profitably exploits gay fantasies of course, but that fact doesn't negate its ability to shift constructions of gender and sexuality. And although the site is obviously targeted at gay men, internet porn is easily accessible to straight men and women. (In fact, there is evidence that the site has a significant number of straight female visitors.) Although the context of broadcast, cable and internet production and consumption differ in important ways (though perhaps in an age of technological convergence and media fragmentation in increasingly subtle ways), SeanCody.com offers an unfettered view of the kind of queer straight masculinity only suggested by its TV counterparts.

8. Similarly, in his analysis of queer straight masculinity in *Swingers*, Justin Wyatt warns that 'not all contemporary films centring on male-bonding demonstrate' the same 'enlightened view' as he feels *Swingers* does. '*Swingers* adopts the model of gay male friendship for its heterosexual characters problematizing rigid classifications of gay and straight,' Wyatt argues, 'while [a seemingly similar male-bonding film like] *The Full Monty*, despite its gay characters, serves to reinforce the lines between gay and straight' (Wyatt 2001: 62).

9. Such a negotiated reading seems harder to make if one also visits the website where video of the football players' reactions help anchor the preferred

gay-panic reading. A protest against the ad campaign eventually led Mars to cancel it. For more on preferred and negotiated reading positions, see Hall (1980).

10. Joe Wlodarz (2005) argues that many of *Oz*'s straight male viewers were turned off when Beecher and Keller's relationship deepened from an exploitative, often violent sexual relationship to a more romantic one. It would not be surprising if many stopped watching, skipped those segments of narrative, or made highly negotiated or oppositional readings.

References

Attwood, F. (2006), 'Sexed Up: Theorizing the Sexualization of Culture,' *Sexualities* 9(1): 77–94.

Battles, K. and Hilton-Morrow, W. (2002), 'Gay Characters in Conventional Spaces: *Will and Grace* and the Situation Comedy Genre,' *Critical Studies in Media Communication*, 19(1, March): 87–105.

Becker, R. (2006), *Gay TV and Straight America*, New Brunswick, NJ: Rutgers University Press.

Bennett, J.A. (2006), 'In Defense of Gaydar: Reality Television and the Politics of the Glance,' *Critical Studies in Media Communication* 23(December): 408–25.

Butler, J. (1990), *Gender Trouble: Feminism and the Subversion of Identity*, New York: Routledge.

Chauncey, G. (1994), *Gay New York: Gender, Urban Culture, and the Making of the Gay Male World 1890–1940*, New York: Basic Books.

Connell, R.W. (2005), *Masculinities*, 2nd edn, Berkeley, CA: University of California Press.

Dow, B. (2001), 'Ellen, Television, and the Politics of Gay and Lesbian Visibility,' *Critical Studies in Media Communication* 18(June): 123–40.

Fejes, F. (2000), 'Making a Gay Masculinity,' *Critical Studies in Media Communication* 17(March).

Gardiner, J.K. (2002), *Masculinity Studies and Feminist Theory: New Directions*, New York: Columbia University Press.

—— (2005), 'Why Saddam Is Gay: Masculinity Politics in *South Park – Bigger, Longer, and Uncut*,' *Quarterly Review of Film and Video* 22: 51–62.

Gilmore, D. (2005), 'How "Gay Style" Was Coopted and Corrupted,' *Gay & Lesbian Review Worldwide* 12(4, July/August).

Hall, S. (1980), 'Encoding/Decoding' in S. Hall, D. Hobson, and A. Lowe (eds) *Culture, Media, Language*, London: Hutchinson, 128–38.

Heasley, R. (2005), 'Queer Masculinities of Straight Men,' *Men and Masculinities* 7(3, January): 310–20.

Joyrich, L. (2001), 'Epistemology of the Console,' *Critical Inquiry* 27(Spring): 439–67 (reprinted in this volume).

Kimmel, M.S. (1995), *Manhood in America: A Cultural History*, New York: Free Press.

McCarthy, A. (2005), 'Crab People from the Center of the Earth,' *GLQ: A Journal of Lesbian & Gay Studies*, 11(1): 97–101.

Miller, M. (2006), 'Masculinity and Male Intimacy in Nineties Sitcoms' in J. R. Keller and L. Stratyner (eds) *The New Queer Aesthetic on Television: Essays on Recent Programming*, Jefferson, NC: McFarland, 147–59.

Pfeil, F. (1995), *White Guys: Studies in Postmodern Domination and Difference*, New York: Verso.

Savran, D. (1998), *Taking it Like a Man: White Masculinity, Masochism, and Contemporary American Culture*, Princeton, NJ: Princeton University Press.

Schlichter, A. (2004), 'Queer at Last? Straight Intellectuals and the Desire for Transgression,' *GLQ: A Journal of Gay & Lesbian Studies* 10(4): 543–64.

Sedgwick, E. K. (1990), *Epistemology of the Closet*, Berkeley, CA: University of California Press.

Sender, K. (2006), 'Queens for a Day: *Queer Eye for the Straight Guy* and the Neoliberal Project,' *Critical Studies in Media Communication* 23(2, June): 131–51.

Shugart, H.A. (2001), 'Parody as Subversive Performance: Denaturalizing Gender and Reconstituting Desire in *Ellen*,' *Text and Performance Quarterly* 21(2, April): 95–113.

Takacs, S. (2005), 'Jessica Lynch and the Regeneration of American Identity and Power Post-9/11,' *Feminist Media Studies* 5(3): 297–310.

Tropiano, S. (2002), *The Prime Time Closet: A History of Gays and Lesbians on TV*, New York: Applause Theater & Cinema Books.

Walters, S.D. (2001), *All the Rage: The Story of Gay Visibility in America*, Chicago, IL: University of Chicago Press.

Westerfelhaus, R. and Lacroix, C. (2006), 'Seeing "Straight" through *Queer Eye*: Exposing the Strategic Rhetoric of Heteronormativity in a Mediated Ritual of Gay Rebellion,' *Critical Studies in Media Communication* 23(5, December): 436–44.

Wlodarz, J. (2005), 'Maximum Insecurity: Genre Trouble and Closet Erotics in and out of HBO's *Oz*,' *Camera Obscura* 20(1): 58–105.

Wyatt, W. (2001), 'Identity, Queerness, and Homosocial Bonding: The Case of *Swingers*' in P. Lehman (ed.) *Masculinity: Bodies, Movies, Culture*, New York: Routledge, 51–65.

Part III

Television itself

Chapter 8

Scheduling normativity

Television, the family, and queer temporality

Gary Needham

Time is so central to the operations of television that several of the foundational writings in television studies are based upon an examination of it. Time has been the lynchpin in television's difference from cinema, in that television has the capacity to produce time as now-ness and immediacy through the live broadcast, or at least television is able to convey the feeling of being live, of being closer to time as it happens. The temporal dimensions of television apparently chime with the rhythms of the everyday, reflecting the life schedules of its viewers in ways that assume an almost unchanging social and domestic organization that is resolutely normative.

One of the goals of this chapter is to explore the efficacy of television's use of time and television's assumptions about the temporalities of its viewers as a process I will call scheduling normativity. It is through the management of time that television is able to produce normativity as one of its desired effects. However, television's capacity to organize time through the practice of scheduling, a system of controlling time that tells us what we can see and when we can see it, also brings normativity into perspective, thus rendering its very existence a tangible concept for queer investigation. Whereas time is central to the television medium and television studies, it is only recently that time and temporality have become, somewhat belatedly, a very fruitful subject for queer theory. Time upholds an ordering of normative relations and structures, not just through television but in everyday practices. Queer theory intervenes here in illustrating not just the normative characteristics of how we both imagine and experience time but also how time itself can be construed, mediated and lived in ways which are fundamentally queer.

What I intend to do in this essay is to bring together television studies and queer theory around the issue of time and temporality and account for the centrality of normativity in television often characterized by discourses of the family. My use of the word 'family' in this chapter refers to an ideal of heteronormative organization. I will first consider the normative character of television that is perpetuated through practices of time that relate to the family. Following that, I will account for how the time debate has been understood in queer theory. To round things off, I want to show how some recent programming has responded to the possibility of imagining time in non-normative ways. It seems coincidental – coincidence itself being a characteristic of queer temporality – that the attempts of recent programming to engage with queer desires and histories during the prime-time schedule confront the issue in an experimental manner, presenting a distorted and perverted sense of time distinct from the synchronous, ordered and linear temporality accepted as the norm.

Family viewing: time and normativity in television

Mary Ann Doane insistently claims that 'the major category of television is time' and that 'time is television's basis, its principle of structuration, as well as its persistent reference' (Doane 1990: 222). The earliest scholarly discussion of time in relation to television is arguably Raymond Williams's concept of flow from *Television: Technology and Cultural Form* (1974). It was Williams's attention to the flow of programming and his experience of US television that ushered in the ongoing theorization of time's mediation and management through audio–visual technologies. Following Williams, several authors, pioneers of television studies, have further developed television as the archetypical twentieth century medium of time. In 1977 Stephen Heath and Gillian Skirrow analysed the ontology of the television image as an electronic transmission, perpetually moving and thus effectively always in a state of being live (Heath and Skirrow 1977). Subsequently, Jane Feuer (1983) provided a compelling argument for time as an ideological force in her influential essay on live television. TV can harness the power of the live broadcast, in which broadcast time and viewing time are simultaneous, which enables the medium to convey liveness by aesthetic means – even, seemingly paradoxically, when television itself is not always live. One of the insights of Feuer's analysis of live television, one that has implications for my own argument, is that the technological basis of the television apparatus is able to 'create families where none exists' (1983: 20).

Liveness is an ideological effect; it is rendered through a very specific textual organization and mode of address that helps to construct familial discourses through the ways in which the family is conjured both on screen and through television's many ways of interpolating the audience as a national family.[1] John Ellis (1982) and Nick Browne (1994) also indicate that the normative character of television is reducible to the ways in which the family becomes central to institutional discourse, and also scheduling, programme content and mode of address. These almost casual observations about television's normative character are in many ways queer theory *avant la lettre* and significant in flagging up the interconnections between television, the family and time, a triumvirate that produces the normativity effect. As Ellis explains:

> Broadcast TV institutions respond by conceiving of this domestic and everyday audience in a specific way. Broadcast TV, its institutions and many of its practitioners alike assume that its domestic audience takes the form of families.

'The home' and 'the family' are terms which have become tangled together in the commercial culture of the twentieth century. They both point to a powerful cultural construct, a set of deeply held assumptions about the nature of 'normal' human existence. (1982: 113)

Television is organized to reflect the assumed temporal coordination of the nuclear family, and the network television schedules both in the US and the UK reflect this through the practice of dayparting.[2] Sections of the schedule correspond to the life timetables of children and child rearing activities (the early morning and late afternoon), mothers, housewives and the elderly (mid afternoon) and eventually the family united every evening in front of the box during prime time's evening hours. This is a well-rehearsed tenet that offers a connective between the temporality of television programming and the temporality of the family. As Anna McCarthy points out, 'the passage of time in home life is measured through the repetitive, segmented structure of the TV schedule, intertwining viewing and other domestic habits and practices' (McCarthy 2001a: 196).

The marginal zones of network television scheduling, such as anything after 10 pm, are the domain of the marginal audience: the un-familial, the singleton, the childless couple, queers. Of particular interest to queer television studies are those programmes which don't fit the normative practices of television scheduling. As Karen Lury notes, those programmes which don't conform to scheduling norms often appear 'wrong, out of sync, disorganized'; they just don't fit (Lury 2005: 104). Two of HBO's series, *Six Feet Under* (HBO 2001–5) and *Oz* (HBO 1997–2003), were both victims of ruthless scheduling on the British terrestrial Channel Four. As hour-long dramas they proved resistant to the commercial logic in which the standard episode length is approximately 42 minutes. Outside of the HBO context *Six Feet Under* and *Oz* defied the scheduling norm needed to accommodate advertising, defiant of the temporal regulation of 30 minutes and 60 minutes scheduling on the half-hour and hour – thus *Six Feet Under* and *Oz* were eventually relegated to the margins of the schedule where they could do no harm. It is no coincidence that *Six Feet Under* and *Oz* are also very queer texts.

Despite television's contemporary existence as an ever expanding multi-channel environment with manifold delivery capabilities, the centrality of the network schedule still remains the benchmark of television's epistemology and allows for frequent and generalized assumptions about television; when we refer to television, unless otherwise specified, this is what is implicitly meant. Furthermore, despite the industrial and technological changes, not to mention the political and cultural shifts that have affected television over the past forty years, it still holds that television, mass medium and commercial entity, imagines that the family audience is the ideological glue that holds it together. The family in front of and on television has been the anchor of this imagined continuity in the face of industrial, technological and cultural change. Even the shift towards demographic thinking in US television during the 1970s has done little to curtail the familial imaginary of television. Take for example the significance afforded to the watershed (UK 9 pm) and the safe harbour (US 10 pm) both of which offer strict divisions between supposedly safe and unsafe viewing for the family.

Regardless of the complexity of the television audience this regulatory practice informs the relationship between content and scheduling, and positions the family, in need of protecting from unsafe viewing before a certain time, as the locus in determining what all viewers are allowed to see at any given time during broadcast. With regard to gay and lesbian content there are fundamental issues at stake in what kind of images, information and pleasures queer viewers have access to before 9 pm and 10 pm, and what in turn is available to others in terms of education and the promotion of acceptance and tolerance. Gay and lesbian storylines are now common in pre-watershed soaps such as *As the World Turns* (CBS 1956–) and *Hollyoaks* (Channel 4 1995–) but queer content and its radical potential, like our queer lives, is still resolutely an evening affair that exists on the margins of the television schedule.

As another example of this practice, the weekly listing in *Radio Times*, the UK's longest running television listings magazine, includes a daily signposting for recommended family viewing. The need for this additional signage for the family audience is indicative of an inconsistency in the familial imaginary since this surely is the point of the watershed and safe harbour. This signalling is achieved through an icon of the family shown next to programmes that are deemed especially suitable for family viewing; these are predominantly drawn from documentaries and non-fiction genres, and include the occasional film. Again this confirms the privileged position of the family in the network television schedule since no other icon indicates any other type of audience or demographic who might be watching television. This gesture also implies the need to protect the family from what must be imagined as potentially unsafe programming, even though the schedule is mirrored by its own ideal.

As an extension of the temporal practice of scheduling, the family is also the cultural expression of television's representational logic played out in most television genres and formats: news items are addressed in relation to their effects on the family and the living-room is a frequent setting for local news reports; families are most frequently contestants on game shows with constant mention of the kids and cutaways to the spouse in the audience; the narrative basis and setting of the soap opera is rooted in domestic family relations; the family also rules the sitcom or at the very least family type structures are the basis of its narrative and genre conventions. The frequent appearances of the family on television offer a mutually supportive and inculcatory discourse for the family who is also imagined to be sitting in front of the television. Anticipating the discussion of queer temporality which follows shortly, it is necessary to also highlight the family's correspondence to concepts of straight time: normative time is mutually reflected by family time, family time is mutually reflected by television's organization of time. I want to consider two recent prime time sitcoms here, *Family Guy* (FOX 1999–) and *Will and Grace* (NBC 1998–2006), because they seem conducive to progressive readings that apparently challenge the normative character of the television family.

Comic timing: families, queers, sitcoms

Family Guy is an animated sitcom that first aired on the FOX network in 1999 on Thursdays at 9 pm in direct competition with NBC's scheduling triumph of 'Must See TV' that once included *Friends* (NBC 1994–2004) and *Will and Grace*. The series was subsequently cancelled after two seasons, yet owing to its continuing popularity on DVD further seasons of *Family Guy* have appeared in an on-and-off-again relationship with FOX. *Family Guy* is much riskier in its humour than its network mate *The Simpsons* (FOX 1989–), with a concerted appeal to a much narrower scope of comedy that is edgier, more vulgar and more sexual (or sexist). What interests me about *Family Guy* here is its insistent focus on familial and patriarchal dysfunction. The mainstay of the programme's comic thrust is partly the awfulness of the politically incorrect father Peter Griffin, yet *Family Guy* also champions the Griffins to be cherished as a television family complete with bigotry and flaws. In a collection on prime-time animation, Michael V. Teuth proposes that animated families like the Griffins and the Simpsons actually offer a 'subversive vision of family life' (2003: 134), yet his claim is not supported much beyond an argument regarding formal aspects of subversion as being something derived through an equation of cartoons with anarchy. I would argue that there is in fact the opposite going on, the formal containment of subversion owing less to the animated form than it does to sitcom genre conventions and television's episodic narratives. The subversive elements of humour in *Family Guy* mostly take the form of cut-away gags and any radical developments in the narrative are curtailed through the episodic structure, a sort of temporal containment of narrative through repetition that starts afresh each new instalment – same characters, different situation – thus resisting the potential for a continuous and ongoing serialization of subversion.[3] While I am not denying that there are other aspects of *Family Guy* which do lend themselves to radical and subversive readings, for example the adult-baby Stewie Griffin, I am maintaining a resistance to the possibility that such claims have anything to do with a counter-discourse against the television family as normative. In what is a contradictory move, Teuth also draws his essay to a conclusion with the less than subversive remark that the 'television family is alive and most assuredly kicking' (2003: 146).

Any discussion of the sitcom in relation to progressive politics may return us to the much-heralded work of Norman Lear in the 1970s, and to *All in the Family* (CBS 1971–9) and *Maude* (CBS 1972–8), the so-called 'relevance' sit-coms. *Family Guy*'s credit sequence refers to the opening sequence of *All in the Family* with its husband and wife singing at the piano. Both of Lear's relevance sitcoms, especially *All in the Family*, represent the family as dysfunctional and bickering, yet comedy and the sitcom form work to contain their critical anti-familial politics not just through the operations of genre but also in practices of reception. Generational and ideological conflict in *All in the Family* allows a number of hot topics to be aired, such as homosexuality, which appears very early on in the first season episode 'Judging Books by Covers' (2 September 1971) (see Wlodarz in this volume).

However, it is worth noting how comedy itself is often the primary generic form of television fiction that has the onus for airing conflicting political positions only for them to be contained by laughter; there is a dialectic in operation here. The *All in the Family* spin-off *Maude* is perhaps the most explicitly political of Lear's sitcoms in its relationship to second wave feminism. The characters of Maude and her daughter vocalized important feminist topics on a weekly basis in well over 100 episodes, most controversially in the two-part abortion episode 'Maude's Dilemma' (14 and 21 November 1972), yet the brevity of such discussions were routinely limited and impeded by Maude's one-liners, as audiences were cued to respond to weighty political issues like abortion through the interpolating effect of the laughter track. Kirsten Martha Lentz cautions against fully embracing the sitcom's progressive politics as she suggests that the pathologizing of the body and voice of Maude herself (majestically portrayed by Bea Arthur) undermine the work of feminism through a brash, bullying and neurotic portrayal of middle-aged white femininity (2000: 71). As a complement to the dialectical impulse of the sitcom to both present and contain its progressive politics, Judith Mayne's analysis of feminism's relationship to *LA Law* (NBC 1986–94) is instructive here:

> *L.A. Law* is by no means the first prime-time series to capitalize on the door that swings both ways. From sitcoms like *All in the Family* to prime-time soaps like *Dallas*, television narrative has relied centrally on principles of multiple identification and of narrative structure in which there is a fine line, if any line at all, between irony and rhetoric, between critique and celebration. (1997: 86–7)

Family Guy offers us the door that swings both ways, bigoted characters brought to life and mouthed by liberal animators. The narrative closure of each episode of *Family Guy*, as with many other sitcoms, is frequently mapped on to a neat, upbeat family togetherness, as the sitcom's generic pleasures work in the service of an ideology of the family: happy families and happy endings are one and the same thing.

The sitcom *Will and Grace* offers a queer variation on the sitcom by having a group of friends, like the co-worker groupings that feature in other instances of the genre, function as a close-knit (yet perverse) family formation complete with similar tensions, conflicts and allegiances. However, *Will and Grace* drew to a close after eight gay seasons with the depressingly heteronormative concluding episodes 'Whatever Happened to Baby Gin?' (5 November 2006) and 'The Finale' (18 November 2006). Those final two episodes are worth commenting on for the way in which a familial logic works to conclude *Will and Grace*, tying up the characters' stories, and informing how straightness, heteronormativity and queerness are positioned in relation to temporality. *Will and Grace* is also exemplary in demonstrating both Lentz and Mayne's arguments concerning the sitcom's relationship to politics; here we can also add the sitcom's relationship to queerness.

The writers and producers of *Will and Grace* were faced with a conundrum in bringing their series to an end; how to conceive of a queer future for their characters? Two of the main characters, Will Truman (Eric McCormack) and Jack McFarland (Sean Hayes), are gay and another, Karen Walker (Megan Mullally), has nil interest in, indeed hostility towards, both children and reproduction. The resolute stasis of the characters of Jack, too camp, and Karen, too nasty and disinterested, remains unchanged on all accounts at the programme's conclusion; the final episode denies them any future and they remain stuck, victims of their resistance to the lure of the family and its connection to a logic whereby the family is the only future possible.

In 'Whatever Happened to Baby Gin?' the pregnancy of Grace (Debra Messing) and her eventual reunion with estranged husband Leo (Harry Connick Jr), father of the child, sidelines gay best friend Will who has sacrificed his potential for a long-term relationship with Vince (Bobby Cannavale) in order to help Grace raise her baby. The desire to create a 'normal family' and the eventual return of Grace's estranged husband breaks up *Will and Grace*'s eight season long relationship in the flash of an episode. As this is a sitcom, we do get a comic glimpse of an alternative future for the queer family, yet this is conveyed as Grace's nightmare rather than an actual possible conclusion to the programme's gay boy/straight girl pairing. Grace's vision offers up a very ugly and unhappy situation; this queer future is depressing, miserable, austere and lifeless; it is no future. However, Karen Walker turns up unchanged after all these years, and her resistance to normativity has in fact preserved her beauty and camp wit from such ills.

In 'The Finale' we are privy to the actual future in the narrative in which many years have passed after the long falling out. Grace and Leo now have a daughter and Will and Vince, back together again (although this is a story elided in the narrative), have an adopted son. Both couples' respective children, now young adults, are getting settled into their first year at university and are moving into dormitories directly across the hall from each other. We soon learn that their children have hit it off and are getting married – and *Will and Grace* (the sitcom) can finally present the straight fantasy of romantic union that Will and Grace (the characters) could never have. This final act is a triumph for heteronormativity in allowing everything to be tied up through a wedding (albeit only in dialogue). As for the other characters, Jack, Karen and Latina maid Rosario (Shelley Morrison), all remain the same and unchanged after all these years; they really have no future to tell. Beverley Leslie (Leslie Jordan), the queerest character in *Will and Grace*'s repertoire, is killed off, blown away by the wind very much like *Will and Grace*'s queer viewers, casually dispatched. All is not entirely lost to a straight future as Jack and Karen are able to offer one last bit of comeback, the alternative to Will and Grace's normality and investment in the family:

Will: I was going to propose a toast to family. Family that loves you and accepts
          you for exactly who you are.
Jack: Boring!
Karen: Too real!

These are the final exchanges of dialogue as the four friends prop up the bar; a token that perhaps conveys the sentiments of the queer viewer's disappointment. What I wanted to draw out of the analysis of *Will and Grace*'s last episodes was the distinction it draws between the familial and the queer, opposed to one another in terms of their relation to temporality, a context defined by having or not having a future.

In time for queer theory

In queer studies the recent turn to time and temporality works from the assumption that normative time is natural for those who are privileged by it (Freeman 2007: 160). The concept of queer time offers alternatives to, and makes visible, normative time; literally and figuratively, normative time is straight time in that its basic structuring principle is linearity, continuity and progression. As this is an emergent strand of queer theory it is useful to briefly outline the scholarship that has taken place and continues to influence current queer thinking around time and its adjuncts, history and historicity. The beginnings of this queer theorization of time can be traced back to Carolyn Dinshaw's work on medieval and pre-modern sexualities where she establishes a case for thinking about queer sexualities in a historical frame as 'affective relations across time' (1999: 138). The pre-modern context continues to be fruitful as is evidenced by Carla Freccero's recent queering of the medieval (2006). Freccero reveals how we can make sense of the queer present through the past as 'a wilful perversion of notions of temporal propriety and the reproductive order of things' (2006: 2). The issue of time is also touched upon, although more implicitly, in Annamarie Jagose's analysis of lesbian visibility as a logic of sexual sequence in which the category 'lesbian' comes to be understood as something that comes after, is secondary and derivative (2002).

The more focused body of scholarship on temporality is in recent work by Lee Edelman (2004), Judith Halberstam (2005) and a special issue of *GLQ: A Journal of Lesbian and Gay Studies* edited by Elizabeth Freeman (2007). This is where temporality comes to take centre place in queer theory. Lee Edelman's *No Future: Queer Theory and the Death Drive* (2004) relates time to the figure of the child, and by implication the family, as the cultural and political fantasy central to imagining a heteronormative nation-state. Edelman coins the phrase 'reproductive futurism', conceptually capturing how the logic of normative time works according to the centrality occupied by the family, reproduction and the creation of children. For Edelman, queerness is positioned and defined through its separation from reproductive acts as the side of those 'not fighting for the children' and therefore not fighting for the future (3). The potential of a queer politics lies in its very resistance to the logic of futurity. Therefore, the crucial definition of queerness as 'future-negating' (26) offers a radical way of working against the ideological role that reproduction occupies as a familial and heterosexual discourse both implicit and explicit in the experience and ordering of normative time. Cultural manifestations of this are the television schedule and television's familial imaginary. The image or figure of the child is a signifier of the family in popular culture and political discourse; it is where the future comes to be projected in a fantasy that Edelman argues is antithetical to those who don't count as normative reproductive families.

> The consequences of such an identification both of and with the child as the pre-eminent emblem of the motivating end, though one endlessly postponed, of every political vision *as a vision of futurity* must weigh on any delineation of a queer oppositional politics. For the only queerness that queer sexualities could ever hope to signify would spring from their determined opposition to this underlying structure of the political – their opposition, that is, to the governing fantasy of achieving Symbolic closure through the marriage of identity to futurity in order to realize the social subject.
>
> (Edelman 2004: 13–4)

Therein lies the problem of *Will and Grace* and what to do about its potentially destabilizing queer elements; a problem that is reducible to Jack and Karen as they are disinvested from the family. One must conclude, as the programme does, that they have no future and thus no story worth telling. This confirms Edelman's thesis and points to the underlying logic of television's normative character as positioned in familial terms.

In *In a Queer Time and Place: Transgender Bodies, Subcultural Lives* (2005), Judith Halberstam approaches time and temporality rather differently from Edelman, eschewing psychoanalysis, but her critical impulse is quite similar in that both question the structures and beliefs that give time its normative character, thus allowing us to make sense of television's relationship to time and in turn the place of queerness within such a debate. As the title of her book suggests, Halberstam also accounts for the alternative temporalities, bodies and spaces of queer lives and subcultures:

> Queer uses of time and space develop, at least in part, in opposition to the institutions of family, heterosexuality, and reproduction. They also develop according to other logics of location, movement. If we try to think about queerness as an outcome of strange temporalities, imaginative life schedules, and eccentric economic practices, we detach queerness from sexual identity and come closer to understanding Foucault's 'Friendship as a Way of Life'.
>
> (Halberstam 2005: 1)

Halberstam characterizes normative time by drawing attention to the different categories through which it comes to be organized and given meaning. These include the interconnectedness of family time, reproduction time and inheritance time (5). Such temporalities are powerful structuring continuities between the past, present and future in which histories and futures are privileged through pregnancy, birth, marriage, legacies, progenies, transmission of wealth and property and child rearing and responsibility. These are the bases of a normative temporal organization and the backbone of an imagined social, cultural and national future that takes the hetero-patriarchal family as its only model. On the other hand:

> Queer subcultures produce alternative temporalities by allowing their participants to believe that their futures can be imagined according to a logics that lie outside of those paradigmatic markers of life experience – namely birth, marriage, reproduction, and death.
>
> (Halberstam 2005: 2)

What Halberstam teases out in her analysis is the efficacy of social, cultural and political discourses of sexuality, gender and identity and the ways they are inextricably linked to the temporal experiences of them – for instance (although these are not her examples), through television scheduling for the family, the regulation of television content and television's mode of address to the family.[4]

Queerness can be understood as a challenge to normative time simply because being queer is experientially outside those definitions of a 'normal lifetime'. Queer time is desire reconfigured to embrace temporal displacements, especially with regard to the past and the future. This is effected through the many ways in which queers themselves can be conceived of as existing outside the logic of linear time, as having no future, as being written out of history. Alternative ways of understanding what has been and what will take place are necessary 'temporal and historical displacements' (Freeman 2007: 159), but even working out how this can be done is also to operate against the apparent logic of time which is inculcated as normative in the ways described earlier.

Queerness is something that is literally out-of-time in the sense of being urgent, immediate and on the outside. Queer time's refusal of normative time instead favours extremes of temporal experience: asynchrony, discontinuity, belatedness, arrest, coincidence, time wasting, reversal, time travel, the palimpsest, boredom and ennui. These are means of negotiating queerness in relation to the experience of time and ultimately impact upon the desire for alternative histories and futures, and experiences of the everyday quotidian temporalities in which we find ourselves living.

Queer travels in television time

As outlined in the beginning of this chapter, television is often thought of as a medium of time. We have programmes that make themes out of television's discursive temporality: reality TV's live transmissions and evictions, *Time Team* (Channel 4 1994–) which popularizes archaeology, genealogy shows like *Who Do You Think You Are?* (BBC 2004–), the countless makeover shows like *Extreme Makeover* (ABC 2002–) and *Ten Years Younger* (Channel 4 2004–) which turn back the years, docudrama's historical reconstructions blurring past and present, the clock-baiting drama *24* (FOX 2001–), the time-travelling *Life on Mars* (BBC 2006–7), not to mention the place of re-runs as television from another time.

In many of these programmes time is bent, the progression of time is reversed and resisted, new temporal moments are re-opened and re-examined; time, like history, is not laid to rest – indeed, perhaps these temporal expressions of television are somehow queer in their refusal to abide by the linear and teleological. (Its also worth noting, as an aside, that, for cultural elitists and film snobs, watching television is often seen as a waste of time, with television studies a waste of intellectual time and scholarly resources; I have had first-hand experience of these attitudes.) More than any other medium or screen based form, I would argue that it is television that can fully embrace the capacity to engage with the concept of queer temporality, quite simply because television's ontology is temporal.

Television is characterized as a domestic media technology and evinces a certain level of engagement and investment that touches on experiences of intimacy, emotion, the familiar and the private. Television viewing can be deeply felt and consoling in a way that corresponds to our levels of commitment, experience and the types of programmes we are drawn to. I am drawing attention to this affective context because a significant number of television moments that express queer temporality operate through intensely emotive means; the asynchronous and the non-linear are deeply felt. I want to explore two television programmes that do this, *Torchwood* (BBC 2006–) and *Cold Case* (CBS 2003–). They differ greatly from one another in terms of genre, style, narration, and the broadcasting context. Despite those differences, their strategies rendering queer temporality are similar to one another, as both programmes cross temporal frames allowing queerness and desire to collapse the non-linear into the affective.

Torchwood is a British science-fiction series, a spin off from the more popular relaunched *Doctor Who* (BBC 2005–); it features a group of paranormal sci-fi investigators headed by the character Captain Jack Harkness (John Barrowman). It is through the character of Captain Jack that *Torchwood* is able to mine its queerness. The gay and lesbian content and sex talk are key to the programme's pitch to a mature audience who are old enough to understand sexuality, and cool and liberal enough to deal with frequent and explicit references to same-sex desire. Captain Jack is defined as omni-sexual by the character himself, the out actor John Barrowman, and the show's gay creator Russell T. Davies, and while Captain Jack desires both men and women, his long-term love affairs and onscreen kisses are mostly with men in the past and present. His character brushes against definitions of queer sexuality in that he resists any sort of classification based on sexual orientation. In fact, the sexual orientation of all the characters is consistently flexible. The episode I want to consider here is called 'Captain Jack Harkness' (1 January 2007), in which the time-travel clichés of the science-fiction genre become integral in defining queer sexual desire across time and reveal the impossibility of imagining such dalliances without recourse to rifts in linear temporality.

While time travel is an ongoing theme in *Torchwood* and science fiction in general, it is in this episode that the implications for queerness of moving around in time are explored in depth. The rules of time travel both open up and close down the potential for same-sex desire; going into the past or the future is inevitably followed by a return to the 'right' time. In this episode the Torchwood team are investigating reports of a haunting in an old dance hall in Cardiff. The exploration quickly leads to Captain Jack and his assistant Toshiko (Naoko Mori) being whisked away in time back to the year 1941 and straight into the middle of a dance for American allied troops. Here, Captain Jack meets his original namesake, the US Air Force hero Captain Jack Harkness (Matt Rippy). They both quickly assert the forbidden nature of their instant attraction for one another and the impossibility of being gay in 1941 – this is post-*Brokeback* television. They fall in love over the course of the evening only for the time rift to be re-opened and pull them apart forever. The Jacks have just enough time to do a slow dance with one another ending with one of the longest gay kisses on television, heightened by swelling music and dizzying camera effects. The time rift is closing; they both take one last and longing look at each other, a close-up of tears running down Jack's (Barrowman's) cheek, my own tears welling too, and finally it's over, time returns to normal.

The Captain Jacks both share the same name and are quite similar in phys-ical appearance, thus literalizing the homo-ness of the situation. Through the time-travel device this points to a narcissistic self-fascination, the old cliché that homosexuality is the love for sameness. The gay romance between the two Captain Jacks is only possible when normative time, as linear and sequential, is bent; the possibility of their romance occurs only through a rift in time. It takes a queer temporality to realize this dilemma, one which opens up a space to explore homophobic oppression in the past and, in so doing, also turns the past into a place of sexual possibility.[5] The final scenes in which the Jacks dance together and kiss is emotive, yet time presents itself as the obstacle to what is otherwise an impossible history; queerness is out of time.

Torchwood is a useful example here because it shows how linear normative time is an obstacle for gay desire and love, which can only be imagined through a queering of the time-travel narrative, producing a temporality in which emotion, sexuality and time coalesce. *Torchwood*'s genre trappings offer travel through time as one possibility for imagining desires across time, both affective and physical, enabled as a queer temporality, one felt by the characters and viewers like myself. The romantic gay kiss is realized through temporal disjuncture, of one point in time and space inhabiting another; it is against the normative logic of time's fixity that queer desire unfolds in *Torchwood*.

Cold Case is rather different from *Torchwood*, as it is a US police procedural drama. The programme centres on Detective Lily Rush (Kathryn Morris) and her team who re-open cold cases. Every episode works with a specific structure that presents the story of the crime through elaborate and stylish flashbacks. The success of *Cold Case* lies in the creative tension between the flashbacks and present day scenes, and the shifts between the two time frames often involve unusual transition devices and editing patterns. The shifts between past and present often use a dual casting system in which two different actors play the same character, one to represent the story of the flashback and the other to represent the character in the present-day investigation.

Every season of *Cold Case* has brought with it gay and lesbian themed episodes, always handled with great affection and care, and through the past–present time structure, *Cold Case* has explored, for example, fatal and violent gay and lesbian hate crimes, institutional and cultural homophobia, an AIDS related storyline and the murder of a teenage boy assumed to be gay for wanting to be a dancer. While criticism is often levelled at crime genres for only including gay and lesbian characters as victims, in *Cold Case* these specific episodes draw attention to the different historical contexts, and ongoing continuities in which homophobia, and gendered and sexualized violence, occur. Upon further investigation the *Cold Case* credits also reveal a number of gay and lesbian personnel, including Jan Oxenberg, who has written a number of episodes,[6] and show creator Meredith Stiehm, who was a writer and executive producer for *ER* (NBC 1994–) and contributed to that programme's lesbian buzz through the Kerry Weaver (Laura Innes) and Kim Legaspi (Elizabeth Mitchell) storyline. *Cold Case*, that is, has queer TV credentials.

Cold Case's episodes follow the conventions I have described above, juxtaposing flashbacks and present day, with the cold case eventually being closed. I want to suggest that for queer viewers of these homophobic crimes of the past, they are understood (and we experience them as viewers) not like the regular one-off crimes presented in each new episode, but instead we see the murders as part of a larger history of abuse enacted upon us, one still ongoing. Unlike the other murders in *Cold Case*, the homophobic crimes are not simply reducible to the individual acts of a sole perpetrator; they are not contained by an episodic narrative format. These are not simply crime-of-the-week episodes but need to be seen as representations of a collective past that includes homophobia, oppression and murder.

The episode 'Best Friends' (8 May 2005) tells the story of a tragic love between two young lesbians in the 1930s, the African–American Billie (Tessa Thompson) and the naïve white Rose (Samantha Streets). The sepia toned flashbacks take us back to the prohibition era, set to the music of Billie Holliday and Duke Ellington. Rose's brother delivers alcohol to a speakeasy where she meets and falls in love with the suave and suited Billie. Various turns of events eventually lead Rose and Billie to flee in a truck from homophobia, racism and prohibition gangsters. They profess their eternal love for one another, and in a scene that quotes *Thelma and Louise* (1991), drive the truck off a pier into the Delaware River; only Rose manages to surface. The older Rose (Piper Laurie), now in her eighties, comes forward to talk to Lily Rush, and in a roundabout way, confesses through her poetry to what originally happened on that night in 1932. The episode's closing few minutes, a montage sequence, show Lily Rush walking away from the elderly Rose sitting on a park bench, case closed. As Rose sits crying, contemplating having spent her whole life saddened and in guilt for how things ended with Billie, we see a hand reach out to Rose; Billie appears as if straight out of 1932, just how Rose remembers her, stunning and dressed in a smart suit and hat, and they both go off walking in the park. The episode's final images show Rose from 2005 and Billie from 1932, walking hand–in–hand, lovers travelling across time, and then in an edit we see Rose as she once was, young and beautiful, the couple back together as they once were. Time becomes meaningless and irrelevant, subsumed in the face of desire and memory; Rose and Billie transcend the logic of time.

As in *Torchwood*, desire manifests itself through impossible temporalities. *Cold Case* offers up a reparative time-travelling fantasy whereas *Torchwood* deals more with genre-defined time-travel. *Cold Case* provides a justly emotive visual trope, an image of an existence in a queer time. The final images of Rose and Billie that *Cold Case* leaves audiences with point to two impossible histories. Not only was the Depression era a problematic time for sexuality and race, one in which a queer interracial relationship was impossible to acknowledge, but the phantasmatically reunited couple, located in a time somewhere 'outside' or 'inbetween', brings the dead and the living, spectral and real, old and young, back together again, walking and loving. Television, for this moment anyway, is able to finally bring the young lovers back together as they once were but never could be. As a queer viewer I can at least imagine and be moved by the occurrence of such emotive reparation – yet only because of and through the persistence of a queer temporality. It is significant that in these concluding moments Detective Rush tells Rose 'it was just the wrong time'.

Remembrance of things future

This chapter has moved through divergent themes around television's relationship to time characterized in terms of both normativity and queerness. I have argued that television is normative through its scheduling and programming practices that correspond to the temporality of the family. While this insight is hardly new in television studies it has never been scrutinized from a specifically queer perspective. Television is fascinated if not obsessed by the family; it is the basis of a good deal of content, and the familial and heteronormative logic of television even pervades programmes like *Will and Grace* that are touted as having something queer about them. *Will and Grace, Torchwood* and *Cold Case* were chosen as examples as they literalize through television the arguments recently developed in queer theory's turn to time; I am taking them as evidence of a wider debate in which television studies and queer studies are able to come into dialogue with one another.

Television's obsession with its own temporality is evidently marked across a number of programmes, but it is precisely because of its time dependency that the medium opens up the possibility that one can both imagine and experience time in ways that are more queer than normative. For a medium characterized by the regulation of time, television has also harnessed time and made it entertainment, and the persistence with which television's time is bent, reversed and complicated hints at a queerness that haunts TV and denies it the full capacity to be as normative as it wishes to imagine.

The queer desires that the *Torchwood* and *Cold Case* episodes raise are relevant here because it is the temporal dimensions of these texts, rather than their representational logic, that allows queerness to manifest. It would seem that in their attempts to represent same-sex desires, they can only do so through recourse to anomalous temporalities – time travel and fantasy. What I am proposing is that we should be looking at the temporal experience of television as a significant location of queerness: how meaning and non-heterosexuality is ordered and disordered, not merely through representation, but through time and its effects. In other words, queerness unfolds and is fashioned through television in what can be understood as time imagined queerly.

Notes

1. For a detailed analysis of liveness see Lury (2005) and Marriott (2007).
2. Dayparting is the dividing of the twenty-four hour television day into the scheduling segments of morning, daytime, early evening, prime time and late evening.
3. Anna McCarthy makes a similar argument in relation to *Ellen* (ABC 1994–8) (McCarthy 2001b; 2003). For McCarthy, *Ellen*'s cancellation owes much to the problem of the character's lesbian life being accommodated by serialized television narrative.
4. Queer-identified heterosexuals might challenge this as a potentially restricting and militant position on the basis that one can be a non-normative heterosexual in practice and desire, articulating a resistance to marriage and child rearing. What must be indicated here is that those resistances are choices rather than impositions.
5. Captain Jack's companion Toshiko who is also trapped in 1941 is of Japanese descent, and this also allows racism and anti-Japanese sentiment to be examined.
6. Jan Oxenberg is better known as an independent lesbian film maker who made several important short films in the 1970s such as *Home Movie* (1972) and *Comedy in Six Unnatural Acts* (1975). For more information see Citron (1981). Jan Oxenberg also appears briefly as one of the talking heads in Rob Epstein and Jeffrey Friedman's film *The Celluloid Closet* (1996).

References

Browne, N. (1994) 'The Political Economy of the Television (Super) Text' in N. Browne (ed.) *American Television: New Directions in History and Theory*, Langhorne, PA: Harwood Academic Publishers.

Citron, M. (1981) 'The Films of Jan Oxenberg', *Jump Cut* 24–25: 31–2.

Dinshaw, C. (1999) *Getting Medieval: Sexualities and Communities, Pre and Post Modern.* Durham, NC: Duke University Press.

Doane, M.A. (1990) 'Information, Crisis, Catastrophe' in P. Mellencamp (ed.) *Logics of Television: Essays in Cultural Criticism*, Bloomington, IN: Indiana University Press.

Edelman, L. (2004) *No Future: Queer Theory and the Death Drive*, Durham, NC: Duke University Press.

Ellis, J. (1982) *Visible Fictions: Cinema, Television, Radio*, London: Routledge.

Feuer, J. (1983) 'The Concept of Live Television: Ontology as Ideology' in E. A. Kaplan (ed.) *Regarding Television: Critical Approaches*, Fredericksburg, VA: American Film Institute.

Freccero, C. (2006) *Queer/Early/Modern*, Durham, NC: Duke University Press.

Freeman, E. (ed.) (2007) 'Queer Temporalities', *GLQ: A Journal of Lesbian and Gay Studies* 13: 2–3.

Halberstam, J. (2005) *In a Queer Time and Place: Transgender Bodies, Subcultural Lives*, New York: New York University Press.

Heath, S. and Skirrow, G. (1977) 'Television, a World in Action', *Screen* 19(2): 7–59.

Jagose, A. (2002) *Inconsequence: Lesbian Representation and the Logic of Sexual Sequence*, Ithaca, NY: Cornell University Press.

Lentz, K.M. (2000) 'Quality versus Relevance: Feminism, Race, and the Politics of the Sign in 1970s Television', *Camera Obscura*, 43: 45–93.

Lury, K. (2005) *Interpreting Television*, London: Arnold.

McCarthy, A. (2001a) *Ambient Television: Visual Culture and Public Space*, Durham, NC: Duke University Press.

_____ (2001b) 'Ellen: Making Queer Television History', *GLQ: A Journal of Lesbian and Gay Studies* 7(4): 593–620.

_____ (2003) 'Must See Queer TV: History and Serial Form in *Ellen*' in M. Jancovich and J. Lyons (eds) *Quality Popular Television*, London: BFI, 88–102.

Marriott, S. (2007) *Live Television: Time, Space, and the Broadcast Event*, London: Sage.

Mayne, J. (1997) 'L.A. Law and Prime Time Feminism' in C. Brunsdon, J. D'Acci and L. Spigel (eds) *Feminist Television Criticism: A Reader*, Oxford: Oxford University Press, 84–97.

Teuth, M.V. (2003) 'Back to the Drawing Board: The Family in Animated Television Comedy' in C. A. Stabile and M. Harrison (eds) *Prime Time Animation: Television Animation and American Culture*, London: Routledge, 133–46.

Williams, R. (1974) *Television: Technology and Cultural Form*, London: Collins.

Chapter 9

Cruising the channels
The queerness of zapping

Jaap Kooijman

I often watch television in bed, just before I go to sleep, switching from channel to channel in search of something good to watch. Yet Dutch television has little to offer around midnight. Most commercial channels only show phone sex advertisements at that time, featuring topless women looking seductively into the camera while playing with their nipples, accompanied by a female voiceover urging me to give them a call. Once in a while a commercial for gay male sex comes by, inviting me to send a text message – 'CRUISING' followed by my postal zip code – to an expensive phone number, with the promise that I will receive directions to the 'hottest' outdoor places in my neighborhood, where I can find anonymous sex with 'willing' men, although 'actual physical contact' is not guaranteed. The commercial consists of footage of cruising at an abandoned parking area, seemingly shot with a hidden camera, showing blurred images of one man watching another from the front seat of a Ford Escort (the car's brand name clearly visible on the dashboard, shown in close-up). The boundary between private and public space appears to be crossed as the opportunity of public sex enters the privacy of my home through the television screen and by a possible connection through my cell phone. One can wonder, however, how 'public' this cruising area really is, as not only are such areas in general hidden from open public view (Califia 1994: 20; Humphreys 1999: 30–1), but the commercial also presents the area as a space that needs to be exposed (hence the hidden camera aesthetic) and that can only be reached by sending an SMS. As a commodity advertised on television, cruising is rendered visible, yet because of its anonymity and the sensation of possible exposure, remains invisible at the same time.

A far more relevant boundary crossing takes place in the opposite direction: from the privacy of my home I come across the depicted parking area by 'cruising' the television channels, with my remote control in one hand and my cell phone nearby. Yet this possible analogy between cruising and zapping did not occur to me when I stopped zapping to watch the gay sex commercial, but instead when, one night a couple of years ago, I stopped zapping to watch a drama series on one of the public broadcast channels. In contrast to the phone sex ads shown on midnight commercial television, the public broadcast channels at that time most often show re-runs of the evening news, art programmes, or high quality drama series such as *Shameless* (C4, 2004–present) and *The Sopranos* (HBO, 1999–2007).

That particular night, after zapping for a while, I stopped at a channel that was showing an American drama series that I did not yet know. I stopped because one of its white male characters stood out. He was not particularly handsome, rather odd looking, and he did not act or say anything specifically gay. Nevertheless, there was something queer about him, which triggered my 'gaydar' and made me stop zapping. Not until later did I learn that I had watched the first season's second episode of *Six Feet Under* (HBO, 2001–5), a drama series about a small funeral home run by the eccentric Fisher family. The 'queer guy' turned out to be David, the youngest adult son. Played by the openly straight actor Michael C. Hall, David is a closeted gay man who, at the time of this particular episode, had not yet come out, not to himself, not to his family, and not to the viewers at home. In other words, my recognition of David's queerness had nothing to do with his public sexual identity or, by extension, with explicit gay visibility. Here I do not want to suggest that David has specific or essential gay characteristics which can only be recognized by other gay men, while remaining invisible to the larger straight audience. To me, David just was the 'odd one out' whom I recognized as being 'queer'; whether or not David indeed would come out as gay (although he did in a later episode) is beside the point. The significance of my zapping experience is the realization that switching from channel to channel and recognizing a queer face among television's talking heads does not differ much from walking through a public space and catching the gaze of another possibly gay man, the cruising glance of queer recognition or misrecognition. My zapping experience suggests that television, like the cityscape, can be viewed as a public space that can be roamed.

In this chapter, I want to explore the usefulness of such an analogy between cruising and zapping. Rather than claiming that all acts of zapping (or the arguably similar act of surfing the internet) should be considered as queer practices, I suggest that perceiving zapping as a form of cruising may open up alternative ways to 'watch television' – both as consumers as well as academic critics. To do so, I borrow Mark Turner's definition of cruising as 'the moment of visual exchange that occurs on the streets and in other places in the city, which constitutes an act of mutual recognition amid the otherwise alienating effects of the anonymous crowd' (Turner 2003: 9), thereby emphasizing the act of exchanging glances that holds the promise of a possible (sexual) encounter instead of the actual practice of anonymous sex, which of course is another definition of cruising. Recognizing zapping as a form of cruising enables us to bring to the foreground different perspectives on the issue of gay and lesbian visibility on both broadcast and narrowcast television and the possible critical stance (or lack thereof) of a queer viewer. I will refer to Turner's writing on cruising, Anna McCarthy's writing on ambient television, and Thomas Elsaesser's writing on zapping to explore whether or not zapping could function as a possible queer practice that can challenge the normative character of television. I will also connect zapping as cruising to the notion of cruising as a form of 'gay spectatorship' and 'queer ways of looking' as has been discussed in film studies (Brasell 1992; de Villiers 2007), and which problematizes the rigid distinction between the cinematic gaze and the televisual glance.

The use of cruising as a theoretical concept to provide an alternative perspective does not mean that questions of identity politics and possible meanings of 'queer' are circumvented. First, cruising does introduce a gay male bias, even if 'anyone familiar with the cultural practice of cruising can obtain access to the spectatorial position [ascribed to] gay men' (Brasell 1992: 55). Second, the use of cruising does imply that 'queer' equals '(male) homosexuality' with the risk of reinforcing the disciplinary categorizations of 'deviant sexualities' that the notion of 'queer' challenges. Commenting on his own use of cruising as theoretical concept, Simon Ofield argues that cruising does not merely provide an alternative perspective but rather 'as a form of practice [is] always already caught up in the disciplines that it attempts to dodge and the understandings that it seeks to displace,' concluding that 'cruising does not provide an escape from these disciplinary regimes, neither in practice nor theory' (Ofield 2005: 351, 362). With these restrictions in mind, I will use cruising to raise relevant questions about the visibility of (more diverse) sexual identities on television and about zapping as a potentially critical tool of television viewing.

Gay and lesbian visibility on television

In recent years, several studies have appeared that examine (the history of) the visibility of lesbian, gay, bisexual, and transgender characters, real-life or fictional, in both broadcast and narrowcast television programmes (Becker 2006; Capsuto 2000; Gamson 1997; Gross 2001). Compared to other countries, including my native Netherlands, the issue of gay and lesbian visibility on television is a relatively active topic of debate in the USA, encouraged by organizations such as the Gay & Lesbian Alliance Against Defamation (GLAAD), which hosts an annual awards gala to 'recognize and honour media for their fair, accurate, and inclusive represen-tations of the lesbian, gay, bisexual, and transgender community and the issues that affect their lives' (www.glaad.org). In spite of its predominantly American character, the debate is relevant internationally, as many American television pro-grammes – soap operas, talk shows, drama series, situation comedies – are also shown in other countries. Most studies recognize a development from invisibility (both the absence of gay and lesbian characters as well as implied homosexuality through the use of negative stereotyping) to visibility (openly gay and lesbian characters), focusing on 'key moments' such as the first gay sitcom character in *All in the Family* (CBS, 9 February 1971), the coming-out episode of *Ellen* (ABC, 30 April 1997), and the mainstream success of the makeover show *Queer Eye for the Straight Guy* (Bravo, 2003–7). Narrowcasting in particular has been perceived as a promising tool in the 'queering' of television, as it enables depictions of homosexuality that are either too 'radical' or just not commercially feasible for mainstream network televi-sion, in series such as *Oz* (HBO, 1997–2003), the American version of *Queer as Folk*

(Showtime, 2000–5), *Six Feet Under*, *The L Word* (Showtime, 2004–present), and *Noah's Arc* (Logo, 2005–6).

As Larry Gross argues in *Up from Invisibility*, the increase of gay and lesbian visibility, both in American society and on television, has resulted in a cultural mainstreaming of gay and lesbian identities. To become visible, gay men and lesbians had to assimilate into the mainstream American culture of 'middle-class normality and respectability,' which becomes apparent when zapping through the channels of American television:

> A few hours of cable-TV surfing, from *The Young and Restless* to Jerry Springer to MTV to *Will & Grace* to *Nightline*, will demonstrate that the [gay and lesbian] cultural mainstream has overflowed the narrow channels in which it once was confined. The newest rating magnets, 'reality' programmes of various sorts, from MTV's *The Real World* to CBS's *Survivor*, take the presence of openly gay people for granted, and this increasingly reflects the real world we live in.
>
> (Gross 2001: xvi)

In other words, the inclusion of gay and lesbian characters does not inevitably challenge the norm (as the notion of 'queering' television implies), but instead may mean that gay and lesbian identities are incorporated within mainstream culture. For example, if the white heterosexual nuclear family is television's norm (Spigel 1990; Taylor 1989), then the openly gay Will Truman of *Will & Grace* (NBC, 1998–2006) still conforms to mainstream culture by being the ideal son in law who just happens to be gay, inviting viewers to secretly long for Will and Grace ending up together regardless of their sexual identities. Will's openly gay best friend Jack, on the contrary, functions as Will's 'deviant' mirror image, harking back to stereotypical depictions of gay men as effeminate, flamboyant, and irresponsible.

The queering of television then is not necessarily to be found in the increasing presence of openly gay and lesbian characters in television programmes. Well-known examples of American sitcoms that have been perceived as 'queer' – even though their main characters are straight – include *The Nanny* (CBS, 1993–9), based on the outrageous 'campy' style and humour of its female main protagonist Fran Fine, and *Frasier* (NBC, 1993–2004), based on the 'queerness' of the two heterosexual brothers, Frasier and Niles Crane, who indulge in 'unmanly' pleasures such as antiquing, wine-tasting, and opera. Jane Feuer makes a distinction between 'gay' and 'queer' sitcoms, suggesting that sitcoms such as *Will & Grace* are 'gay' as they feature 'already fully formed gay main characters,' whereas *Frasier* is 'queer' as it challenges dominant depictions of masculinity and heterosexuality (Feuer 2001: 71). Although such a distinction may be too strict (or even implies that 'fully formed' gay characters cannot challenge the norm), it does emphasize that queerness on television is not explicitly connected to gay and lesbian visibility. Elsewhere I have argued that, if there is anything 'queer' about *Queer Eye for the Straight Guy*, the queerness is to be found in the role of the straight male contestants rather than the openly gay stars of the show. Moreover, the show uses 'queer' as just another fashionable commodity, signifying good taste and a refined sense of style, thereby depoliticizing its critical potential (Kooijman 2005).

Although narrowcast television has enabled a more diverse depiction of gay and lesbian sexual identities with shows such as *Queer as Folk* and *The L Word*, narrowcasting can also result in strict categorization, as is shown by the difficulty of the black gay series *Noah's Arc* in securing a place on television. Created by Patrik-Ian Polk, *Noah's Arc* is about the daily lives of four African–American gay men in West Hollywood, described on Amazon.com as '*Sex and the City* [meets] *Queer as Folk* and *The L Word* – with an all-male, all-black, all-gay cast.' As it proved difficult to sell the series to cable channels, *Noah's Arc* was to be released on DVD only (which raises the question of whether or not a television series that is neither broadcast nor narrowcast can still be considered television). In 2004, the announced DVD release was promoted with a *Noah's Arc* website and the showing of the pilot episode in cinemas in large American cities. The website advertised *Noah's Arc* as 'America's first black gay series' that is 'too hot for colour television,' thus making fun of the notion that the series was deemed too 'gay' for black television channels, but also too 'black' and 'gay' for other cable channels. Whereas, with series such as *Soul Food* (Showtime, 2000–4) and *Queer as Folk*, Showtime had shown that there was room for, respectively, a black drama series and a gay drama series on narrowcast television, there seemed to be no room for a series that was both black and gay. Eventually the series was bought by Logo, the gay and lesbian cable channel owned by MTV and launched in 2005, which promises the 'LGBT world ... a place all its own ... [bringing] you the stories, shows, and news you won't see anywhere else' (www.logoonline.com). After two seasons, however, *Noah's Arc* was cancelled, with no specific reason given. Obviously, there are many reasons why a television series might be cancelled, yet here one cannot help but wonder whether or not the cancellation had something to do with the difficulty of catering to a niche audience based on two minority cultural identities: black and gay. Narrowcasting may provide room for alternative cultural identities as long as they fit within the clearly defined and commercially profitable boundaries of the targeted niche market.

If on both broadcast and narrowcast television the presence of openly gay and lesbian characters tends to be integrated within – rather than challenge – television's normative structure, where can queerness on television be found? To address that question, two shifts of focus are needed. First, instead of perceiving the 'queering' of television as a progressive movement from invisibility to visibility of gay and lesbian characters in specific programmes, the queerness of television is to be looked for in those televisual moments that challenge normative depictions of both heterosexuality and homosexuality, as well as other forms of cultural and sexual identities. Second, instead of merely focusing on the representation of 'queerness' in television programmes, attention should be paid to the practice of watching – a shift from questioning who is being represented (or not) on television, to questioning how television is or can be 'queered' through the way television is watched.

The flâneur, the cruiser, the zapper

In *Backward Glances*, Mark Turner takes cruising between gay men as a starting point to explore alternative histories of New York and London in an attempt to recover a counter-discourse in these cities of modernity. Although cruising is 'the stuff of fleeting, ephemeral moments not intended to be captured' (Turner 2003: 10), Turner locates such moments in literature, poems, photographs, and historical records. Since the nineteenth century, the city has come to be perceived as a site of alienation and anonymity, in which the flâneur often functions as the most telling embodiment of the modern urban experience. Referring to Charles Baudelaire and Walter Benjamin, Turner sees parallels between the flâneur and the cruiser as urban street walkers who anonymously participate within the larger urban structure through observation. Yet there is a clear distinction between the flâneur and the cruiser, as the former does not make contact with others among the urban crowd, whereas the latter is actively seeking connections with others, even if such contact remains anonymous:

> The cruiser … is one of the alternate ways of reading the urban street walker who exists in an environment of uncertain, ambiguous signification. Like every other street walker, the cruiser writes his own text of the city, but it may be a text not all of us can read equally. He is the anonymous wanderer who bathes in the multitude (*pace* Baudelaire) or botanizes on the asphalt (as Benjamin would have it) in order to seek out another individual – to find that other whose gaze will meet his own.
>
> (Turner 2003: 36)

What Turner suggests then is that the cruiser is a queer alternative to the flâneur, who can be used similarly to conceptualize the experience of urban modernity, yet thereby incorporating queer readings of the city. Moreover, such queer readings do not only provide alternative perspectives, but may also function as counter-narratives, challenging existing conceptions of the urban experience. 'Cruising is a practice that exploits the ambivalence of the modern city, and in doing so, "queers" the totalizing narratives of modernity, in particular, *flânerie*' (Turner 2003: 46). The 'queering' Turner identifies is to be found in the exchange of glances, the way cruisers make anonymous contact, often invisible to the crowd of other city dwellers.

This is not to suggest that 'queering' is the only way to provide alternative readings, or that only the homosexual male cruiser challenges the position of the flâneur as embodiment of the urban experience. Obviously, there are many other forms of exchanging glances that establish short moments of anonymous recognition, ranging from appreciative looks based on a shared cultural background between pedestrians while passing each other on the street to adulterous flirtation between passengers (of all genders and sexual orientations) on the subway. Moreover, both the flâneur and the cruiser as concepts reinforce the male bias that they contain, and which has been challenged by studies of the flâneuse and the lesbian flâneur (D'Souza and McDonough 2006; Munt 1995). Taking that into consideration, the focus on the cruiser as an alternative to the dominant perspective of the flâneur as conceptualization of the urban experience is effective, as such a 'queering' explicitly problematizes the oppositions between public and private, outside and inside, visibility and invisibility, and norm and deviancy (Fuss 1991; Sedgwick 2008). Cruising as a cultural practice seems more 'queer' than 'gay male' in the sense that, in contrast to contemporary, relatively visible, and normative 'out-and-proud' gay culture, cruising remains in the shades of deviancy, harking back to pre-Stonewall times when homosexuality was forced into relative invisibility, at least in mainstream straight culture. Cruising consists of secret glancing that seeks recognition invisible to the outside world, resulting in anonymous contact, either out of necessity (closeted homosexuality) or sheer pleasure (the thrill of secrecy and the danger of exposure), or both. Richard Dyer recognizes such ambiguity as well in the pre-Stonewall 'culture of queers,' which encompassed 'subversion, play, passion and irony,' forms of resistance to dominant straight culture that might be read as empowering in their transgression, yet which also 'may either mask the reality of the oppressiveness of the category queer or accept too high a price in the name of intensity of feeling and refinement of expression' (Dyer 2002: 7). By extension, 'queering' is not just a liberating act of recovering hidden traces of homosexuality that can challenge existing grand narratives, but also an ambiguous practice that can both reinforce and undermine normative structures.

Whereas Turner makes a connection between the flâneur and the cruiser, in Anna McCarthy's *Ambient Television*, which focuses on the use of television outside of the home, the flâneur is (eventually) connected to the television viewer. As McCarthy notes, 'spectatorship – visual culture's discursive positioning of subjects – is part and parcel of modern life, activated in the succession of consumer spectacles that punctuate the everyday itineraries of the shopper, the customer, the tourist, the commuter' (McCarthy 2001: 3), and, I would add, the cruiser and the zapper. Television viewing is not limited to watching at home, but also includes encounters with television on the street, in bars, in waiting areas, or on planes – in spaces where the private and the public often overlap. Although McCarthy is explicitly talking about non-domestic television (which is the groundbreaking aspect of her study), her perspective also has an impact on the way we perceive television inside the home. Rather than placing it in opposition to television outside of the home, domestic television can be seen as part of the larger televisual media landscape, both outside and inside, both public and private. Yet, with respect to zapping, there is an important distinction. While the television viewer outside of the home 'zaps' by moving from one television screen to another, the television viewer inside the home zaps by changing the channel. Although in this chapter I focus only on domestic television (the television set at home, though not necessarily located in the family living room), McCarthy's concept of ambient television challenges the conventional relationship between television and its viewers, enabling different perspectives on the viewer's subject position in relation to the television set. In this way, the television viewer can take on different roles, including the one of flâneur.

Like the modern city, television can and has been perceived as a product of modernity (or perhaps even as a modernist project), one of the technological inventions 'that *made* modern man and the modern condition' (Williams 2003: 5). As a powerful technology, television was often believed to be a potential instrument of nation building. Particularly in the times of broadcast television, when American television was dominated by the three major networks (ABC, CBS, and NBC) and European television was controlled by national public broadcast services, television could serve as a normative force, providing structure to both the nation-state as well as the nuclear heterosexual family (Spigel 1990). Two technological developments challenged television's power over its viewers. First, the introduction of the remote control in 1950 gave viewers literally more control, enabling them to switch quite easily from one channel to another. Second, the steady growth of cable and satellite television since the 1970s has offered viewers many more channels to choose from. As a result, television no longer functions merely as broadcaster, but, in addition to its mainstream programming, also presents alternative programming as narrowcaster to specific groups of viewers (which, as discussed earlier, has had a great impact on gay and lesbian visibility on television). With the risk of presenting a too simplistic picture of the normative character of television, such a perspective does enable us to make a connection between the zapper who cruises the channels of television and the cruiser who roams the streets of the modern city. In other words, paraphrasing Turner, zapping may be perceived as a practice that exploits the ambivalence of television, and in doing so, 'queers' the totalizing narratives of modernity, of which both the modern city and television are intrinsic parts.

Obviously, such an assumption is rather ambitious, but it does provide a guideline to think about the critical potential of zapping as a queer practice. Television may be compared to the modern city, in which broadcasting constitutes the larger public space accessible to all or most of us, while narrowcasting constitutes a specific assigned area targeted at a particular user. To take New York City as an example, broadcast television is like Times Square, catering to a broad audience with strict regulations of what is publicly acceptable, whereas narrowcast television is like Christopher Street, catering to a specific niche (in this case, queer) audience, with more room for cultural expressions that tend to be considered unsuitable for a broad and mainstream audience. In such a comparison, MTV's gay and lesbian channel Logo functions as a specific designated space catering to the 'LGBT world,' in the same way as gay and lesbian bars and other LGBT social places do within the city.

If television is like a modern city, can the television viewer be compared to the flâneur, representing the televisual experience in a similar way as the flâneur represents the urban experience? If zapping is like cruising, can the television viewer be compared to the cruiser – the zapper who challenges television's normative character in both its function as broadcaster and narrowcaster, similar to the way the cruiser challenges the normative structure of the modern city? Like in the cityscape, queerness on television is not located in one specific spot: a single television programme featuring openly gay and lesbian characters or one narrowcast channel targeted at a specific gay and lesbian audience. Rather, as Alexander Doty has suggested, queerness in popular culture is often to be found in the in-between spaces, 'in that mass culture twilight zone between mall multiplex and art house, or between network television and PBS' (Doty 1993: 103). Similar to the flâneur and the cruiser, who pass through the in-between spaces while walking across the city, the zapper might find queerness while switching from one television channel to another.

Toward a queer zaptitude

Ever since television has ceased to be dominated by broadcasters such as the American national networks or European public broadcast services, often deciding what 'quality television' its audience needed, viewers have gained more control over what they themselves consider worthwhile. In his essay 'Zapping One's Way into Quality,' Thomas Elsaesser argues that quality television is to be found amidst the flow of commercial images and messages:

> It does seem impossible to discuss quality on television without detecting the virus of commercialization and commodification infecting everything, the arts, culture, news, information, and even the weather report. The alternative, however, is the illustrative lecture, promoting an idea of quality and culture that reproduces the worst feature of public service television, when its self-appointed job was to improve its audience by deciding, if necessary on their behalf, what was good for them. Only a broadcasting system that still enjoys a monopoly over its viewers ... can be so well-meaning and paternalistic. Otherwise, zapp ... zapp ... zapp ...
>
> (Elsaesser 1994: 57)

Rather than suggesting that television has become a sheer commercial cultural wasteland, Elsaesser sees zapping as a tool that viewers can use to shift through the televisual images in search of quality. The power of both television and its viewers lies in the moments when the zapping stops. Film scholar Wanda Strauven, for example, recounts a zapping experience she had when staying one night in a cheap Route 66 motel. Although preferring to see herself 'not as a couch potato, but as an active "homo zappens" who is taking control over the multiplicity and the simultaneity of signs (or channels),' Strauven ends up switching mindlessly from one channel to another until she comes across images from an old French black-and-white film with English subtitles: 'In my zombie mood (or mode) I zapped forward; then, abruptly, I stopped and went back. I had to go back to those images' (Strauven 2005: 125). Being both disciplined by and in (remote) control of the televisual flow, Strauven is prompted by this moment when the zapping stopped to question how these cinematic images work differently when viewed on a small television set as a part of a larger flow of images, instead of being viewed within the conventional setting of the cinema. In other words, here the practice of zapping, more than the images themselves, invites critical reflection.

Conceptual artist Johan Grimonprez, known for his documentary *dial H-I-S-T-O-R-Y* (1998), has coined the term 'zaptitude' to describe the critical potential of zapping. He recognizes the commercial value ('the supermarket ideology') of narrowcast television, which divides the audience into niche markets. 'With 600 channels soon provided on New York cable, might the overall homogeneity not desire the other part: the urge for an extreme diversity, a kind-of-supermarket-idea with specialized departments, evidently to push the viewers' quota' (interview with Obrist 2003). Applied to the queerness of television, the popularity of programmes with high gay and lesbian visibility, such as *Will & Grace* and *Queer Eye for the Straight Guy*, targeted at a mainstream and predominantly straight audience, and the shows of channels such as MTV's Logo, specifically targeted at a gay and lesbian audience, fit within the supermarket ideology of commercial television in which 'queerness' is used as cultural capital. However, like Elsaesser, Grimonprez ascribes power to television viewers, who can use their remote control to decide what they want to watch and do not want to watch: 'The very act of watching television contains already a participatory nature in itself, the way we receive, contextualize, and re-contextualize images. It's exactly what we do with the zapping tool (say: "zaptitude"). Zapping buys into the supermarket ideology, but at the same time it can embody a critical distance as well.' Again, the practice of zapping both overpowers and empowers viewers of television. If indeed, within the televisual cityscape, there is room for a critical perspective, can such a 'zaptitude' also constitute a queer critical stance, a specifically queer zaptitude?

In his search for quality television, Thomas Elsaesser finds it through the practice of zapping: 'Quality television, quite simply, is a programme that stops the zapping and makes me stay put, because I recognize it, and because it recognizes me' (Elsaesser 1994: 63). Here a connection can be made to the earlier quoted definition of cruising by Mark Turner as 'the moment of visual exchange … which constitutes an act of mutual recognition,' inviting a comparison between cruising and zapping. Similar to the way Elsaesser finds quality television through zapping, I encounter television's queerness in that moment of mutual recognition. Queerness may be located in such an unexpected connection between viewer and televisual image, character, or moment, revealing an in-between space encountered through the practice of zapping. By replacing 'quality' with 'queer,' I paraphrase Elsaesser, thus suggesting that television's queerness can be found in that moment when I stop zapping and stay put, 'because I recognize it, and because it recognizes me.'

Obviously this raises the question of how such an encounter can consist of mutual recognition, as that implies that television can 'look back' at its viewer.

Writing about queer cinema, film scholars R. Bruce Brasell and Nicholas de Villiers have both applied cruising to investigate, respectively, 'gay spectatorship' and 'queer ways of looking,' showing that the glance of cruising is quite different from the conventional cinematic gaze. Both authors suggest that the cruising approach enables a more ambiguous position of the viewer, creating room for different interpretations and engagements with the text. Following Roland Barthes, de Villiers argues that such an approach creates a distance, one which is not necessarily critical but can also be based on fascination or abjection, which 'might enable other forms of queer desire and vision' (de Villiers 2007). In his analysis of Andy Warhol's *My Hustler* (1965), Brasell also refers to Barthes when he suggests that cruising positions the film's viewers within a larger community of gay men, regardless of the gender or sexual identity of the viewers. 'In the second half of the film, we are positioned as participants in a cruise – as Joe cruises Paul, he also begins to cruise me/you/us. He eyes us through the bathroom mirror, inviting us to eye him back. To continue to look at him on the screen is thus to become implicated in the process of cruising' (Brasell 1992: 62). Although these scholars write about film rather than television, a similar argument can be made for the glances that are exchanged on television; one could even assume that television can more effectively implicate its viewers within such a process of cruising, as, unlike cinema, addressing viewers – directly or indirectly – befits the conventions of television.

By perceiving the zapper as a cruiser who moves across the television channels in search of a gaze that will meet his own in mutual recognition, the in-between places where queerness is found can be made explicit, thereby inviting alternative interpretations that may alter or counter conventional conceptions of television watching. Rather than being contained within the boundaries of specific gay and lesbian programming, or specific gay and lesbian channels, the zapper as cruiser can move throughout the televisual cityscape, recognizing queerness in particular fictional and non-fictional programmes, television personalities, the 'collage' of different images within the flow of television, advertising, etc. However, the difficulty obviously lies in the subsequent articulation of such moments. Whereas the call for gay and lesbian visibility can be translated into explicit political actions (as the work of GLAAD and other organizations shows), the recognition of queerness by the zapper as cruiser remains an individual act, which may result in alternative interpretations yet does not alter the actual televisual cityscape itself. The control that the individual zapper may execute through the remote control is limited, perhaps presenting a false sense of control that does not reach beyond the power of not watching at all. Yet that is too cynical a view on how television works. Although undoubtedly not as politically effective as organized activism promoting gay and lesbian visibility (which, although not always intended, often results in the cultural mainstreaming of queer identities), recognizing the queerness of television through zapping as cruising can at least provide a critical stance, a queer zaptitude, thereby helping to prevent the reduction of the 'LGBT world' to just another commercial niche market.

Making television's queerness explicit (and thus visible) starts with identifying those fleeting moments of mutual recognition when zapping, as I have done with the account of my personal viewing experiences at the opening of this chapter: both the gay male 'cruising' phone sex advertisement and my first encounter with David from *Six Feet Under*. These moments may include expressions of explicit gay and lesbian visibility, in all its varieties, in drama series, sitcoms, reality television shows, soap operas, talk shows, and news programmes. More important, these moments may also include expressions of invisibility, of implicit queerness, found in the in-between spaces of the televisual flow, like my encounter with David. I still do not know what exactly made me stop zapping, what I recognized when David's glance met my own. All I know is that I did stop, a moment that would lead to my thinking about the analogy between cruising and zapping, eventually resulting in this chapter, because I recognized queerness, and because queerness recognized me.

References

Becker, R. (2006), *Gay TV and Straight America*, New Brunswick, NJ and London: Rutgers University Press.

Brasell, R.B. (1992), 'My Hustler: Gay Spectatorship as Cruising,' *Wide Angle* 14(2, April): 54–64.

Califia, P. (1994), *Public Sex: The Culture of Radical Sex*, 2nd edn, San Francisco, CA: Cleis Press.

Capsuto, S. (2000), *Alternate Channels: The Uncensored Story of Gay and Lesbian Images on Radio and Television*, New York: Ballantine Books.

de Villiers, N. (2007), 'Glancing, Cruising, Staring: Queer Ways of Looking,' *Bright Lights Film Journal* 57 (August). Online: http://www.brightlightsfilm.com/57/queer.html [accessed 3 May 2008].

Doty, A. (1993), *Making Things Perfectly Queer: Interpreting Mass Culture*, Minneapolis, MN and London: University of Minnesota Press.

D'Souza, A. and McDonough, T. (eds) (2006), *The Invisible Flâneuse?: Gender, Public Space and Visual Culture in Nineteenth-century Paris*, Manchester: Manchester University Press.

Dyer, R. (2002), *The Culture of Queers*, London and New York: Routledge.

Elsaesser, T. (1994), 'Zapping One's Way into Quality: Arts Programmes on TV' in T. Elsaesser, J. Simons, and L. Bronk (eds) *Writing for the Medium: Television in Transition*, Amsterdam: Amsterdam University Press, 54–63.

Feuer, J. (2001), 'The "Gay" and "Queer" Sitcom' in G. Creeber (ed.) *The Television Genre Book*, London: British Film Institute, 70–1.

Fuss, D. (ed.) (1991), *Inside/Out: Lesbian Theories, Gay Theories*, London and New York: Routledge.

Gamson, J. (1997), *Freaks Talk Back: Tabloid Talk Shows and Sexual Nonconformity*, Chicago, IL and London: University of Chicago Press.

Gross, L. (2001), *Up from Invisibility: Lesbians, Gay Men, and the Media in America*, New York: Columbia University Press.

Humphreys, L. (1999), 'Tearoom Trade: Impersonal Sex in Public Spaces' in W. L. Leap (ed.) *Public Sex/Gay Space*, New York: Columbia University Press, 29–54.

Kooijman, J. (2005), 'They're Here, They're Queer, and Straight America Loves it,' *GLQ: A Journal of Lesbian and Gay Studies* 11(1): 106–9.

McCarthy, A. (2001), *Ambient Television: Visual Culture and Public Space*, Durham, NC and London: Duke University Press.

Munt, S. (1995), 'The Lesbian *Flâneur*' in D. Bell and G. Valentine (eds) *Mapping Desire: Geographies of Sexualities*, London and New York: Routledge, 114–25.

Obrist, H.U. (2003), 'E-mail interview with Johan Grimonprez,' *dial H-I-S-T-O-R-Y: An art project by Johan Grimonprez*, Brussels: Argos.

Ofield, S. (2005), 'Cruising the Archive,' *Journal of Visual Culture* 4(3, December): 351–64.

Sedgwick, E.K. (2008), *Epistemology of the Closet*, 2nd edn, Berkeley, CA: University of California Press.

Spigel, L. (1990), *Make Room for TV: Television and the Family Ideal in Post-war America*, Chicago, IL: Chicago University Press.

Strauven, W. (2005), 'Re-Disciplining the Audience: Godard's Rube-Carabinier' in M. de Valck and M. Hagener (eds) *Cinephilia: Movies, Love and Memory*, Amsterdam: Amsterdam University Press, 125–34.

Taylor, E. (1989), *Prime-time Families: Television Culture in Postwar America*, Berkeley, CA: University of California Press.

Turner, M.W. (2003), *Backward Glances: Cruising the Queer Streets of New York and London*, London: Reaktion Books.

Williams, R (2003), *Television: Technology and Cultural Form*, 3rd edn, London and New York: Routledge

Chapter 10

Hearing queerly

Television's dissident sonics

Glyn Davis

In May 1988, the night before Section 28 of the Local Government Act – a clause which was introduced in order to prevent local authorities from 'promoting homosexuality' – was passed by the British parliament, four members of an activist group known as the Lesbian Avengers invaded the BBC's 6 o'clock news. Presenter Sue Lawley continued reading the headlines over a routine montage as shouts of 'Stop Section 28!' could be heard in the background, along with other whoops and indecipherable utterances; off camera, her co-presenter Nicholas Witchell leapt from his desk and (allegedly) sat on one of the women, putting his hand over her mouth to stifle the yells. The shot framing Lawley behind her desk momentarily lost its balance, the corner of her head obscured by a superimposed image, as she ad-libbed an apology, saying 'we have rather been invaded by some people'.

The relationship between sound and image in television news is often somewhat disjointed – the time-lags stuttering through the conversation between studio presenter and live reporter in the field, which are covered by the reporter's nodding; sudden marked jumps in volume, up or down, as pre-recorded inserts begin; misdirected or inoperative microphones in the studio; and so on. However, these are habitual glitches, fairly regular interruptions in the quotidian flow of the news broadcast which, although unplanned, may actually operate to assure audiences of the programme's 'liveness'. The Lesbian Avengers incident, in contrast, facilitated a marked breakdown between sound and image, a confusing disruption for those on the sofa at home: who was making the noise? what was that thump? And though Lawley struggled gamely on, the programme had become unhinged: was that odd rumpus going to start again – whatever it was?

I open the essay with this sequence as I want to identify it as a notably 'queer' moment in television history. Significantly, its queerness is not solely related to the fact that it was caused by lesbian activists. Rather, the scene's warped and unpredictable textures – the brief disintegration of the relatively reliable parameters and components of a generic form of programming – opened up television as a medium, exposing some of its workings and operations, and gesturing towards other possibilities. Central to the argument of this essay (and, indeed, of this book as a whole) is that such moments are not rare. The Lawley–Lesbian Avengers scene has become an entertaining sequence for television to re-screen – it is routinely replayed on clips shows, and can be easily sought out online at www.youtube.com.

But as these particular sources, which often revel in the mess of television, serve to reveal, the medium is riven with incidents of perverse and unpredictable disruption – from diva extraordinaire Grace Jones ranting over and then slapping talk show host Russell Harty, to the Fox News presenter Shepard Smith describing how actress/pop star J-Lo's ex-neighbours would rather give her a 'curve job than a blow job, er, blo- block party'. (As an aside, could TV clip compendium programmes, from Dennis Norden's *It'll Be Alright on the Night* series to the *It Shouldn't Happen To* ... franchise [both screened on ITV], be seen as repositories of disruptive sequences of television, many of which may be understood or enjoyed queerly? 'Are you one of those people ...?' asks Norden, in perhaps his best-known catchphrase; yes, Dennis, I am). And the moments extend beyond the live – and putatively 'live' – forms of broadcasting, such as news and chat shows; some drama series, for instance, have featured (and continue to feature) 'what just happened there?' moments, intrusions that operate to tear apart the generic predictabilities of the text.

The recently rejuvenated *Doctor Who*, for instance, has contained a number of such notable disturbances, usually consisting of fleeting allusions to non-heterosexual pleasures or other unspecific perversities. In the season two episode 'Tooth and Claw' (22 April 2006), for instance, the Doctor (David Tennant) and Rose (Billie Piper) meet Queen Victoria (Pauline Collins), who is travelling with her entourage to the Torchwood estate in Scotland, home of Sir Robert (Derek Ridell) and his wife Lady Isobel (allegedly 'away in Edinburgh'). When the building's sinister shaven-headed staff turn out to be hiding a werewolf in the basement, Robert asks the Doctor 'Did you not think there was something strange about my household staff?', to which the Doctor replies, 'well, they were bald, athletic, your wife's away ... I just thought you were happy'. (Further, as Michelle Henning suggested to me in a personal communication, isn't there something queer about the wheezing, groaning sound of the Doctor's spaceship, the Tardis? I would add that this noise seems especially perverse when it accompanies images of the Tardis spinning down an anal wormhole in time and space). What connects together all of these interruptions, I want to argue, is that they frequently operate via the aural channel, or, more accurately, bring the aural and visual streams into a dissonant – and dissident – relationship to each other.

Before considering the operations of some of these disruptively queer moments in more detail, however, it is necessary to set in place a theoretical framework that enables a more complex understanding of the workings of television sound, and its relationship(s) to non-normative sexualities. First, I want to outline some of what has been previously written regarding television's aural qualities and characteristics; second, I will offer a brief survey of some of the writings that have addressed the connections and intersections between queerness and sound, especially the voice. Then, bringing these fields of enquiry into discourse with one another, however fractious or partial, I will explore some instances of queer TV and their sonic textures, as well as their pleasures and politics.

Sound in television studies

In film studies, there was for some time a lack of critical attention paid to the operations of the soundtrack; indeed, it was a commonplace for theorists of the audio components of cinema to decry the lack of work produced on the subject, and to criticise the tyranny of the visual. However, arguments regarding the 'image bias' of most film theory are now less easy to maintain, as there exists a significant (and ever expanding) library of books and articles on film sound – most of which are about music, but a considerable number of which address dialogue and the voice (see, for instance, Lastra 2000; Kozloff 2000; Sergi 2004).

This is in marked contrast to television studies, where there is a notably smaller volume of writing on the medium's sonic qualities and textures. Three key pieces of work are worth highlighting for their detailed focus on TV sound. One chapter of John Ellis's book *Visible Fictions* (1992), which focuses on broadcast sounds and images, provides a provocative overview. Rick Altman's 1986 essay 'Television/ Sound' focuses on the links between sound use, Raymond Williams' notion of flow, and the imperatives of commercial television. Although providing some strategic insights – that much TV viewing is distracted, that television audiences may only engage with the screen for around half of the time that they are 'watching' – the essay is rather constrained by its exclusively US focus. And Karen Lury's book *Interpreting Television* (2004) offers a detailed consideration, through a range of examples of programmes, of the manifold different ways in which sound can operate in relation to television – as music, as speech, as silence, and as concrete sounds.

Of course, these are not the only published texts which explore TV's audio landscape. Analyses of specific performers or personalities sometimes grapple with the ways in which physical performance abilities relate to, or connect with, the skills of vocal delivery (see, for instance, Vernallis 2004). Music on television – from pop promos, to live performances, to the classical scores for nature documentaries – has received sustained attention (see, for example, the essays collected in Frith et al. (eds) 1993). Articles on (so-called) 'quality' television drama often rhapsodise about the literary textures of the script, in a manner which solidifies or shores up the notion of the TV-writer-as-auteur but often ignores the skills of the actors (and the rest of the creative team) in breathing life into those words (see, for instance, far too many of the essays written about *The Sopranos*, or *Deadwood*, or *Six Feet Under* – or, indeed, much of the work collected under the rubric of 'Whedon Studies' at slayageonline.com).

However, sustained interrogations of TV sound *qua* sound, in all its manifold forms and varieties, are rather rare. Frequently, lip service is paid in writings about TV to the fact that the medium has a different sound/image relationship from cinema, with sound positioned and constituted as more important than the image with television. But that 'importance' has not led to the proliferation of a critical library of writings on the topic, the creation of a specific sub-field of study, of the form that film studies has produced.

The arguments regarding the significance of sound for television as a medium are clearly articulated by Ellis in *Visible Fictions*, and are worth reiterating here in some detail. 'The image is the central reference in cinema', he writes.

> But for TV, sound has a more centrally defining role. Sound carries the fiction or the documentary; the image has a more illustrative function. The TV image tends to be simple and straightforward, stripped of detail and excess of meanings. Sound tends to carry the details (background noises, music). This is a tendency towards a different sound/image balance than in cinema, rather than a marked and consistent difference. Broadcast TV has areas which tend towards the cinematic, especially the areas of serious drama or of various kinds of TV film. But many of TV's characteristic broadcast forms rely upon sound as the major carrier of information and the major means of ensuring continuity of attention.
>
> (Ellis 1992: 129)

This quote is now more than 25 years old, but remains pertinent. Of course, it is necessary to think through the ways in which alterations in the size and shape of television screens, and the development of home cinema systems with their complex multi-speaker arrangements have reconfigured not only domestic spaces and the sound/image relationships in television, but also the relations of audiences to television's sounds and images. Some of these issues are addressed in Barbara Klinger's 2006 book on home entertainment, *Beyond the Multiplex*. However, it is unknown what percentage of homes now have 'home cinema' systems (a relatively small number, probably), and how many viewers still rely on the weak speakers built into TV sets themselves. Even with these technological transformations, it remains the case that with television sound is a more dominant channel of information than the image. Indeed, Ellis describes sound as television's 'major carrier of information' – calling to mind, perhaps, the pejorative critical perspective on television that perceives the box in the corner as 'radio with pictures' – in a manner that assumes a particular level or degree of sonic clarity. (Another aside: might aural muddiness, an inability to make out clearly what is being heard – which is itself surely a fairly regular aspect of television's airing and consumption – occasion semantic [or a more general] confusion, of a form that might afford queer possibilities?)

Ellis continues:

> Broadcast TV can be left on with no one watching it, playing in the background of other activities in the home. This is perhaps a frequent event; certainly, it also makes impossible the construction of a voyeuristic contract between looker and representation. Instead, broadcast TV uses sound to appeal to its audience, using a large degree of direct address whose function is to attract the look and

> attention of the viewer, and to hold it. The separation that this practice implies
> is different from that of cinematic voyeurism.
>
> (Ellis 1992: 138–9)

The separation that Ellis identifies here is *both* between image and sound, and as a correlative, between television as a medium and its audiences. This is not to suggest that television's sound/image relationships aren't often or even usually neatly integrated – as with cinema, there is frequently an attempt to disguise the 'material heterogeneity' of television broadcast material. Rather, the dominance of the aural over the visual channel with television produces a gap between the two that – however inadvertently – can serve to *reveal* that 'material heterogeneity'.

Fundamentally, the gaps between image and sound, and between the medium and its audiences, are ontological components of the medium. For cinema, neat suture – of the text as an audiovisual whole, and of the spectator to the film – remains the ideal form to strive for, especially in the commercial realm of production. This tidiness has ideological implications. As Mary Ann Doane has identified, strategies of post-production sound design in cinema contribute significantly to the classical film text's semblance of being hermetically sealed, but this seamlessness is always in danger of cracking apart.

> Because sound and image are used as guarantors of two radically different modes
> of knowing (emotion and intellection), their combination entails the possibility
> of exposing an ideological fissure – a fissure which points to the irreconcilabil-
> ity of two truths of bourgeois ideology. Practices of sound editing and mixing
> are designed to mask this contradiction through the specification of allow-
> able relationships between sound and image. Thus, in the sound technician's
> discourse synchronization and totality are fetishised and the inseparability of
> sound and image is posited as a goal.
>
> (Doane 1985: 56)

Television, on the other hand, with its speedy modes of production, ephemerality, dependence on live broadcasting, and sheer volume of output, is regularly split open by chasms and pillars of noise and light.[1] As the viewer travels through the televisual landscape, these interruptions may be minor – potholes in the tarmac, unforeseen speed-bumps – or they may be more considerable and unexpected, a herd of noisy cows on the road.

For queer theory and theorists, such formations and deformations – absences, gaps, ellipses, holes, folds, overlaps, swellings, obfuscations – whether material or metaphorical, are places of possibility, ripe for appropriation and intervention, their shapes and mechanics chiming or squaring with the experience of sexual alterity. Take, for instance, this definition of the 'queer' by Eve Kosofsky Sedgwick:

> one of the things that 'queer' can refer to [is] the open mesh of possibilities, gaps,
> overlaps, dissonances and resonances, lapses and excesses of meaning when the

constituent elements of anyone's gender, of anyone's sexuality aren't made (or *can't be* made) to signify monolithically.

(Sedgwick 1993: 8)

Although she is discussing the operations of sexuality, Sedgwick's quote can also, I believe, be usefully applied to, or mapped onto, in a structural and formal manner, the workings of a medium like television. (Pushing this argument to its furthest limit, could it be proposed that queer audiences might feel more of an affiliation with television as a medium per se, than with cinema, due to the former's unavoidable and constituent rickety form?) Certainly, the mucky and often faultering textures of television – the rough cuts, the sudden silences, the disconcerting loss of transmission, the discombobulations experienced while zapping between stations and shows – provoke specific theoretical questions that can be inflected queerly. What does the aural channel reveal or suggest that does not 'fit' with the images witnessed – and how, phenomenologically, is this discordance experienced? In what ways are the images presented to us complicated by the things we hear? If the image/sound relationship is fragmented with TV, then what does this fracture expose about the ideological operations of the medium, and the narratives, messages, and fictions it presents to us? Which specific aspects of television sound – colour, volume, intelligibility, timbre – can be read, or understood, or brought into coterminous comprehension, with and through queer theoretical writings and concepts?

Examining a more concrete example at this juncture may serve to highlight ways in which television's sounds can be understood queerly. In his book *The Voice in Cinema*, Michel Chion identifies the power of the acousmêtre in fictional film – that is, the voice that is heard, but not anchored in a depicted body. As Karen Lury notes, the acousmatic voice is prevalent in all sorts of television programming, from dramatic fiction narrators to continuity announcers, from adverts to the 'Voice of God' voice-overs that accompany state events such as royal weddings or funerals (Lury 2004: 59–64). Many voice-overs on TV, of course, are those of known individuals, people whose bodies and physical appearances audiences are familiar with; many others, however, are not – and the absence of knowledge of their physical presence provides their vocalisations with a particular power.

Thomas Waugh, writing about some of the films of Andy Warhol, has noted the separation of their audio and visual tracks, with campy voice-over narration commenting on what is depicted (this appears in, for instance, *Beauty #2*, *Bike Boy* and *Harlot*). Widening his frame of reference, Waugh writes that

> Voice-image separation extends as well, of course, to the post-Stonewall canon of homoerotic narrative cinema – from Curt McDowell's *Loads* to *The Law of Desire* ... The popularity of this technique, I would argue, reflects more than its logistic and economic suitability for artisanal and underfinanced industrial cinema. The voice-off or voice-over, emitting from the body of author-subject as he/she retreats once more behind the camera or mixing console, may articulate a level of retroactive self-reflexivity or simply a sportscasting-style simultaneity,

descriptive or directive, diegetic or extra-diegetic. This dynamic is at the centre of the erotic give-and-take, the tease of the viewer's response by the controlling yet unpossessing author.

(Waugh 1996: 57)

In other words, in queer cinema the acousmatic voice is regularly used as a formal and stylistic device; for Waugh, the prevalence of the queer acousmêtre in film is connected to the particular erotic dynamics it enables. Given the prevalence of the disembodied voice across television per se, it is likely that these queer dynamics also inflect a variety of audience TV viewing experiences.

Further, Chion himself highlights the potentially disruptive effect that the acousmêtre can have:

For the spectator ..., the filmic acousmêtre is 'offscreen,' outside the image, and at the same time *in* the image: the loudspeaker that's actually its source is located behind the image in the movie theatre. It's as if the voice were wandering along the surface, *at once inside and outside*, seeking a place to settle. Especially when a film hasn't yet shown what body this voice normally inhabits.

(Chion 1999: 23)

Although Chion is here talking about cinema, his observations arguably apply with even more force to television, a medium across which the acousmatic voice prolif-erates. Chion suggests that the acousmêtre has the power to threaten or trouble the inside/outside binary. As a point of theoretical overlap, queer theorists have iden-tified the ways in which queerness and non-hetero sexualities can undermine or problematise binary modes of thought (see, in particular, Fuss 1992 and Sedgwick 1990). This is not to suggest that the acousmatic voice in television is always nec-essarily queer. Rather, TV's acousmêtres have the potential to operate to produce effects – both aural and affective – that can be experienced as queer.

Queer sounds

At this juncture, it is necessary to redirect discussion a little, and to consider the connections between specific sorts of sounds and sexual 'otherness'. I will not give space here to the affiliations between queerness and music, largely because this is well-trodden ground; for those interested in this realm, from classical to pop, texts by Brett et al. (1995), Gill (1995), Hubbs (2004), and Smith (1995) serve as invaluable starting points. Rather, I want to explore other areas of sound – the voice, ambient noise, silence – and their relationships to queerness, that have been less explored by theoretical texts.

There is a long-standing cultural association between sexuality and the voice. As Wayne Koestenbaum has suggested in his book *The Queen's Throat*, Western understandings of the voice and of sexuality arguably resemble each other, in ways which can cause confusion and conflation of the two. Although it is a cultural myth, it is often assumed that having a voice equates with having an identity; that the voyage of a voice, from outside to inside, is equivalent to the story of sexuality (Koestenbaum 1994: 155). Coming out, for instance, almost always involves vocalising one's hidden identity, confessing, admitting; the voice, interpreted (or operating) as a repository of truth, reveals who you really are, sexual orientation neatly (and possibly cathartically) expressed in words. As Koestenbaum puts it, 'Queers have placed trust in coming out, a process of vocalisation. Coming out, we define voice as openness, self-knowledge, clarity'. (1994: 158)

In particular, Koestenbaum notes the historical connections between gay male sexuality and the voice:

> Cultural folklore convinces us that we can tell someone is gay by voice alone. Decadent novelist J.-K. Huysmans wrote in a letter to Marc-André Raffalovich that 'sodomy changes the voice, which becomes almost identical in all of them. After several days study in that world, from nothing but the sound of the voice of people I did not know, I could infallibly predict their tastes. Do you not think there would be research to be done on the influence of one organ on another?' And Earl Lind, the remarkable author of *Autobiography of an Androgyne* (1918), believed that 'the voice is one of the chief criteria by which to determine abnormal sexuality. I fancy that I can diagnose a man sexually simply by having him sing'. (1994: 14)

Although such examples may seem comical now, their present-day versions are perpetuated and assumed widely – that gay men lisp, or are overly sybillant, or that the registers of their voices reach, perhaps uncontrollably, shrieking levels beyond the limits of heterosexual men. In situation comedies, the 'humour' of the gay stereotype is often located in the voice, and its difference from the heterosexual male's voice; thus, in *Gimme Gimme Gimme* (BBC, 1999–2001), the pyrotechnics of James Dreydus as Tom Farrell run the range from mockney drawl to glissando purr; in *Will & Grace* (NBC, 1998–2006), Jack McFarland (Sean Hayes), when especially infuriated, yelp and shrieks at such a pitch that comprehension of what he is saying is almost impossible.

Across the twentieth century, gay men have often been noted for – or identified, or marked by – their voices, for their wit and verbal dexterity, their impersonation abilities, their crooning, their falsetto. Even a cursory list of relevant well-known individuals here would include Oscar Wilde, Noel Coward, Andy Warhol, Truman Capote, Kenneth Williams, Julian Clary, Frankie Howerd, Stephen Fry, Boy George, Jimmy Somerville, Rufus Wainwright, and Neil Tennant. (This may actually be my 'fantasy dinner party' list of invited guests.) Television interviews with Andy Warhol from the 1960s, for instance, are remarkable not only for the lack of information he gives away ('gee, I don't know, what do you think?'), but also for the rather high-pitched, delicate quality of his vocals, often scuffed or grazed by primitive or ineffectual recording and transmission technologies, his voice seeming to almost float independent of his body. Frankie Howerd, when delivering his stand-up routines, would cut up the flow of the lines with verbal and physical twitches and tics; as Andy Medhurst puts it, 'Howerd's whole career rested on the inflections wrung from non-words, half-words, stranded words, noises, interjections, and pauses – "ooh … ah … no … listen …"' (2007: 3).

Or take, as another emblematic moment equal in historical significance to the Lawley–Lesbian Avengers incident, the appearance of Julian Clary on the 1993 British National Comedy Awards, which were hosted by Jonathan Ross. Taking to the stage to present an award, Clary stated, in his distinctive gentle, camp purr, that he had 'just been fisting Norman Lamont backstage'; following a shocked-laughter response from the audience of celebrities (including, the camera revealed, comedian Mark Lamarr, and daytime hosts Richard Madeley and Judy Finnegan), he delivered his punchline: 'Talk about a red box'.[2] Ross briefly talked over the top of Clary, smudging the payoff; after a subsequent brief halting exchange, Clary unruffled, the crowd evidently unsteady, Ross asked 'Are we still on?' Not only was Clary's joke outwith the proprieties of television – a moment of unexpected queer rupture in the cheeky-but-harmless ebb of the awards ceremony – but the effect of his line arguably lay in the jarring discord between his soft, mellifluous tones and the violence of his language.

The association between gay men and the voice also manifests in subcultural uses of language – for instance in polari, the gay lexicon used most famously by Sandy and Julian from the BBC radio series *Round the Horne*. Further, coming-of-age narratives in autobiographical tomes often note how, at school, gay men have avoided confronting their own sexual identities (and a wider culture of oppression) by throwing themselves into academic study – developing a skill with language, with words, which is later used as a defence, a weapon, a shield (see, for instance, Fry 1998). In addition, gay men are often connected to the realm of gossip (see Abelove 2005). Gavin Butt, in his book *Between You and Me* (2005), has elucidated some of the ways in which the circulation of gossip in the post-war American art scene enabled the establishment and identification of a queer world, pre-Stonewall. And although gossip is evidently not the exclusive privilege of gay men, the cultural affiliation is often assumed – and is propagated in such places as Kenneth Anger's scurrilous *Hollywood Babylon* books (1979; 1984) and Perez Hilton's scandalous website (www.perezhilton.com).

Evidently, these observations regarding sexual difference and the voice do not merely apply to gay men. A similar historical string of links and observations could be put together relating lesbians and bisexual women to their distinctive vocal textures and cultures. This might include: Marlene Dietrich's husky burr; Greta Garbo's almost affectless intonation; the lesbian Weimar subculture that centred around specific performance spaces; k. d. lang's deep and seductively sonorous delivery of her songs; Sandra Bernhard's snappy, yappy delivery (combined as it is with her New York Jewish accent and captivating mouth).

The potentially disruptive queerness of Bernhard's voice, in fact, seems to be commented upon in the two episodes of *Will & Grace* in which she appears as herself. In season three's 'Swimmin' Pools … Movie Stars' (11 January 2001), for instance, Will and Grace attend an open viewing of Bernhard's apartment, which is up for sale, out of sheer nosiness. When Bernhard is friendly towards the pair, they rashly offer to buy the place from her, attempting to maintain the pretence that they were always interested in the property. Will and Grace finally confess to Bernhard that they don't want the apartment, which arouses the performer's ire. The volume of Bernhard's delivery begins to rise – but her words are intermittently drowned out by the grinding of a blender that is being used by her pianist to make smoothies. Although this is partly a comment on her vulgarity and use of blue language, it also intimates that the dangerous power of her voice needs to be drowned out – for reasons of television's conservatism, certainly, but also, intra-diegetically, for the delicate ears of the oh-so-safe Will Truman and Grace Adler (although Grace, snapping back at Bernhard, does get one little blast from the blender for herself).

Finally, although trans voices are not as prevalent on television as those of gay men, lesbians, and bisexuals, there are particular arenas in which they flourish. Appearances in drama series and sitcoms may be rare – although Kathleen Turner's performance as Chandler's father on *Friends* (NBC, 1994–2004) is worthy of inter-rogation, if only for Turner's use of her vocal range, and Candis Cayne's role in *Dirty Sexy Money* (ABC, 2007–) provided a rare moment of visibility and audibility for a trans actor in prime time – but it is talk shows that enable the proliferation of trans voices on television (on which subject, see Gamson 1999).

Arguably, the transsexual voice is one that is regularly perceived as dissonant; that is, it is the problematic fit between vocal tone, register, and colour, and the body from which it emanates, that casts suspicion on the speaker's gender and/or orien-tation. Might it be that the trans voice on television is particularly representative of the medium's queer sound textures? The fragility of the voice/body relations in the popular understandings of trans identities seems to echo, in their material pres-ence, the frailty of television's sound/image relationships – that is, the medium's seemingly eternal threat of falling apart, crumbling at the core, its pretence at suture a precariously maintained fiction that many (if not all) audiences know to be smoke and mirrors.

Television sound, of course, manifests in forms other than vocalisations and music, including ambient sounds and silence. In relation to ambient sound, tele-vision – when not battering viewers with a barrage of voices, acousmatic and otherwise – often emits non-specific sounds, lacking concrete referents. Here I am not thinking of the whine of the dying cathode ray, or the buzz rattle of a duff speaker, but of the wow and flutter lodged in the background of everyday trans-mission, located behind the voices or in the spaces between words: hums and clicks, echoes and whispers – what the band Stereolab might seductively call, in the words of one of their song titles, 'The Noise of Carpet'. Could it be here, behind and beyond the quotidian voices that fill the airtime, that we find television's queerest sounds? Ambient music, from Brian Eno to Slowdive, has been seen by some authors as enabling regression to a pre-gendered existence, or as hinting at the pleasures of allowing gendered identities to blur and dissolve (see Reynolds and Press 1995). Certainly, ambient sound, as diffuse and positioned against (and around) concrete noises, could be read as analogous to models and understandings of sexuality which refuse restrictive, hard and delimited notions of 'correct' gender and sexual identities – a topic which deserves more consideration than I can give it here.

Finally, a few words on silence. Television is rarely silent; Michel Chion writes that 'silent television is inconceivable, unlike cinema' (1994: 165). As Karen Lury notes,

> When television is silent, it would seem that it is either a deliberate intervention by the home viewer – via the mute button – or an accidental, technical fault in transmission. Even during a technical fault, however, it is rare to hear nothing, as usually the first thing viewers note is the sound of music, accompanied by an explanatory sign, which promises that 'normal service' will be resumed shortly.
> (Lury 2004: 86)

Might it be possible to argue that television's rare silent moments – dramatic removals of sound, that is, rather than those caused voluntarily by the remote-wielding viewer – are the medium's queerest moments? Here, I do not wish to suggest that we equate queer TV with broken TV; rather, that we should think through silent television as disruptive, as drawing attention – perhaps in the same way that some direct action political interventions aim to do. Certainly, some queer theorists have attempted to think through the political ramifications of silence for queerness. Jonathan Katz has explored, for instance, John Cage's silences:

> if silence was, paradoxically, in part an expression of Cage's identity as a closeted homosexual during the Cold War, it was also much more than that. Silence was not only a symptom of oppression, it was also, I want to argue, a chosen mode of resistance. This silence is not the passive stratagem of a closeted homosexual unwilling and unable to declare his identity within a hostile culture. On the contrary, in contrast to the codes of the closet, if the point of Cage's silence was to escape notice, its effect was surely the opposite. (1999: 238)

That is, the public attention Cage's silences received – and the position that they have subsequently come to hold in the modernist/avant-garde canon – invite sustained analysis and interpretation (as well as emotive responses) from audiences and critics, despite being essentially constructed out of absence. Taking Cage's silences as a model, perhaps, with television, the most provocative and political of queer sounds are the ones that simply aren't there, or the ones that just stop.

Stop, hey, what's that sound?

Bringing together the observations made so far into a multidimensional framework, I want to turn my attention to two extracts, from very different sorts of television.

Although, up to this point, I have been suggesting in this essay that queer sounds proliferate across television, appearing in divergent programming contexts and beyond such parameters, evidently certain sorts of television enable the manifestation of some queer sounds more than others. Liminal forms of programming – those hidden away in the schedule and/or with tiny audiences, those less ruthlessly policed by the guardians of broadcasting, those in genres of programming where anarchic content is welcomed (such as children's TV and animation) – can arguably include queer lines of dialogue and noises with less fear of criticism or detection. Scripted drama – which often commands television's largest audiences – may be more of a closed shop, inevitably more conservative. On the other hand, the association of (some of) such programmes with 'quality' may provide the opportunity for artistic licence and creativity – not that queer moments on television are ever necessarily the most 'artistic'. Live television, in all its glorious and florid messiness, may provide most opportunity for transgression. Evidently, these are not fixed or closed categories; however, when considering television's queer sounds, it is necessary to identify the ways in which programming parameters impede or support the production of such noises.

In episode twelve of the first season of the drama series *Six Feet Under*, David Fisher (Michael C. Hall) finally comes out to his mother Ruth (Frances Conroy). Alan Ball's series for HBO, which ran for five seasons from 2001 to 2005, was a notably 'authored' text; part of this authoring was its stylised uses of sound. Not only did the show contain long stretches of silence or ambient noise (conveying, for instance, the dry, clinical sounds of the basement preparation room, or the muffle of the space in which caskets are presented for potential purchase), but numerous scenes featured characters talking about talking, talking about not talking, singing, throwing their voices, and so on. To a certain extent, discussing this programme in the context of this essay is rather obvious; as a 'quality' drama series created by a gay man, and which featured overtly gay/queer characters, the show is exceptional. However, David's coming out scene is worthy of exploration for its queer sonic textures, which combine lines of dialogue with ambient sounds and moments of silence.

Indeed, David's coming out purposefully counters the predictability of most coming out scenes in film and television texts, in which a bold declaration is followed swiftly either by angry rejection or emotional acceptance. David walks into the TV den to find his mother lying with a cloth over her forehead. After a lengthy pause, he declares that he is gay. Ruth wants to know why he didn't tell her earlier; she declares that she couldn't choose to love him and not his sexual orientation, as though he was a chicken from which she only selected the parts she liked. Both Conroy and Hall have quite extraordinary voices – ones which, moreover, lack consistency. Hall's is sometimes deep and velvety, at other points barking and clipped; he also emits 'giveaway' high-pitched shrieks. Conroy, similarly, pinballs between gentle susurration and abrasive cries. Both actors are able to shift texture and tone quite radically from one sentence to the next. (Here's a game to play in your own time: which actor has the queerest voice on television – and what audio characteristics determine or contribute to that status?) The visuals may anchor these noises in the bodies of specific actors, to some extent, but the instability of the sound, semiotically and affectively, somewhat unhinges the concretisation of character.

That is, unlike, say, Nate (Peter Krause) or Claire (Lauren Ambrose), whose voices are more predictable, less variable, and occupy a narrower range of expression, Ruth and Michael both have unusual voices with a broad range that they can (and do) manipulate. If David's voice reveals his queerness (whether or not he is actively coming out), this scene seems to ask us what the textures of Ruth's voice also unveil. That the dialogue itself does not adopt an even flow, or the predictable generic form of the coming out scene – with silence and clumsy pauses interrupting the brittle outbursts and unexpected phrases ('We're having veal' is the last line of the scene, quietly delivered by Ruth) – produces an odd discord between the rather humdrum framing, and the unpredictable sound. And although Ruth's recourse to talking about meat, chicken and veal, may represent a resort to safety – she is used to playing the role of maternal provider for her clan – it also, in the context of a coming out scene, serves as a perverse interruption.

To move to another example, an interview with the band Frankie Goes to Hollywood conducted by Jools Holland for the music programme *The Tube* (Channel 4, 1982–7) reveals the queer potential of unscripted television. Following a performance of a demo version of 'Relax' – the sequence was recorded before the group had signed a record deal – singer Holly Johnson suffers through a number of clumsy questions from Jools. (Despite decades in front of the camera as a presenter, Holland has never gained interviewing skills or technique.) Johnson is dressed in a cropped black mesh vest, leather cap, bright red shiny trousers and straps around his biceps; Holland, in striking visual contrast, wears a Mickey Mouse t-shirt, under a wide-lapelled camel-coloured coat. The rest of the band, standing around, share jokes and banter outside of the audible range of the microphones. The question-and-response mode stutters along, with Johnson and the rest of the band attempting to enliven proceedings – Johnson tells Holland that the interview is Holland's audition to join the band, before campily asking 'did he pass?' to someone off-camera. Holland is provoked into confessing a history as a ballroom dancer. At the end of the sequence, Holland's attempts to retain control of the interview collapse; the voices of the other band members become a sustained whirr in the background, and Holland has his clothing augmented: a leather cap is pushed onto his head, someone hands him a whip and then, looking off to one side, he says (with some surprise) 'in the mouth!', then, more embarrassed, 'as they say', and a fake gun enters the frame.

The queerness of this sequence is located less in the gay fetish wear – although the clash of these clothing items, the faded grandeur of the ballroom in which the band are interviewed, Jools Holland's bland attire, and Holly Johnson's husky Liverpudlian burr serves as quite a heady brew – than in its inaudible fragments and their evident impact on the unpredictable direction of the interaction.

What are the rest of the band getting away with saying out of the range of the microphones? How does this lead to Holland's transformation into a (partial) makeshift clone? What exactly is he going to have to take in his mouth? That the scene's editing is messy, suggesting that stretches of interview have been excised, only adds to the shambolic nature of the interview and hints at its illicit content; something about this band and their behaviour, it would seem, is beyond the purview of conventional television and its regular recording technologies. Certainly, *The Tube* was often rickety and messy, its lack of sheen part of its appeal. However, the interview with Frankie Goes To Hollywood is especially chaotic and confusing, its aural clutter difficult to follow as a regular interview, its queerness lurking just out of vision and earshot, always threatening to erupt and disrupt.

Now you hear it

Queer sounds on television are prolific; they appear in scripted series, in live broadcasts as improvisations or mistakes, as well as in an array of other programme formats. These noises are difficult to categorise – and the experience of them as queer may depend to a significant extent on the audience(s) watching. Although they may produce a jolt in viewers – 'what did he just say?', 'can you hear that noise?' – this does not necessarily entail a sort of Brechtian distanciation from the programme and the medium, a crowbar violently separating the viewer from what they are seeing and hearing. Indeed, in contrast, such moments may enhance the relationship with the television, producing a purposeful heightened level of attention to the qualities of the text. They may, however, be correctly described as perplexing, destabilising, perhaps even disorienting.

Sara Ahmed, in her book *Queer Phenomenology* (2007), riffs on the meaning of the 'orientation' in 'sexual orientation', asking what it means to lack an orientation, to be oriented differently, or to be disoriented. This essay has focused, especially in its examples, on moments of sound–image rupture in television, instances of dislocation – incidents which are themselves often disorienting. Ahmed suggests that for many, being disoriented is a fleeting experience that makes sense only in relation to the habitual experience of being 'correctly' oriented (2007: 5–6). Trapped in the habitual and normative, even conceptualising of the differently oriented could be difficult. And yet, for those who live their lives differently oriented – and in her book Ahmed discusses women, queers, and non-white ethnicities and races – thinking and living obliquely is not surprising or disconcerting.

Television, with its ontological gaps, is often perilously close to falling apart: in the spaces between its sounds and its images, I'd like to suggest, spaces of queer possibility lie – spaces in which a male newsreader gives J-Lo a blowjob, Jools Holland gets it in the mouth, and Nicholas Witchell noisily sits on a lesbian. When the gaps are exposed, the workings of the medium temporarily yawning open, all audiences are offered the opportunity to consider, if only fleetingly, another realm of existence, in which things are wired differently.

Notes

1. Of course, there are significant obstacles to applying Doane's argument directly to television. The material heterogeneity of cinema is closely bound up with film's existence as celluloid stock; television, in comparison, although regularly pre-recorded on film or video, is most often beamed through the ether via less tangible technologies such as fibre-optic cables and satellite transmissions. Discussing film's materiality in contrast to that of TV also requires engagement with differing apparatuses of consumption. Further, cinema's denial of its fabrication as text and product involves effacing the labour behind its creation, whereas television regularly exposes its own workings. I do not have enough space to consider these concerns in great depth here. However, I would maintain that television's clumsiness, its tendency to disintegrate whilst being produced or aired, can productively be read in relation to Doane's argument.
2. Norman Lamont is a former Conservative MP who served as the Chancellor of the Exchequer from 1990 to 1993; in 1992, he was the focus of various 'sleaze' allegations by the tabloid press, and thus was regularly the target of comedians. The Chancellor of the Exchequer is responsible for all of the nation's economic and fiscal concerns. When the Government's annual budget is announced, the Chancellor traditionally parades the paperwork along Downing Street in a small red case – hence Clary's reference to a 'red box'.

References

Abelove, H. (2005), *Deep Gossip*, Minneapolis, MN: University of Minnesota Press.

Ahmed, S. (2007), *Queer Phenomenology: Orientations, Objects, Others*, Durham, NC and London: Duke University Press.

Altman, R. (1986), 'Television/Sound' in T. Modleski (ed.) *Studies in Entertainment: Critical Approaches to Mass Culture*, Bloomington and Indianapolis, IN: Indiana University Press, 39–54.

Anger, K. (1979), *Hollywood Babylon*, New York: Random House.

_____ (1984), *Hollywood Babylon II*, New York: Arrow Books.

Brett, P., Thomas, G.C., and Wood, E. (eds) (1995), *Queering the Pitch: The New Gay and Lesbian Musicology*, London: Routledge.

Butt, G. (2005), *Between You and Me: Queer Disclosures in the New York Art World, 1948–1963*, Durham, NC and London: Duke University Press.

Chion, M. (1994), *Audio-Vision: Sound on Screen*, New York: Columbia University Press.

_____ (1999), *The Voice in Cinema*, trans C. Gorbman, New York: Columbia University Press.

Doane, M.A. (1985), 'Ideology and the Practice of Sound Editing and Mixing' in J. Belton and E. Weis (eds) *Film Sound: Theory and Practice*, New York: Columbia University Press, 54–62.

Ellis, J. (1992), *Visible Fictions: Cinema, Television, Radio*, London: Routledge and Kegan Paul.

Frith, S., Goodwin, A., and Grossberg, L. (eds) (1993), *Sound and Vision: Music Video Reader*, London and New York: Routledge.

Fry, S. (1998), *Moab is my Washpot*, London: Arrow Books.

Fuss, D. (1992), 'Inside/Out' in D. Fuss (ed.) *Inside/Out: Lesbian Theories, Gay Theories*, London: Routledge, 1–10.

Gamson, J. (1999), *Freaks Talk Back: Tabloid Talk Shows and Sexual Nonconformity*, Chicago, IL: Chicago University Press.

Gill, J. (1995), *Queer Noises: Male and Female Homosexuality in Twentieth Century Music*, London: Cassell.

Hubbs, N. (2004), *The Queer Composition of America's Sound: Gay Modernists, American Music, and National Identity*, Berkeley, CA: University of California Press.

Katz, J. (1999), 'John Cage's Queer Silence: Or, How to Avoid Making Matters Worse', *GLQ: A Journal of Lesbian and Gay Studies*, 5(2): 231–52.

Klinger, B. (2006), *Beyond the Multiplex: Cinema, New Technologies, and the Home*, Berkeley and LA, CA: University of California Press.

Koestenbaum, W. (1994), *The Queen's Throat: Opera, Homosexuality and the Mystery of Desire*, London: Penguin.

Kozloff, S. (2000), *Overhearing Film Dialogue*, Berkeley, CA: University of California Press.

Lastra, J. (2000), *Sound Technology and the American Cinema: Perception, Representation, Modernity*, New York: Columbia University Press.

Lury, K. (2004), *Interpreting Television*, London: Arnold.

Medhurst, A. (2007), *A National Joke: Popular Comedy and English Cultural Identities*, London and New York: Routledge.

Reynolds, S. and Press, J. (1995), *The Sex Revolts: Gender, Rebellion and Rock'n'Roll*, London: Serpent's Tail.

Sedgwick, E.K. (1990), *Epistemology of the Closet*, New York: Prentice-Hall.

_____ (1993), *Tendencies*, Durham, NC and London: Duke University Press.

Sergi, G. (2004), *The Dolby Era: Film Sound in Contemporary Hollywood*, Manchester: Manchester University Press.

Smith, R. (1995), *Seduced and Abandoned: Essays on Gay Men and Popular Music*, London: Cassell.

Vernallis, C. (2004), *Experiencing Music Video: Aesthetics and Cultural Context*, New York: Columbia University Press.

Waugh, T. (1996), 'Cockteaser' in J. Doyle, J. Flatley, and J. E. Muñoz (eds) *Pop Out: Queer Warhol*, Durham, NC and London: Duke University Press, 51–77.

Index